THE KONKOMBA OF NORTHERN GHANA

David Tait with two Konkomba elders

THE KONKOMBA
OF NORTHERN GHANA

DAVID TAIT

EDITED FROM HIS PUBLISHED AND
UNPUBLISHED WRITINGS
BY JACK GOODY

FOREWORD BY DARYLL FORDE

Published for the
INTERNATIONAL AFRICAN INSTITUTE
and the
UNIVERSITY OF GHANA
by the
OXFORD UNIVERSITY PRESS
LONDON IBADAN ACCRA

1961

Oxford University Press, Amen House, London E.C.4

GLASGOW NEW YORK TORONTO MELBOURNE WELLINGTON
BOMBAY CALCUTTA MADRAS KARACHI LAHORE DACCA
CAPE TOWN SALISBURY NAIROBI IBADAN ACCRA
KUALA LUMPUR HONG KONG

PRINTED IN GREAT BRITAIN
BY W. & J. MACKAY & CO LTD, CHATHAM, KENT

Foreword

I FIRST met David Tait when he came to University College, London, in 1946, at the age of thirty-four, to read Anthropology in the department we had just established there. He was one of a group of exceptionally able students, several of whom have, like himself, since made signal contributions to the work of the younger generation of anthropologists. Most of them had also had overseas experience during the war years and were correspondingly mature in their intellectual and social outlook. Among them Tait was frequently accorded a moral leadership in student affairs. For he combined great seriousness of purpose and intellectual curiosity with a deep but unsentimental affection for his fellow men, which was shown not only to his fellow students and teachers, but extended also to the lives of the peoples who were the object of their studies in Social Anthropology. His seniority in years and his unhurried deliberation in discussion matched his large frame and gentle, if sometimes quizzical, expression.

His earlier life had afforded an unusual and in many ways advantageous preparation for the intensive study of strange societies. He left school early—without enthusiasm for further academic study at the time—to train as a textile designer in the north of England. Then, as his wife has since told me, his interest in art, philosophy and history developed and, in connection with one of the extra-mural courses he was pursuing, he was awarded a Gladstone Memorial Prize for an essay on the history of education. He had been planning to prepare himself for a career in social work, probably as a probation officer, when war broke out and he joined the Friends Ambulance Unit with which he worked in the East End of London during the early years of evacuation and air raids. Later he went with one of the units to Palestine where, despite a severe handicap of ill health, for which he was later invalided home, he organized labour and works projects in a camp of 7,000 refugees near Gaza.

Back in England he assisted Miss Eleanor Rathbone, M.P., in her work for refugees, and after her death served himself for a time as Secretary to the Parliamentary Committee on Refugees. It was the experience of these years that directed his interest to Anthropology and the opportunities it offered for deeper understanding of other cultures and social values and also for the systematic studies that he felt were needed for effective work in social rehabilitation.

The deep humanitarian sympathy that lent both pertinacity and warmth to his later field studies is recalled by Mrs. Tait when she wrote in a letter to me: 'When I saw David among the old women and children of a Konkomba hamlet, I was strongly reminded of his time among the evacuees, mostly old and very young. He had a special gentleness, fun and imaginative understanding in such circumstances.'

When, after taking his degree in 1949, he was offered a Lectureship in African Studies in the Department of Sociology, newly established under the direction of Professor Busia in the University College of the Gold Coast, David Tait accepted with alacrity, more especially as it offered opportunities for a field study. Most of his research was among a people in the Northern Territories who were materially poor and had so far shared little in the economic developments of the country. The Konkomba were also a people among whom the small scale and uncentralized character of the social organization offered opportunities for the study of unspecialized forms of social control and adjustment in which he was particularly interested. Tait remained in the Gold Coast over several of his leave periods in order to push ahead with his field research, and in 1952 he obtained his Doctorate in the University of London for a thesis on the political organization of the Konkomba. This first substantial contribution, and the papers he published subsequently in elaboration of some aspects of the study, established his reputation for field research and theoretical analysis in Social Anthropology.

He had in the meantime begun research on the political organization of the Dagomba chiefdom whose raiders had, in the period before the Pax Britannica, harried the Konkomba. He had long-term plans for a full study of all aspects of Dagomba culture and social organization and of the historical development of relations between centralized and segmentary societies in that part of the Western Sudan. These were cut short by the motor accident in which he was killed in April 1956.

The death of David Tait was a great loss not only to the development of anthropological studies in West Africa. It deprived the young University College which he served of an inspiring teacher for whom his students and colleagues had the greatest affection and admiration. For Tait had not gone there for a tour or two. He had identified himself closely with what has now become the University

College of Ghana and with the future of the country it was founded
to serve. The College has recognized the importance of his work and
of his contribution to the early years of its own development in the
generous grant that it has made towards the costs of publishing this
collection of his studies on the Konkomba. For its part, the International African Institute is most grateful to the Publications Board
of the College for responding so readily to a request for a grant to
enable it to undertake this publication. It is also greatly indebted to
Dr. Jack Goody, who has contributed the Introduction to this
volume and whose own field researches among neighbouring peoples
have enabled him to bring to the task of collating and editing the
texts of the several studies his intimate knowledge of the region and
its peoples. A full list of David Tait's publications and a bibliography
of other works on the Konkomba will be found at the end of this
volume. Although, inevitably, it cannot be the polished and definitive
study that Tait would have hoped to have written himself, we believe
that the book will prove valuable to students and scholars as well as a
fitting memorial of the work of a very able and much loved anthropological field worker.

DARYLL FORDE

International African Institute
October 1960

Contents

Foreword by Daryll Forde   v
List of Illustrations: Plates, Maps, Figures, Genealogies   xi
Tables   xii
Introduction by Jack Goody   xiii

PART I. THE POLITICAL SYSTEM

  I   Relations with neighbouring peoples   I
 II   Ecology: with an additional note on the growth of some
        Konkomba markets   13
III   The territorial organization   32
 IV   The clan and lineage system   72
  V   Marriage and the extended house   93
 VI   The lineage over time   114
VII   Links between clans   127
VIII The tribal system   151
 IX   Conclusion   156

PART II. THE DOMESTIC ORGANIZATION

  X   The family, household, and minor lineage   160
 XI   Friendship relations   210

PART III. SOME FEATURES OF KONKOMBA
RITUAL INSTITUTIONS

XII   Divination and sacrifice: (i) The role of the diviner;
        (ii) Spirits of the bush; (iii) Libation   221
XIII Konkomba Sorcery   232
        Bibliography of the Konkomba   246
        Bibliography of the writings of David Tait   247
        Index   249

List of Illustrations

PLATES

David Tait with two Konkomba elders		*Frontispiece*
I (*a*)	A compound	*facing page* 14
(*b*)	Inside a compound	14
II (*a*)	In Kakã market	24
(*b*)	A sacrifice in a compound: Mada sacrifices to his *ungwim*	24
III (*a*)	The young men dance at Kenatshu	90
(*b*)	A dead woman's co-wives dance at her funeral	90

MAPS

The position of the Konkomba in Ghana	3
Distribution of Konkomba tribes in Dagomba and east of the river Oti	5
Distribution of Riverain Konkomba	37

FIGURES *page*

1.	Seasonal activities	16
2.	Market space	19
3.	Structural space of Konkomba	22
4.	Marriage prohibitions	101
5.	Relationship between a husband and wife	104
6. 7. 8. 9.	Illustrations of marriages between extended houses	106–7
10.	Births in agnatic and uterine generations	109
11.	Betrothals in agnatic and uterine generations	110
12.	Links between clans	129
13.	Matrilateral kinship terms	134
14. 15.	Affinal kinship terms	135
16.	Plan of a compound	164

GENEALOGIES AND HAMLET PLANS

I.	The Benangmam of Kitiak	
II.	The Bekumbwam of Saboba	
III.	The Benalog of Nalogni	*at end of book*
IV.	The Bwakwintib of Bwakwin	
V.	The extended house of Dongwi	

Tables

I	Marriages arranged by tribe	99
II	Marriages arranged by distance	100
III	Population of three districts	118
IV	Numbers of lineage members, living and dead	121
V	Composition of households in three clans	165
VI	Wives of household heads	166
VII	Marriages of men of three clans showing first marriages and re-marriages of women alive and dead	167
VIII	Relation of first husband to second in widow inheritance	169
IX	Percentage of relationships of first husband to second in widow inheritance	169
X	Disparity of age between husband and wife: all marriages	171
XI	Disparity of age between husband and wife: first marriages only of the wives	171
XII	Disparity of age between husband and wife: remarried widows only	172
XIII	Marriage frequencies of men by age set	174
XIV	Range of marriages by age set	176
XV	All marriages and betrothals of men of one major lineage by age set of men	174
XVI	Households grouped by age set of the head	186
XVII	Composition of households on a common basis of ten households per age set	187
XVIII	Kin of household head: cumulative totals	189
XIX	Kin of household head: percentages of total	189
XX	Average of marriages by age set	192

Graphs

I	Marriages of men by age set reduced to ten men per set	175
II	Mothers of compound heads in households by age set of the heads	175
III	Range of actual marriages against the mean	177
IV	Showing all marriages and all betrothals for the men of Kotodo by age set on a common basis of ten men per set	178
V	Mean size of household against the range by age set of the heads	185
VI	Means of family, extended house, and minor lineage kin in households by age set of the heads	188
VII	Cumulative totals of family, extended house, minor lineage, and total kin in households by age set of the heads	190
VIII	Cumulative totals of family, extended house, and minor lineage kin shown as percentage of total household by age set of the heads	191
IX	Minor lineage kin in households by age set of the heads	192
X	Wives, sons, and daughters of compound heads by age set of the heads	193
XI	Younger brothers and their wives in households by age set of the heads	193
XII	Sons and daughters of younger brothers and elder brothers in households by age set of the heads	194

Introduction

THE aim of this book is to make available in one volume David Tait's writings on the Konkomba, published and unpublished. This means that two of his most interesting articles 'An Analytical Commentary on the Social Structure of the Dogon' and 'History and Social Organisation', as well as his entertaining 'Food in the Northern Territories', have been omitted from this selection.

The first part of the book consists of the doctoral dissertation on the political system which he submitted to the University of London in September, 1952. This was briefly summarized in an article 'The Political System of Konkomba' published in *Africa* the following year and not reprinted here. Much of the third and some of the fourth chapters appeared posthumously in his contribution to *Tribes Without Rulers* (1958), a book which he planned and edited together with Dr. J. Middleton. I have here used the text of the thesis, but I am most grateful to Messrs Routledge and Kegan Paul for their permission to include two passages from that article (*Tribes Without Rulers*, p. 186, lines 10–15 and p. 189, line 40 to p. 190, line 6). The remainder of this volume consists of published papers on various aspects of Konkomba life, but mainly on the domestic organization and the religious system. I am indebted to the editors of *Africa*, the *Bulletin de l'Institut français d'Afrique Noire*, *Man*, *The Journal of the Royal Anthropological Institute*, *African Studies* and *Universitas* for permission to reprint these articles.

The first ethnographic survey of Northern Ghana was carried out by R. S. Rattray and published in 1932 as *Tribes of the Ashanti Hinterland*. A few years later Meyer Fortes began his fieldwork on the Tallensi, the first intensive study by an anthropologist of any of the peoples of this region. After the Second World War, David Tait was appointed to a lectureship at the new University College of the Gold Coast and started work in the important chiefdom of Dagomba. However at this time the Government of the Gold Coast were more interested in research among the non-centralized peoples on their borders, the 'Lobi' in the west and the Konkomba in the east. I myself had applied to the Colonial Social Science Research Council for a grant to work among the Lobi, but the Administration preferred to have a study done on the eastern side. David Tait had already been greatly attracted by the Konkomba, some of whom live under the jurisdiction of the Dagomba, and he had thought of doing fieldwork among them at some time in the future. Hearing of the possibility that I might be asked to go to the Konkomba, he suggested that he alter his timetable and first turn his attention there, a plan which was thoroughly agreeable both to the Administration and especially to myself, who was now free to undertake the research I had planned.

I mention this matter in order to explain the sequence of David Tait's periods in the field, which were as follows:

April, 1950–January, 1952. From April until about August of 1950 he worked in Dagomba, for the remainder of the period with the Konkomba.

Easter vacation, 1953. One month in Dagomba and Konkomba with J. D. Fage and A. Spicer recording languages and traditions.

During the academic year 1952–53 he is thought to have made a further visit to the Konkomba and also to have worked on the descent groupings of the Gã (Accra region).

Christmas vacation, 1953. He made an expedition around the perimeter of the Oti plain to study special aspects of some of the larger Basare and Konkomba clans.

Easter vacation, 1954. In Dagomba.

Christmas vacation, 1954. Among the Wala, the inhabitants of a small Mossi-speaking state in the north-west of Ghana.

April–October, 1955. In Dagomba, which he again visited for very short periods during the following Christmas and Easter vacations.

I have not found it an easy task to edit the uncompleted work of a fellow anthropologist. On the one hand, I desired to print as much as possible of his material and to place his thesis before the reader exactly as it was written. Several reasons caused me to modify this attitude and to introduce some small changes. Every anthropologist, as he becomes more experienced, improves upon his first analysis of the fieldwork data, and David Tait was no exception; even during the few years he was publishing he made changes of this sort, and doubtless would have made others too. While I cannot specify the latter, I can attempt to make consistent, either in the text or by footnote, the earlier and the later formulations. In the second place, we do not work as isolated individuals but as members of an academic community, and, as in all societies, communication is only made possible by the adoption of common forms. I have therefore made some changes to conform with the usage of other writers. For example, although David Tait had previously written of the local shrine in a district as a Land Shrine, I have substituted the phrase Earth Shrine which has been used by Fortes and myself for a very similar phenomenon. It seems to me of great importance to draw attention to the common features of societies, otherwise ethnographic reports will become more and more difficult to read, not because of increasing depth of analysis but merely because of variations in terminology.

My third reason for introducing minor changes has been an attempt to make understanding easier. I found parts of Chapter 6, 'The Lineage over Time', difficult to follow, and I have tried to clarify this by employing distinctions of my own between fission, partial and definitive, and segmentation. It seems confusing to use the term segmentation, as some have done,[1] both for a process of change within a lineage system as well as for that regular process, which characterizes any merging series, whereby sub-groups distinguish themselves, or stand opposed, in certain contexts of action, and are identified in other situations when confronted with groups of greater inclusiveness, of a higher order of segmentation. I have discussed these definitions in earlier publications; but I believe I there obscured the issue by accepting a distinction between fission and segmentation, which spoke of the first as a process and the second as a state.[2]

One other change that I have made has been in the term used for the main ritual officiant among the Konkomba, the *otindaa*. In his survey of Northern Ghana, Rattray translated the Nankanse equivalent *ten'dana* as Chief-Priest or Priest-King, though he gives as the literal translation 'owner of the land'. This he regards as similar to the Ashanti *asasewura*, the title sometimes given to Akan chiefs in respect of certain of their ritual functions.[3] Fortes in his analysis of the Tallensi spoke of virtually the same ritual officer as the Custodian of the Earth shrine. In my own accounts of the LoDagaa I have followed Fortes' usage; for the phrase provides a good translation of

---

[1]e.g. J. Barnes, *Politics in a Changing Society*, 1954, p. 49. The same usage is adopted by Middleton and Tait in *Tribes Without Rulers*, 1958, p. 7.

[2]Barnes, op. cit., says in a footnote that Mrs. U. P. Mayer pointed out to him that Fortes distinguished between the two concepts in this way. On further consideration, I feel that this needs some modification. Fission is certainly used for a process, one leading to a change of state; but while we may think of segmentation as a *state* of subdivision, of a particular sort, perhaps, it is characterized by a segmentary *process* by which groups oppose themselves in some contexts and merge in more inclusive ones. But this does not lead to any permanent or semi-permanent change of state.

[3]Rattray, op. cit., p. xix and p. 255.

the term *teŋgaansob*, *sob* meaning 'owner' or preferably custodian, *teŋgaan* being the name of the Earth shrine. Among the LoDagaa *teŋgaan* also refers to the land associated with a particular Earth shrine, which forms an area of ritual jurisdiction I have called a parish. An equally acceptable translation might therefore be 'owner (custodian) of the parish (local Earth)'. Following Fortes I use Earth with an initial capital to indicate that here it is primarily the mystical aspects of the earth or land which are referred to.

In his previous papers on the Konkomba, Dr. Tait referred to the Earth shrine as the Land shrine and the Custodian of the Earth shrine as the Owner of the Land. I want to make the point that despite the differences in usage, the offices called by these various names are strictly comparable. It seems advisable therefore to retain one term, so that the task of the student of West African social systems is not rendered more difficult than need be. With this in mind I have substituted the phrase 'Earth shrine' for 'Land shrine'. Perhaps inconsistently, I have not replaced Owner of the Land by Custodian of the Earth shrine but by Owner of the Earth. This I have done because I did not want to depart too radically from David Tait's previous usage, as it might have led some readers to think that two different offices were being spoken of. Secondly, the phrase which Fortes and I have employed is certainly rather cumbrous for continual usage, and thirdly, the Konkomba word, like the Nankanse and Ashanti cognates but unlike the LoDagaa, does not contain any specific reference to the shrine but only to the Earth. 'Owner of the Earth' is better than 'Owner of the Land' for it emphasizes that the office is essentially a religious one. 'Earth priest', or the 'Master of the Earth' of French ethnographers, would in some ways have been still more appropriate, for they avoid the possible error of suggesting that the office has anything to do with the ownership of the land in the usual sense of the phrase. On the other hand, Rattray's 'Chief-Priest' or 'Priest-King' seem to me unacceptable in that they imply another sort of political functionary; indeed these terms clearly represent a momentary glimpse of the Golden Bough in the orchard bush of the West African savannah.

There is a final point which requires an editorial comment. The reader will notice that in his first paper to refer to the subject of witchcraft and sorcery, 'The Role of the Diviner', here reprinted as Chapter XII, Dr. Tait speaks of the Konkomba *osuo* as a witch. Subsequently, in his article called 'Konkomba Sorcery', he translates the word as sorcerer. The point is that the Konkomba, like the nearby

Gonja, refer to the practitioners of what Professor Evans-Pritchard, and the Azande, distinguish as the techniques of witchcraft and sorcery by one and the same word. Hence both are possible. I believe that Dr. Tait changed his terminology because he felt that Professor Evans-Pritchard had laid great stress on the hereditary nature of Azande witchcraft, whereas among the Konkomba transvection, like the use of harmful medicines, is learned. I have left the different usages as I found them, and I merely draw attention to what might otherwise appear to be an inconsistency.

Orthography

In his doctoral thesis, Tait employed the Roman alphabet to transcribe Konkomba sounds, adding that the letter 'j' should be given the value of the 'y' in the English 'you' and 'z' that of 'ge' in the French 'rouge'. Subsequently, in his published work, he employed the simple phonetic alphabet recommended by the International African Institute. This means that certain tribal names are differently transliterated in the later sections. I have not attempted to rationalize this situation; to introduce the phonetic spellings into the earlier section would mean that the names on the maps would be partly in one alphabet, partly in another. I am clearly unable to reduce all the Konkomba words to the phonetic script; and although I could have made the reverse change from phonetic to Roman script, I have thought it advisable to leave the more accurate forms unchanged.

Acknowledgements

In a footnote to his article on 'The Family, Household and Minor Lineage', David Tait makes the following acknowledgement, which may also serve for this book.

'The research on which this paper is based was carried out, in the main, from August 1950 to January 1952, under the auspices of the University College of the Gold Coast. My thanks are due, in the first instance, to the Principal, Mr. D. M. Balme, C.M.G., and later to the Council of Senators and Professor K. A. Busia for generous grants and assistance in many other ways. As regards this paper, I am grateful for advice and comment to Professor Meyer Fortes, Professor K. A. Busia, Dr. G. Jahoda, Dr. J. R. Varley, and, as always, to the Editor of *Africa*, Professor Daryll Forde.'

In addition I myself would like to thank Dr. Marjorie Tait for making the manuscript available and Mrs. P. M. Bassindale for the photographs reproduced in Plates II*a*, III*a* and III*b*. I am also indebted to Dr. John Fage, Dr. Paul Baxter, M. J.-C. Froelich and M. R. Cornevin for helping in various ways. The assistance of Miss Barbara Pym of the International African Institute has made my task very much easier. I would also like to thank H. E. Goody for reading the proofs and Esther Newcomb Goody for preparing the index.

In conclusion I would add that in a few cases I have been unable to reconcile genealogical data (names and relationships) given in the text with that shown in the Genealogies themselves. There may also be some inconsistency in the spellings of proper names. Part of the difficulty lay in typing errors and obscurities in the copy of the Ph.D. thesis which I was using. The reader who wishes to check on these, and upon various emendations I have made, can of course examine the original copy which is deposited with the University of London.

JACK GOODY

Cambridge, 1959.

PART I. THE POLITICAL SYSTEM

I. Relations with neighbouring peoples

THE Konkomba people live in what was formerly the French
and British Mandated Territory of Northern Togoland[1] and
principally about the banks of the Oti river and on the Oti
plain north and west of the Basare and Kotokoli hills. Their territory
lies between 9° 10' and 10° N. and 0° and 1° E. The total population
of the Konkomba, if both French and British censuses be added, is
put at about 45,000.[2]

Their territory is in the Northern Guinea zone but because it lies
so little above sea level (it is below the 500 ft. level) conditions are
more severe than in other parts of the zone to the west and east.

Konkomba speak of themselves as *Bekpokpam*, of their language as
Lekpokpam, and of their country as *Kekpokpam*. I will speak of them
as Konkomba, a term used by previous writers and derived from the
Dagbane form *Kpakpamba*. Their country I will speak of as 'Konkombaland', that is, the Konkomba-held region of the Oti plain and
the low hills to the west. This follows their own usage. Though they
were expelled from the regions of Yendi and Sambu by the Dagomba
they do not now claim these regions as their own. It is the land which
they now occupy and which in Konkomba thought is independent of
Dagomba rule that is meant by the term *Kekpokpam*.

Their neighbours to the west are the Dagomba. This people is
known to Konkomba as the *Bedagbam*; they speak of themselves as
Dagbamba, of their language as *Dagbane*, and of their country as
Dagbong. The country is divided into two regions: *Tumo*, or western
Dagomba, and *Naja*, or eastern Dagomba. To the south-west of

---

[1]It was in the British Mandated Territory, now included in the Northern Region
of Ghana, that Dr. Tait worked (ed.).

[2]The Gold Coast census, 1948, gives 59,640 as the Konkomba population.
R. Cornevin, *Histoire du Togo*, 1959, pp. 92–93, gives the Konkomba population of
Togo as 18,605. The total, according to these sources, would be about 78,000. (ed.).

Konkomba lie the Tobote (*Bedzelib*), to the east the Kabre (*Beka-birum*) and to the north the Tshakosi (*Betshakwo*).

The relations of Konkomba with the Tobote (*Angl.* Basare) and Kabre differ from those with the Dagomba and the Tshakosi. With the exception of the latter, who are Akan speakers, all these peoples speak Gur languages. Like the inhabitants of the centralized states of Mamprusi, Mossi and Nanumba, the Dagomba speak a language belonging to the Mossi or Mole-Dagbane sub-group. The Konkomba and the Basare speak a language of the Gurma dialect cluster, which takes its name from a people situated in the vicinity of the Niger, far to the north-west. The Kabre speak a language of the Tem sub-group. The Tem and Gurma sub-groups appear to have more affinity with each other than either with the Mossi sub-group. Certainly as far as their culture is concerned the Basare and Kabre are similar in many ways to the Konkomba. For example, the type of compound of the Basare is more like that of the Konkomba of northern Gushiego—the Bekwom, Benangmin and Benamam tribes —than like the type of compound built by the Konkomba of the Oti plain. Both the Konkomba of northern Gushiego and the Basare apply the same term to a Konkomba of the Oti plain—*umwaridza*. In the dialect of the Betshabob this is *umwadza*, man of the river people. It is the singular form of the term *Bemwatib*, the river people, applied to the Konkomba of the plain by those living on the low hills west of the plain.

The Basare of the hills live in much larger settlements than do Konkomba: some of their settlements have more than one hundred compounds and this is many times more than the largest Konkomba settlement at the present time. Though of the same cultural type as Konkomba, the Basare differ in certain ways: for example, their diviners are all women whereas all Konkomba diviners are men; their household shrines are of a kind not found among Konkomba. Their social organization appears to be not unlike that of Konkomba but, since they do not practise infant betrothal of girls as do the Konkomba, their marriage system and domestic organization may be very different. Their kinship terminology is very like that of Konkomba.

Kabre settlements in both pattern and scale are more like those of Konkomba than they are like those of the Basare. To the casual observer, the most striking feature of their compounds is the astounding number of medicines and shrines.

To the east of Konkombaland, then, lie people of similar culture

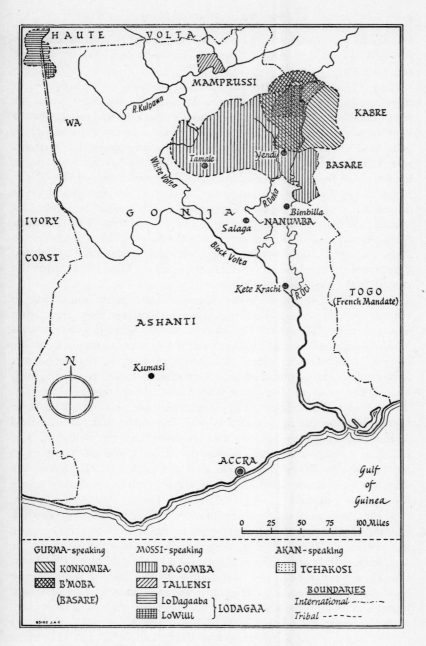

MAP 1. The position of the Konkomba in Ghana.

and social organization to Konkomba and there is nothing that can properly be called an eastern frontier. To the west and north lie very different peoples.

The Tshakosi or Anufo are said to have originated from Akan mercenaries hired by the Mamprusi to assist the Nalerigu Na in his wars. Such wars or armed raids as the Tshakosi carried out appear to have been directed to the east and south outside the state of Mamprusi and not against those Konkomba who live along the southern slopes of the Gambaga escarpment within Mamprusi state. Relations between the Benjembob, Bejikpab and Bekwom tribes of the Mamprusi Konkomba and the invading Mamprusi are reported by administrative officers to be quite unlike the relations between Dagomba and Konkomba and to be generally friendly. The Tshakosi spread to the east of the Oti river as far as Sansane Mango and south along the Oti to Nambir where they meet the Betshabob Konkomba. The Tshakosi carried out intermittent raids on Konkomba until the arrival of the Germans in 1896.

Of all their neighbours the Dagomba are most important to Konkomba, since it was the Dagomba who expelled them from what is now eastern Dagomba. The story of the invasion is briefly stated by Konkomba and recited at length in the drum chants of Dagomba. I quote a Konkomba elder. 'When we grew up and reached our fathers they told us that they (our forefathers) stayed in Yaa [Yendi]. The Kabre and the Bekwom were here. The Dagomba were in Tamale and Kumbungu. The Dagomba rose and mounted their horses. We saw the horses, that is why we rose up and gave the land to the Dagomba. We rose up and got here with the Bekwom. The Bekwom rose up and went "across the River". We go, rising up to go "across the River"; we leave and drive back the Bekwom. We drive back the Bekwom and when we settle here they run away taking the road to Nangma.'

If we allow an average duration of ten years to the reign of each Dagomba Paramount, the Dagomba invasion of eastern Dagbong from western Dagbong, according to one account, occurred in the early sixteenth century in the reign of Na (Chief) Sitobu. This invasion thrust the Konkomba and Basare to the east of their former locations. From Yendi the Dagomba advance went east to Zabzugu, north-east to Sunson and north into Gushiego and, at a later date, south to create the present state of Nanumba.

The eastern and northern thrust created three special chiefdoms in the Dagomba State. I do not propose to give a detailed account of

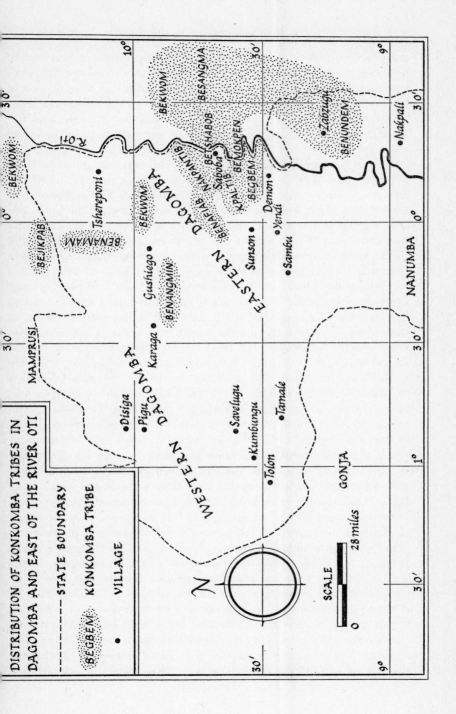

DISTRIBUTION OF KONKOMBA TRIBES IN DAGOMBA AND EAST OF THE RIVER OTI

------- STATE BOUNDARY

BEGBEM: KONKOMBA TRIBE

• VILLAGE

SCALE

0   28 miles

N

the political organization of Dagomba but an outline of the higher levels of the political hierarchy is essential to an account of Konkomba-Dagomba relations. The political system of Dagbong is a hierarchy of chiefdoms of which there are two principal kinds— 'royal chiefdoms' (*YaNabihinama*) and 'elder chiefdoms' (*YaNa-Kpambalnama*). Both kinds of chiefdom are ranked in an order of seniority.

Of the royal chiefdoms there are two principal categories—chiefdoms for sons of former paramount chiefs (*YaNanema, s. YaNa*) and chiefdoms for grandsons of former paramounts—*YaNabihinama*, in the stricter sense, and *YaNajansinama*, respectively. The latter are not of great importance here, though it is recognized in Dagomba that grandsons of Paramounts whose fathers have not risen far in the hierarchy are a great nuisance; they are men who make importunate demands for skins to which they are not entitled. Chiefdoms are metaphorically known in Dagbane as 'skins', and the skin (*gbong*) symbolizes the office. On elevation to a chiefdom a man is said to 'eat the skin' (i.e. become chief). All chiefs sit on piles of skins, in these days cow skins, though the Paramount sits on a lion skin. The royal chiefdoms proper are those to which only sons of former Paramounts have a claim. There are many of these and they are ranked in an order of seniority within the politico-territorial divisions of Dagomba. Three principal royal chiefdoms are the 'gates' (*dunjoli*) to the paramountcy. That is, the successor to the Paramount, who resides at Yendi, must be chosen from the three royal chiefs of Miong, Karaga and Savelugu. Within each of these chiefdoms lie other and lesser royal chiefdoms whose holders aspire to the higher chiefships. But even within one of these three chiefdoms the ladder of seniority is not a single line, since the smaller chiefdoms are grouped under three 'gates' to the higher skin. For example, in Gushiego the junior chiefdoms lead to one of the three skins of Kamshiego, Vugo or Bogo, themselves the 'gates' to Gushiego. Many chiefships are therefore 'gates' to higher offices, and the highest of all is the paramount chiefship of Yendi itself, the incumbent of which is known as the Ya Na. But not all royal chiefdoms lead to Yendi. Chiefdoms are also classified as either 'day-time' or 'night-time' chiefdoms. That is, if the chief is installed by night on his skin then that skin is his terminus and he can advance no farther: but if he is installed by day on his skin then that skin is not the highest to which he may aspire. The royal skins of Miong, Karaga and Savelugu are day-time chiefdoms; the skin of Yendi is the night-time skin *par excellence*. Unlike Miong,

Karaga and Savelugu, the royal skins of Sunson, Demon and Zabzugu are 'night-time' chiefdoms and their holders can advance no
farther. These chiefdoms are virtually military outposts against the
Konkomba and Basare.

In sum, there are a great many royal chiefdoms held only by sons
or exceptionally by grandsons of former Paramounts and these men
seek to rise ever higher and higher in the system until they finally
reach Yendi. In practice, the recent tendency has been for the men
elected to Tampiong to go to Gbungbaliga, thence to Miong and
thence to Yendi. The right to appoint to any royal chiefdom is in the
hands of the Paramount; consequently there are no homogeneous
territorial divisions wholly under the control of a royal chief. Within
each chiefdom lie certain smaller chiefdoms of men who can look
only to the Paramount for advancement and are unlikely to join in a
rebellion under their senior chief against the Paramount. This is not
to say that rebellions are unknown in the history of Dagomba. Each
principal royal chiefdom has its own elder chiefdoms at the disposal
of the royal chief. It also contains royal grandson chiefdoms at the
disposal of the royal chief to sons of former holders of his office who
did not reach Yendi.

Over against the royal chiefdoms are the elder chiefdoms. Some of
these are like the royal chiefdoms in that they are to some extent
territorial units lying far from Yendi; others are divisions of the
capital itself. They do not lie within the boundaries of the royal
chiefdoms. Some of the outlying elder chiefdoms and all the chiefdoms that are sections of Yendi were formerly held by eunuchs. There
can therefore be no rights of succession to these or other chiefdoms
to be enjoyed by descendants of former holders. The YaNa appoints
freely to them from among his junior and senior elders. Again some
of them are 'day-time' chiefdoms and the others are 'night-time'
chiefdoms. There are two further sub-categories of elder chiefs. In
the first category are the *Worizahonema* (s. *Worizahe*). Strictly
speaking there is only one *Worizahe* who is an elder to the YaNa and
he is the chief of the *Worizahonema*, the Tolon Na, who is also *Wulana*
or principal elder to the YaNa. The Tolon Na has a chiefdom distant
from Yendi from which he must pay frequent visits to the capital to
sit in council with his Paramount to whom he is *Wulana*. The term
wulana is reserved for that elder who is closest to his chief and in all
cases save that of the YaNa and the Tolon Na a *wulana* lives near by
the chief. All descendants of a former Tolon Na through two generations of both males and females, as well as descendants of other chiefs

who follow the Tolon Na, are called *Worizahonema*. These people
have two special duties. The Tolon Na himself is head of the Dagomba cavalry, for the Dagomba army was divided into cavalry and
infantry in a battle array of a centre and two wings. Secondly, all
Worizahonema may and many do serve as elders to important chiefs;
especially as *Wulana*, principal elder and *Kpanalana*, literally spear-
owner, or second elder, to such chiefs as the Savelugu, Karaga and
Miong *Nanema*. The second sub-category of elder chiefdoms are the
YaNabelahe—the slaves of the YaNa—and among these are found
the chiefs of the *Kambonsi*, the infantry of the Dagomba army. The
head of these is the Kambong Nakpema who has a chiefdom near
Yendi. Each royal and elder chiefdom has its own infantry and when
called out the divisional *Kambonsi* chief knows the chief to whom he
must report in the State army.

There are also two Tshakosi chiefdoms that are included in the
Dagomba State: the Tsheriponi Feme and the Malba are both
Tshakosi and their people are Tshakosi. How it happened that these
two chiefdoms came to be attached to Dagomba rather than to
Mamprusi, I do not know.

It is in eastern Dagomba that Konkomba and Dagomba meet.
Only two royal chiefdoms lie on the eastern bank of the Oti; the
capital of one is Zabzugu and its chief the Jelzorilana; the capital of
the other is Nakpali and its chief is the Kworlilana. Four Dagomba
chiefdoms lie along the western bank of the Oti. From south to
north they are: part of Kworli, Demon, Sunson and Tsheriponi.
Many Konkomba are found in all but the last of thse chiefdoms. One
other chiefdom contains many Konkomba and that is Gushiego, the
chiefdom of the Gushi Na, the second Elder to the YaNa (and in some
ritual contexts his principal Elder). This outline of the distribution of
Konkomba ignores, for the moment, the recent drift of Konkomba
into the royal chiefdom of Miong and elsewhere in Gonja and Krachi.
It is in these chiefdoms that the bulk of the Konkomba of Ghana will
be found. The Dagomba invasion pushed the Konkomba to the east,
on to the Oti plain, and the Dagomba claim that they established their
rule right up to the river itself and at two places over the river.

It is difficult to estimate the former power of Dagomba east of
Yendi. The Germans distinguished the independent and the conquered Konkomba, a division that followed the course of the Oti
river; those on the west were regarded as conquered by Dagomba.
With the imposition of British rule the power of Dagomba chiefs in
eastern Dagbong was strengthened and the claim of the Dagomba to

rule the western Konkomba was upheld. It is very doubtful if their claim had much validity. As recently as the 1920's there was sporadic fighting between Konkomba and Dagomba of adjacent villages. In this sort of fighting the Konkomba could more than hold their own and today, man for man, it is hardly too much to say that the Dagomba fears the Konkomba. But Konkomba had no form of regimental system, no co-operation of segments on a wider than tribal scale and could put nothing into the field comparable to the Dagomba cavalry. Equally, the Dagomba had no administrative system or standing army with which to control those Konkomba whom they neither absorbed nor expelled. The eastern chiefdoms of Zabzugu, Sunson and Demon are, even today, Dagomba outposts in a predominantly Konkomba territory and Sunson village, at least, is still separated from Konkomba settlements by a stretch of empty bush. This empty land covered, until recent times, a much wider area but has been filled by Konkomba drifting west from the riverain tribes.

Relations between the two peoples have long been hostile and remain so today. Dagomba 'rule' was limited to sporadic raids to obtain the slaves needed for the annual tribute to Ashanti. The Dagomba drum chants speak of this or that Paramount making war against Basare and add 'he pushed pepper up the noses of the Konkomba'. Today, sporadic raiding continues in a different form. From time to time collectors are sent into Konkomba territory to collect corn, which is sold in the markets to raise money. When the YaNa was fined in the District Commissioner's court in 1950, no fewer than two lorry loads of sorghum were collected in the Saboba region alone on the grounds that, 'The European says it has got to be paid'. In the same year some Konkomba were stopped by Dagomba on their way into Yendi market and their headloads of new yams taken, on the ground that they had paid no tribute to the YaNa. In Dagomba the tribute of New Yams is only a ritual payment made by a certain chief who lives not far from Yendi. There appear to be no grounds for supposing that there was ever any traditional payment to the YaNa devolving on all who inhabit Dagbong or enter the Yendi market. Of these particular yams one headload went to the District Commissioner's interpreter, one to the sergeant of police in Yendi, and the rest to the YaNa's household. The total value was about £18. It is rare for a Konkomba to appeal to the District Commissioner though instances of this sort of extortion are frequent.

The riverain Konkomba, at least, and probably all the Konkomba except those in the chiefdom of Gushiego, never admitted Dagomba rule. In 1944 the Benafiab, who live around Wapul, rebelled against continual extortion. One of the Dagomba sub-chiefs of Sunson, the Dzagberi Na, had long extorted from the neighbouring Benafiab. Those Konkomba living near Dzagberi raided the house of the chief and killed him, his elders and his wives. A policeman who tried to stop them was pinned to a tree with arrows. The ringleader was finally shot evading arrest by police near Lemwabgal after months of searching. As a further punishment Konkomba were compelled to build the Wapul–Saboba road. And a police station was built in Saboba.

It is all but impossible to get a Konkomba to speak of this affair. But they are wholly unrepentant. When I asked why they had killed the women too the answer was a rhetorical question: Who was getting the yams? Who incited the Dzagberi Na to extort from Konkombas?

This rising has not been without its effect. The Jelzorilana, Chief of Zabzugu, in 1951 was compelled by Konkomba to divide the remitted 10 per cent of the poll and cattle tax among the Konkomba elders instead of keeping it all himself. In a year or two the Sunson Na may be driven to follow suit.

It is in Gushiego that extortion by the chief is said to have been most severe and continuous in the last year or so. There is a dispute still going on over the succession to the skin, for the former chief died in January 1951. The Dagomba of Gushiego will not accept the YaNa's appointee and the Konkomba of Gushiego will accept no one of the line of the dead chief.

It is in this chiefdom that the Konkomba are most closely integrated into the Dagomba system. They number more than half the population of the chiefdom and were neither expelled nor assimilated by the Dagomba. It is here and only here that they hold offices under the chief. They act as his *Kambonsi*, the infantry of the chiefdom, though not all the *Kambonsi* are Konkomba. Twenty-one out of thirty titles are held by Konkomba.

The history of the Dagomba invasion may be summed up as follows: the invasion expelled many Konkomba from their former homes and this retreat to the east in turn pushed back one group of Bekwom as well as the Kabre. Other Konkomba were absorbed by the invaders. Along the eastern front of the Dagomba advance no precise boundaries were established comparable to that on the west against the Gonja State, but a number of military chiefdoms were created as outposts against the Konkomba and Basare on whom periodic slave and other raids were made. In Gushiego alone was there an attempt, only partially successful, to draw the Konkomba into the structure of Dagomba society. Even this must have been a late attempt, since the infantry of the Dagomba army was not created until the nineteenth century.

Under British rule the Dagomba chiefs have appointed Konkomba sub-chiefs in the Konkomba areas. These sub-chiefs are of very little importance for the most part, unless they are also elders. Such chiefs are found in Kpaliba, Saboba and Saangul; each of these has a number of subordinate Konkomba sub-chiefs, but they are of no consequence. A Konkomba chief is known as such only to the Dagomba royal chief in whose chiefdom he holds office. The only exception is the Kpaliba Na. The present chief of Kpaliba lives to some extent like a Dagomba in that he dresses like one, keeps a horse and wears the type of medicines prepared and sold by Dagomba mallams. But like other Konkomba chiefs, he has little authority among his own people: the important men are still the elders. The Chief of Saboba, appointed by the Chief of Sunson, is a man in middle age. When there is something to be done, such as the conscription of boys for the newly built Saboba school, he cannot call the clan elders of his supposed chiefdom to a meeting in his house but must himself walk to each hamlet in turn to discuss matters with the various elders. This would be unthinkable behaviour in a Dagomba chief. Furthermore, agreement or non-agreement lies wholly with the elders and the chief has no authority to command them in anything. Within his own clan he is perhaps a little more powerful, in that some disputes have recently been taken to him, but he is as yet in no position to act as more than a mediator.

Despite the long juxtaposition of Dagomba and Konkomba in Eastern Dagomba there are no marked differences between the Konkomba of the western bank of the Oti and the Konkomba of the eastern bank. Only in Kpaliba and some other places near Demon are there any marked signs of cultural borrowing. So far as I know there are as yet no Konkomba Muslims.

A far more potent instrument of change than Dagomba coercion is the growing trade carried on in some of the Konkomba markets. To Konkomba markets come lorries bringing prospective buyers of sheep, goats, fowl, grain and yams. Yoruba traders bring cloths, beads, bicycle parts, hoe blades, and so on, to sell in these markets, while Mossi butchers and weavers have settled near them.

The Konkomba have lived close to the Dagomba for some

hundreds of years, unable to defend themselves against the organized army of Dagomba, but only too well able to take their revenge on nearby Dagomba communities. In this may lie the explanation of the territorial gap between them, which has only recently been closed by a westward drift of Konkomba who have maintained their own social structure and religious system, their own beliefs and culture throughout the centuries. Infinitely loyal to a fellow clansman, instantly aggressive to an outsider, they have preserved their own way of life to this day.

II. Ecology

KONKOMBALAND has little to recommend it to the stranger. Between the low hills of eastern Dagbong to the west and the hills of Kotokoli and Basare to the east, the Oti plain is alternately a swamp and a dust-bowl. During harmattan visibility drops to a few hundred yards; shade temperatures rise to over 110° by day and drop perhaps to 50° at night. But the Oti river is a perennial delight where it runs in its deep channel; in this arid plain it is a joy to the eye no less than to the parched body. In the wet season the plain is flooded to such an extent that for about three months some hamlets can be reached only by boat and may be wholly cut off until the floods recede. At the height of the wet season, day temperatures are low and may rise no higher than 75° and they do not drop very far at night. The rainfall of the region is not excessive for it seldom exceeds 50 inches a year. The bulk of this rainfall comes between late July and mid-September, after the Volta, into which the Oti flows, has already risen. The floods of the Oti plain often appear to rise from the south as the Oti is unable to drain away. Even though the rains over the plain may all but fail, as they did in 1950, the region is still flooded though not as severely as it was in 1951. These floods are of no use to Konkomba farmers; it is rainfall on the plain that is essential to good crops. Indeed they may be actually harmful, for the soils must be severely leached and the annual flooding may account, in part, for the severe exhaustion of the soil which occurs in many regions.

The annual flooding and the ever-flowing river make communication between hamlet and hamlet difficult. Between hamlets on different sides of the river it is always a lengthy business. The walking distance between any two hamlets is seldom the length of a bee-line between them because paths have to detour to follow ridges lying above flood level. Konkomba also build paths across the flood plain to a height of about four feet, and even these may be under water at the height of the floods. These paths also serve as dams into which fish traps are set and as banks into which lung fish burrow and are dug up in the dry season. The paths are individually owned and are inherited from father to son.

The hamlets stand on ridges in the plain surrounded by the compound farms on which sorghum, millet and hunger rice are grown. The yam farms and plots of rice, groundnuts, and other crops are also placed on ridges of high ground. Yams are never grown near the compounds. Most Konkomba farmers are therefore separated from their bush farms by stretches of land that will be under water for part of the year.

The land and the crops are the primary interests of Konkomba. Their rites are principally directed to making the land fruitful and the power of elders rests on their relation to the ancestors and to the land. Yet Konkomba are not, as are Dagomba, all the year round farmers. There are fairly long stretches when there is little or no farm work to be done and they then hunt, fish, carry out Second Burial rites and, if they are young, go off to work on the Krachi farms where money is to be earned. Their main crop and preferred food is guinea corn (sorghum) which is eaten with meat or fish stews seasoned with red pepper and herbs or, in a meagre season, with herb stews alone. Yams I take to be a comparatively recent introduction and they are certainly not as well liked as are the grain foods. The river produces fish in abundance but game is not plentiful in the region, though several kinds of antelope are known and hunted. Elephant and the larger game, though known to Konkomba, are more plentiful north of the head waters of the Oti. Wild guinea fowl are usually to be found and in the wet season duck and teal abound; there are many kinds of water bird. Despite the apparent abundance of fish added to the game and other meats eaten, protein deficiency diseases are reported to be frequent among Konkomba. The worst cases I saw were men, though one would not be surprised to find protein deficiency among the girls because unmarried women do not eat meat.

Cattle are kept and each compound head has one or two. Only once did I hear of a man who was said to have 100 head. Only elders possess more than three or four cattle. Only two men known to me have as many as thirty and they hired a Fulani to tend their combined herds. Cattle are usually herded by small boys and girls between the ages of 10 and 14 years and then only in the growing season between the planting of the sorghum and its harvest. After that the cattle

A compound

Inside a compound

wander freely and are even left to find their own water in the river. They grow very lean in the hot season and many are killed off each April in Second Burial rites. Sheep, goats, innumerable fowl, guinea fowl and ducks are kept, and it is these that are most commonly used in sacrifices at shrines and to the ancestors.

Konkomba are primarily farmers and the farm is the centre of interest in rites and in labour. Supplication of the ancestors commonly takes the form of prayers for rain but they are also asked to keep away the wind. The sudden fierce storms that sweep over the open plain do enormous damage in a few moments. These storms break down the corn, tear the roofs off houses, batter down house walls and, on one occasion, swept away my tent.

Despite the importance of farming, Konkomba know nothing of soils and do not assess farm soils directly. Much of the soil is clay and there are stretches of lateritic gravels with outcrops of laterite rock and some sandy patches. Konkomba choose land for farms by the grasses growing on it, and as a guide the grasses appear to be more than adequate. Hunting and fishing are pleasurable pursuits which add a valuable animal protein to the diet in which the staple is sorghum. There is no very marked hunger season in Konkombaland, as there is to the north of the Gambaga escarpment, and this may be due to the introduction of yams. On the other hand it is probable that Konkomba are always on the verge of hunger and only by frugal living can their food be made to last until a new crop is in.

The year has two principal seasons, the dry season—*lepir*—and the wet season—*kesie*. These major divisions are subdivided. The end of *lepir*, when the harmattan wind (*oningum*) dies down and before the early rains when the southerly rain winds come, is called *ketetu*, literally, sweat. The season of early rains is called *onale*, the season of the heaviest rains is *kesie* proper, and the end of the rains is called *ketakuu*.

The farm cycle may be taken to begin with the digging of the yam mounds in January. A Konkomba counts the years since an event by the number of times he has dug yam mounds. The method is accurate for little more than half a dozen years and beyond that time is counted only by reference to outstanding events, such as the Dzagberi affair or a fight between clans. This planting of yams yields the early crop in June and provides the principal food through what is elsewhere a hunger season. Second yam plots are dug in early May. After the January yam plots are dug come the hunting season and the net fishing season in February and March. April is the time of Second

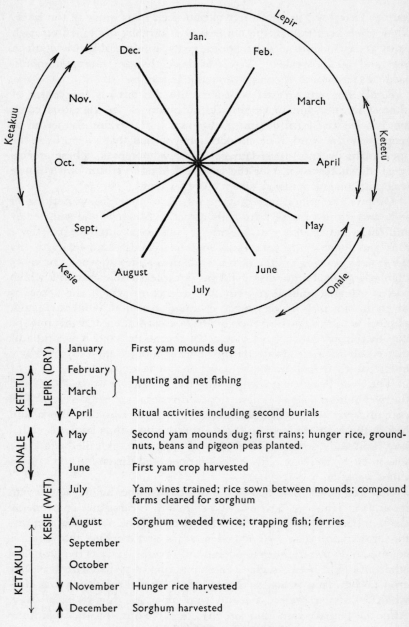

		January	First yam mounds dug
		February ⎫	
		March ⎭	Hunting and net fishing
		April	Ritual activities including second burials
		May	Second yam mounds dug; first rains; hunger rice, ground-nuts, beans and pigeon peas planted.
		June	First yam crop harvested
		July	Yam vines trained; rice sown between mounds; compound farms cleared for sorghum
		August	Sorghum weeded twice; trapping fish; ferries
		September	
		October	
		November	Hunger rice harvested
		December	Sorghum harvested

FIG. I. SEASONAL ACTIVITIES

Burials, a period given over largely to ritual activities. In May the late yams are planted and by mid-May the first rains begin to come. Once the first rains come the hunger rice is planted, as are ground-nuts, beans and pigeon peas. As the time of the heavy rains approaches in June and early July the yam vines are trained on sticks and rice is sown between the mounds; the compound farms are cleared for sorghum. In mid-July farm work is at its most concentrated when the active men are clearing the grain lands. By mid-August the sorghum is well advanced in growth and the rains are at their height. There is now a pause in farm work, though the yam farms need attention and the sorghum is weeded twice, yet there is time for trapping fish. Men with boats are out at ferries where there is good money to be earned. It is said that at one time the charge at one ferry over the Oti reached 10s a passenger; this is an outrageous amount, yet at the height of the floods a charge of 5s to strangers is not unusual. As the rains decline in September, the hunger rice crop ripens and is harvested by mid-November. Once this harvest is gathered in, many young men go off to Krachi to work on the yam farms, where they can earn up to £10 in four to six weeks' work. The yams from this area are traded to the larger centres of population such as Accra and Kumasi. Before they return in mid-December the sorghum harvest is brought in by the women and by the men who remain behind and stored in large, tripod granaries. With the return of the young men the cycle begins again with the digging of the yam mounds.

This annual cycle of farm and hunting activities is the cycle of ecological time. Time is also counted by the moon. The cycle of ecological time does not appear to be closely tied to the time of lunar succession. There is no counting of a year of named moons as there is by the Islamized Dagomba. Lunar time is, however, used over a short space for determining ritual activities. For example, in calculating when to perform their Second Burials, clan elders calculate from the rhythm of farm work and decide that they will carry out these rites in the moon after certain tasks are completed. They do not calculate two or three moons ahead. Rites are performed in the second and third phases of the moon to give the best light for the evening activities.

Far more important than lunar time is the cycle of the six-day week. Dagomba now use a seven-day Muslim week, but all over Dagomba as in Konkombaland the old six-day week persists in the market cycle. The Konkomba week is one of six days and on each day of the week there is a market somewhere in the vicinity. The days of the week are often, though not invariably, named after the market. These markets give a second space and time dimension. We may ignore the visits of the young men to Krachi, for they are a very recent innovation, and say that ecological space-time is a cycle of farm activities within the boundaries of a clan's lands in one solar year. The markets give a much wider extension in space though a shorter cycle in time, unless the different products of the farm year and their appearance on the market is held to make the market cycle also an annual one. Market space varies from clan to clan according to the actual markets that a clan regards as in its cycle. In the following lists the names of the days of the week are those used by four different clans; the list of markets shows which ones each clan regards as in its cycle.

Day-names used in Saboba District:	Market held at:	Day-names used in Sagban District:	Market held at:
Kakã	Saboba	Kakã	Saboba
Njakpa	Yendi	Tshampo	Yendi
Lamo	Saambwer	Lamo	Saambwer
Sakpa	Saangul	Ndzo	Ndzonando
Kpengen	Mange	Pumpumda	Mange
Bitshejela	Demon	Batiekpo	Demon

Day-names used in Sobib District:	Market held at:	Day-names used in Lemwol District:	Market held at:
Kakã	Saboba	Kakã	Saboba
Bewa	Bewado	Mandza	Kudzo*
Lamo	Saambwer	Lamo	Saambwer
Laban	Saangul	Kpatengben	Kutwer
Kpengen	Ngamwe	Kpengen	Mange
Lekpakwo	Bengbepo	Laafi	Natshanyuni*

*The markets marked thus are discontinued.

These market cycles are presented in the diagram on p. 19. It will be seen that a clan does not make its selection solely on the basis of distance; the choice is partly conditioned by the prestige of the market and partly by the nature of the intervening terrain. The Yendi market draws on people within a radius of about fifty miles.

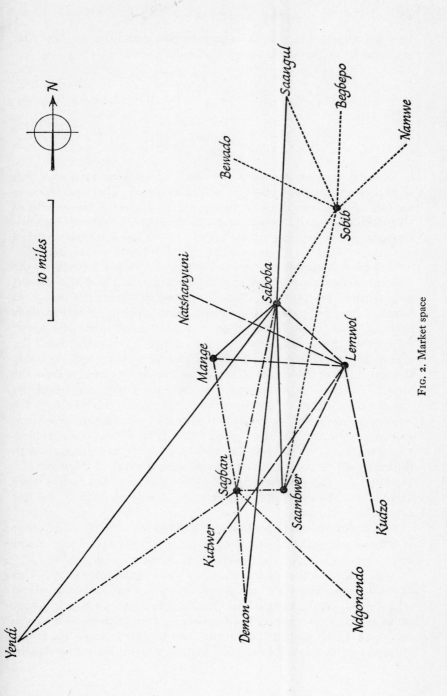

FIG. 2. Market space

It is the principal market of eastern Dagbong and the markets that are regarded in Yendi as the six of the cycle are:

Yendi market
Gushiego market
Karaga market
Mange or Wapul market
Demon or Bimbila market
Saboba market

Yendi is the major market of a cycle of markets, each of which stands as the major market of a smaller cycle. The cycles do, of course, overlap, especially in recent times with the rapid growth of all markets along the western bank of the Oti. In western Dagomba the series of overlapping market cycles is much more precisely worked out around Tamale, the major market of the Northern Region.

The growth of such markets as Saboba and Mange is probably the reason for the disappearance of smaller markets like that of Natshan-yuni in the Lemwol cycle. But it is noteworthy that the people of Lemwol have not replaced the lost market of Natshanyuni in their cycle, partly because Natshanyuni was the market of the Nakpantib tribe to which the people of Lemwol belong. On the other hand the reason why they do not yet include Yendi in their cycle is probably the actual distance plus the fact that they would first have to cross the river. The river again is probably the reason why the people of Saboba do not include Ngangen market in their cycle. Though the Saboba people are of the Betshabob tribe they include the Bemokpem market at Saangul in their cycle: this market lies some sixteen miles to the north of Saboba and can be reached, though with difficulty, all through the wet season, whereas that of Ngangen, on the same day and run by people of Betshabob tribe, lies twelve miles away across the river and is extremely difficult to reach in the wet season.

Of Konkomba markets proper the two most important are those at Saboba and at Saambwer. Two more of considerable, but perhaps not equal, importance are those at Mange and Wapul.

I do not mean that people frequently attend the different markets of their cycle; but they are always aware of them either as places where goods can be bought and foodstuffs sold to raise a little money or as points in a time cycle. Konkomba from Saboba seldom, in fact, visit Yendi market though they can be driven to do so. In the spring of 1950, when they learned that bags of kapok sold in Saboba market for 3s were being resold in Yendi market for 10s to 12s, they began to carry kapok to Yendi to sell it there themselves. They thus forced the Saboba price up to nearly the Yendi rate and in 1951 prices rose again to 12s. The Yendi price is now about 18s.

Konkomba markets are far from being purely economic occasions and perhaps the majority of the attenders go there to drink beer, meet people and enjoy themselves. Market day is not merely a day off work but a day out. Friends meet and lovers make assignations, while the business of trading goes on at the same time.

Every clan has two days of the week set apart. One of these is the market day itself (*kenjandaa*), the day on which the majority of people of that clan go to market in the afternoon, a day of rest, a holiday. The other day is *lekwobil* (*kwo*, to forbid), a holy day, a day on which work on the farm is forbidden; it tends to fall on the third day after market day. Men will collect sticks for yam vines on this day but would not permit me to visit the farms. It is on these two days that occasional rites are done, especially on market day when the necessary beer is available. It is on market day that longer ritual activities begin, to end on the holy day.

The market cycle yields a second dimension of space and time, the one which Konkomba most frequently use in their thinking. It may be called market space and market time. Is market space and time just another sort of ecological time or is it something different in kind? Ecological space and time are expressions of the relation of a people to their habitat and this is a fairly simple relation in terms of farm work and the solar cycle. If markets were purely economic occasions for carrying on trade in the products of the farm cycle against such goods as cloths and hoe blades, then the market cycle would be another expression of the ecological cycle. But markets are also social occasions. If Konkomba went only to their own tribal markets then market space and time could be regarded as expressions of structural space and time. It therefore seems that they must be treated as a separate dimension in the total social space of Konkomba.

Just as ecological time has its ritual points in the cycle—the new food rites, the annual purification of the Earth—so too market time has its ritual points in its cycle—*kenjandaa*, market day, and *lekwobil*, holy day.

I do not further discuss these dimensions of space and time now but turn to consider structural space and structural time. Structural time in the lineage system of Konkomba is exceedingly short, since

major lineage depth does not exceed three to four generations back
from the living elders. The time depth of lineages I deal with in the
sections on the lineage system. Since there are no structures of
greater time depth than those I call major lineages, the lineage gives
the greatest extension through time known to Konkomba, and the
apical ancestor of many major lineages is dated, in Konkomba
thought, to the time of the Dagomba invasions.

Structural space in the sense of distance between structures is of
several kinds. Political distance and political relations, the principal
subject of this study, are dealt with in later sections and are approached through a discussion of the lineage system. We may say
that the Konkomba political system is one of relations between clans
which are localized, unilineal structures with political functions.
Clans of one tribe may and do fuse in opposition to clans of another
tribe to give a tribal system. But it is more difficult to define relations
with other people of similar culture and structure to Konkomba,
since there is no alliance of Konkomba tribes in opposition to, say,
Basare and Kabre. Konkomba are aware of a distinction, especially
in the case of the Kabre who speak a language of a different sub-
group. These relations can be represented diagrammatically as a
series of concentric circles. The relations between Konkomba and
Dagomba cannot be so represented. A diagram of Konkomba structural space must be an asymmetrical one. This asymmetry is not
simply an expression of territorial distribution but of political and
other values.

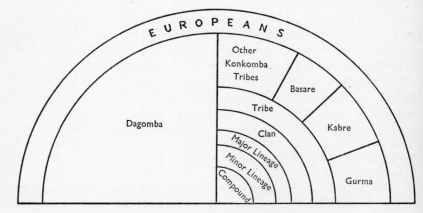

FIG. 3. Structural space of Konkomba

Figure 3 crudely represents the structural space of Konkomba. Each unit is a localized one but the diagram is not solely an expression of local units but of units of common values.

Each part of the diagram has a territorial connotation, yet, beginning in the compound, two or more compounds fuse in a hamlet or minor lineage; two or more minor lineages fuse in a major lineage; two or more major lineages fuse in a clan; clans fuse in a tribe. All these processes can be observed. Once we compare the Konkomba as a people *vis-à-vis* their neighbours, the criteria to be used are variations in custom and language more extreme than those between one Konkomba tribe and another; there is no alliance of Konkomba tribes against another people. Further, Kabre and Basare are like Konkomba, people who suffered at Dagomba hands; they are of the same kind. Dagomba are of a different kind; they are the mounted invaders, the raiders, the extortioners who will not live in peace alongside their neighbours. The structural distance between a Konkomba clan and a Dagomba community is therefore greater than that between the same Konkomba clan and a Basare clan, even though the Basare clan may lie sixty miles away across the plain while the Dagomba community lies only a few miles off to the west. This is only another example of structural distances at lower levels, since a clan is closer to another one that is its offshoot than it is to a third clan of the same tribe, even though in physical distance the offshoot is twenty miles away and the third clan almost a neighbour. Similarly, clans of one tribe are nearer to each other than are clans of different tribes, no matter what may be the ecological distance between them.

Above, I spoke of ecological space and time and of market space and time. These two dimensions are alike in so far as they are both cyclical and are both related to physical distances in Konkombaland. Structural space extends beyond Konkomba territory to include non-Konkomba peoples, and structural time is not cyclical but may be said to begin with the Dagomba invasions. Structural, ecological and market space do not together make up the total social space of an individual, since he also stands in kinship relations. While ecological, market and structural space are expressions of group relations and group values, kinship space is an expression of relations between categories of kin or relations between persons and personal values. The clans and lineages are based on agnation and therefore agnatic kinship has a simple and direct relation to the lineage system, but it is related to the political system only through the lineage system.

Matrilateral kinship lacks this direct relation to the lineage system. But, because of the prescribed relations of amity between certain categories of affinal kin, matrilateral kinship is in fact linked to the Konkomba political system. For example, in inter-clan feud and inter-tribal war it may operate to mitigate or prevent brawls and fights and so to obviate a feud. Some consideration of affinal kinship is therefore necessary in a discussion of the Konkomba political system.

I do not seek to analyse agnatic kinship, for to attempt to do so would be very greatly to extend the length of this discussion. In any case, though the political relations with which I am principally concerned are relations between agnatic groups, I do not think a full analysis of kinship is necessary to an understanding of the political system.

While affinal relations range widely in structural space to cross clan, tribal and national boundaries, they do not range widely in structural time but endure only through the life time of the individual who stands at the centre of a set of such ties. A network of affinal relations is different for each individual, even for the children of the same parents. The sets of affinal relations of the men of one minor lineage range almost at random throughout the structural space of that minor lineage.

Matrilateral kinship relations, since they do not express the values of permanent or long enduring groups, are not those which form the structural space of Konkomba, but range widely through that space at any specific point in time.

The concepts used in this account of Konkomba ecology, of the relation of this people to their environment and some of the effects of that environment on their modes of thought are, it must be emphasized, merely concepts. Market time and space is merely a way of looking at particular contexts of activity and is not the only way of considering those actions.

In what follows I first give a general account of the settlement and territorial pattern. This is followed by an analysis of the lineage system as it appears at a particular point in time, and then by an account of the age-sets. In the next chapter I describe the marriage system and its relation to the lineages and this leads to a discussion of lineage growth, fission and elision. I then give an account of several different kinds of relation which link clan to clan within the framework of the tribe. I conclude by describing the tribal system and by attempting to outline the political system of the Konkomba.

In Kakă market

A sacrifice in a compound. Mada sacrifices to his *ungwin*

AN ADDITIONAL NOTE
ON THE GROWTH OF SOME KONKOMBA MARKETS[1]

The markets are all partially under the control of the Native Authority in Yendi. In practice only the larger markets—those that are growing in importance—have attracted any attention in Yendi. Only those attended by the market officer are subject to market tax.

There is great variation in the numbers who attend Konkomba markets. At some there are never more than fifty people in a day while the larger ones may in these days be visited by up to 2,000 people.

There are few or no specialists in Konkomba. I know of only one weaver and one leather worker, both of whom learned their trades from Dagomba. The terms for loom, shuttle, pulley, and so on, are Dagbane words. I know, also, of only one Konkomba blacksmith. Yet Konkomba does have words for smith, blacksmithing, hammer, etc., which are not borrowings from Dagbane.

In the region once occupied by Konkomba, the region that is now eastern Dagomba, old foundries and smelting sites are found on now unoccupied land. It may be that, in the past, Konkomba smiths were more common than now but that they disappeared because no ore was found on the Oti plain. Other craftsmen, e.g. wood-carvers and boat makers, are not specialist, full-time workers, but are men with some skill who do this work during slack periods on the farms.

All Konkomba are farmers, principally sorghum and yam farmers who also grow some rice, millet, maize, beans, peas and cotton. Groundnuts and okro are grown on the women's farms. Konkomba also keep cattle though they do not pay a great deal of attention to them. The largest herd I know of is thirty head, while many men have no more than two or three. They also keep sheep, goats, pigs and innumerable hens and guinea fowls. All males over the age of about seven have some livestock of their own, usually fowls, but many boys not yet old enough to herd cattle have also a number of sheep of their own.

To Konkomba markets, then, come small surpluses of grain, yams, livestock, and so on, to be sold (and sometimes bartered) in order to buy the products of craftsmen.

In many of the smallest markets the only produce on sale is entirely

[1]This was published in the Proceedings of the Annual Conference of the West African Institute of Social and Economic Research, Sociology Section, held at Ibadan, in March 1953.

locally produced. But in the largest markets, those with which I am principally concerned, not only local produce is sold but also imported goods brought from urban centres by Yoruba and other traders.

There are three markets which are growing with astonishing rapidity. They are at Saboba, Galimata and Saambwer. Until a few years ago—until 1948 or 1949 and certainly until after the war (in the case of Saambwer until 1951)—these markets were, on the whole, just local markets. They were always large markets by Konkomba standards but it is they which now attract traders from outside. In these markets trading has two phases. In the morning the traders from Yendi are buying in such bulk as the market affords foodstuffs which they sell in Yendi and Tamale and possibly as far away as Kumasi. After 2.30 p.m. the market fills with local people who are buying and selling in small quantities and many of whom are simply there to drink beer and enjoy themselves.

In the dry season of 1950, one or at the most two lorries drove from Yendi to Saboba carrying traders to the market. In the dry season 1951–2, seventeen lorry loads were regularly attending this market. In two years this market jumped from being a small and almost entirely local market to the position of the second most important market in eastern Dagomba. It now exceeds in importance, judged by the number of traders from outside who attend it, the by no means negligible markets of Gushiego and Tsheriponi.

This and other markets in the region have attracted Mossi weavers and butchers who have settled round the markets as permanent settlers. No Yoruba have as yet settled near a Konkomba market but, from a base in Yendi, they do five-day trips visiting the larger Konkomba markets and return to Yendi for the day of Yendi market. No southerners—Ashanti and so on—have yet set up stores near these markets. While there is no marked tension between Konkomba and Yoruba, between Konkomba and Mossi tension is acute. Konkomba accuse Mossi of charging extortionate prices and it is true that the same products can be bought more cheaply in Yendi. Konkomba themselves, when working a ferry, take a clansman over free of charge, a Konkomba of another tribe for 3d, and a Mossi for 1s. During the floods a Mossi travelling with a bundle of cloths for sale may have to pay as much as 10s at a ferry crossing. Recent developments have neither exacerbated nor diminished the long-standing tension between Konkomba and Dagomba. For Dagomba, the Konkomba are still the despised people their cavalry invasion swept before them 400 years ago. But, though the Dagomba may despise the Konkomba, he also fears him and avoids hand-to-hand fighting. The tiny Konkomba clans could not stand up against the organized cavalry of Dagomba, but the Dagomba were no match for the Konkomba on the ground and they never settled in small villages near to Konkomba villages. For the Konkomba, the Dagomba is still the evicter, the raider, the extortioner.

In Saboba market the goods sold by Konkomba are still the produce of the local farms but the traders now bring in hoe-blades, cotton goods, beads, talcum powders, bicycles, fruits, kolanuts, kerosene, lamps, cigarettes and soap. The lorries bring their goods from Yendi and take back guinea corn, yams, livestock, cotton and kapok in season. Blacksmiths bring knives, hoes, spears and iron crooks. Barbers come and tailors bring their sewing machines to work in the market. Bicycle repairers set up workshops.

The traders who come to buy in bulk are all Muslims and are mainly Dagomba. They tend to come from the families of the butchers who are the wealthiest class in Dagomba. They are far wealthier than the chiefs. Further, they invest money, not so much in other trading ventures, but in house property. It is they, for example, who build the stores found around Dagomba markets which are rented out to southern storekeepers.

These men buy sheep and goats by the dozen or more to sell to their kinsmen who slaughter the animals and sell the meat. They also buy guinea corn which is measured in 4-gallon kerosene tins. Since the people who come to sell the corn bring it in a great variety of measures, a number of sellers group together to make up a tinful and divide the price later. A tin sold in December 1951 at 17s.

Prices showed an intermittent rise over the two years I was in Saboba. The prices obtained for grain and yams, for example, rise in every season of shortage. But the new harvest does not bring a real fall in prices. The higher price is maintained through the season of plenty with perhaps a slight fall, though it never falls to the previous harvest price. With the next dry season and shortage the rise begins again. Further, Konkomba are able deliberately to force prices up sometimes, since they know that higher prices obtain in Yendi than in Saboba. For example, in Saboba in 1950 a sack of kapok was selling for 3s; in Yendi it sold at 10s. Konkomba began to carry their kapok to Yendi to sell it there until they forced the Saboba price up to 8s and the Yendi price went up to 12s and 14s. The 1952 prices were 12s to 14s in Saboba and up to 18s in Yendi.

When Konkomba learn that a yam fetches up to 2s in Tamale, we may expect a rise in the Saboba price of 4d (December 1951).

Though the bulk of goods passing through Saboba market has greatly increased in this period there has been no increase in farm production in that locality. The increased sales are wholly the result of sellers coming from greater and even greater distances to that market, each seller bringing a small quantity.

Attendances at this market, and this is true of Galimata and Saambwer markets also, show that while some people arrive from places lying up to five miles west of the market, many more came from up to thirty miles to the east of them. All these markets lie on the western bank of the Oti river. Saboba and Galimata are connected with Yendi by two roads and the people of Saambwer themselves built a road linking their market with one of the Saboba–Yendi roads. These roads therefore provide an outlet for the small surpluses of the Konkomba farmers of the Oti plain, and each market lies not only near to or on a road but it also lies on the western side of a good ferry or ford over the Oti. There is no easy outlet to the east for this produce. The Kabre markets which lie on the Sansane Mango–Sokode road are barter markets and do not offer the trade goods Konkomba want. This is not true, of course, of Basare market but, since sellers even carry their goods the forty miles from Basare itself to Yendi, I can only suppose that the prices offered in Yendi make worth while the labour involved in walking that distance. In sum, the Oti plain is contributing to the feeding of Yendi and Tamale and perhaps of Kumasi. Not even for Yendi, the smallest of these towns, can I offer any figures on the quantities of grain, yams and livestock imported other than the crude figures of the lorry movements I have already given.

Some of the money gained by the sale of these surpluses is saved and most of the rest is spent on clothing and bicycles. It is difficult to say when cloth first reached the Konkomba. The Dagomba say that weaving came to them with Islam, that is, in the early nineteenth century.[1] I do not regard this assertion as very reliable since the Muslims ascribe all civilization to Islam. It is true, however, that the older Konkomba women do sometimes discard their cloths and put on leaves to go on the night fishing expeditions. But these are ritual occasions, carried out by the light of the full moon, so this fact is not necessarily evidence that cloth is a recent introduction. The cloths bought now are not only the production of the Mossi weavers

---

[1] This appears to me too late a date for the coming of Islam to Dagomba (ed.).

but also imported cotton cloth. Other clothing bought nowadays
includes white topees and shoes. These articles are bought not so
much for wear, but for display at burials and it is elders who buy them
so that their bodies may be displayed in them before interment.
Bicycles are now found in every Konkomba compound and some
households possess two or three. Some guns are also bought, while
the next thing that I expect to be in demand is the gramophone.
Men do not sell grain or yams to get money to invest in cattle or
sheep. Cattle, especially, are kept principally for slaughter during
Second Burials, and though they are a form of wealth, in fact, Konkomba do not seem to think of cattle as an important capital invest-
ment. They breed their own and a son acquires some from his father
but they are not yet bred for sale. Most cash derived from sales is,
without any doubt, buried.

   This form of hoarding is an ancient Konkomba custom. Not a year
passes but that some pot of long buried cowries is dug up on the
farms, a reminder of the days when cowries were the medium of
exchange in this region. They can still be used in Bawku market.

   The greater part of the money from these sales goes to the heads
of compounds. Few Konkomba men marry before the age of forty,
and until they marry, or until their fathers die, whichever is the later,
they are under the control of a senior man. All produce from the
land, all fish and all game is shared among the compound heads. It is
they who hold the money gained from the sale of this produce. But
they, in turn, have to provide for their sons and other young men
living in their compounds. None the less, much of the money gained
is buried. It is impossible, as yet, to say how much, on an average,
each head has got. I suspect one or two of the elders of having buried
up to £20 in two years. They are not, after all, responsible for clothing their wives unless there is some special necessity. The women
clothe themselves out of the money they earn by the sale of beer.
Many young women get additional money from the sale of groundnuts, which are grown on farms their lovers hoe for them.

   With the growth of the markets has come an increased activity at
the ferries. Some fords (and the ferries are always at points where
there may be dry season fords) are shrines and consequently they
are under an elder's control. All fords are property of one or another
clan. Consequently, the income from a ferry goes exclusively to the
clan that owns it. If the place of the ferry is a shrine the income goes
to the elder who controls the shrine. At other ferries any clan member
can operate a ferry or, rather, anyone who can get a boat. But since

the only persons who can make a boat are senior men, this income again goes to the compound heads. Yet this income is not limited to clan elders. Clan elders hold all dawa-dawa trees on clan lands, but any land holder may own a kapok and any man who has a suitable kapok may fell it and make a dugout canoe.

Since the recent growth of these markets is due not to increased production but to drawing on an ever-widening area, can the expansion of the markets be continued? I think it can. But not by further expansions of the producing area. The Oti plain is an area of severe soil exhaustion. During the past thirty years exhaustion of the soil has driven many Konkomba out of their native regions to settle elsewhere. Konkomba were always highly mobile on the ground and lineage fission is an almost continuous process in this society. Yet it is only in the past thirty years that Konkomba have begun to move from the riverain areas and press to the west and only in the last ten to fifteen, at the most, that they began to move to the Krachi-Salaga regions. Their principal area of settlement is in a great triangle of formerly unoccupied territory between Salaga, Bimbila, and Krachi. It is said that the place known as Saboba had 500 compounds forty years ago. It now has under 100. Whole clans have moved off together from this region. In Saambwer and Kedzabo the ruined and empty houses outnumber the occupied ones. This rapid depopulation of the region has given the land a much needed rest and some of it is recovering. Of course, where some soil erosion has occurred it will take hundreds of years to recover, but some land is already coming back into use. Further, not all a clan's land is exhausted when the clan is driven out. Konkomba farm in two principal ways—compound farms and bush farms. Compound farms are grain farms and bush farms are yam farms and it is the grain lands that are exhausted. The grain lands ideally are worked for two years and fallowed for one, while bush farms are worked for three successive years and fallowed indefinitely. There is always more bush than compound land. It is therefore possible, given that the soil is rested and that the population has been greatly reduced by migrations, that cash crops may be grown on some of this land that is recovering.

In the area I mentioned earlier it is the migrant Konkomba who are growing the yam crops that go to feed the southern centres of population. The Konkomba of the Oti region seldom if ever go to work on the cocoa farms. Few go as town labourers—Dr. Busia found two in his survey of Sekondi-Takoradi against over 100 Farafaras. They are never domestic servants though many join the

army and the escort police. Yet the young men do go from the plain
to the Krachi region, when they work for short spells of three to four
weeks on the yam farms of their fellow Konkomba. They usually
go to the farms of fellow clansmen or, at the very least, a fellow tribesman. In this short spell of work they earn up to £10. Three-quarters
of this sum goes to the 'father' of the young man, the rest goes on
clothing and perhaps on bride price.

Since Konkomba are taking to cash crops in the south, it may not
be long before they begin to work cash farms on the restored land of
their homeland.

I have not yet been able to work among the Konkomba who have
moved south. It may be that social change will be observable there.
In their homeland there are no observable changes as yet between the
value systems of the clans affected by the economic changes I have
mentioned and the clans unaffected by them. The pattern of authority
is the same in both. The only change that I observed was the practice
of hanging cloths round a compound in which a corpse is being prepared for burial. This began in the compound of a man who had been
to Krachi and it is spreading rapidly. There is, then, with increasing
income, an increase in burial display. Yet Konkomba always displayed what they had at burials. There is as yet no structural change
as the result of these other changes. More potent in structural change
is the depopulation of the riverain areas. The clans are almost
certainly less complexly segmented than they were in the past; they
are also less complexly segmented now than are the larger clan
aggregations of the Basare in their upland environment. It must be
remembered, however, that the changes I refer to have taken place
since the recent war and principally in the last five years.

III. The Territorial Organization[1]

I BEGIN the analysis of Konkomba society with an account, largely in descriptive terms, of the unit which I will call a district. The district is a territorial term and denotes the stretch of land which is occupied by the social unit I will call a clan.

The Konkomba people is made up of a number of tribes which may be distinguished in the following ways: they occupy territorial units, in that tribal territory is the totality of the districts occupied by clans of one tribe; they have different face marks; clans of one tribe may stand in ritual relations to each other; clans of one tribe accept the rite of 'They bury the fight' through which feud between clans can be ended; and finally, clans of the same tribe assist each other in inter-tribal warfare. It is in inter-tribal war that one sees the co-operation of segments on the widest scale known to Konkomba. The tribe is the largest unit of common values and though the tribe is not a corporate body, there is a strong sense of tribal loyalty. At the other end of the scale is found what I call a lineage. The major lineage, the largest segment of the Konkomba system in which descent from one common ancestor is asserted to be known and is genealogically demonstrated, is itself a segmented structure. Major lineages are the units with which all the larger structures may be said to be built, since from lineages clans are formed and from clans tribes are formed.

Between the major lineage and the tribe is found that unit of

[1]A version of Chapter III and parts of Chapter IV have appeared under the title 'The Territorial Pattern and Lineage System of Konkomba' in *Tribes Without Rulers* (ed.) J. Middleton and D. Tait, London, 1958.

structure which I call a clan; this is the unit which occupies the territory I call a district. I use the term district to denote a continuous territory and the hamlets in which live the inhabitants of that territory. Nevertheless, there is no Konkomba term translatable by 'district'. Konkomba speak of 'this land' (*keteng ke*) in contexts in which the phrase refers to the total area of cultivated land over which the speakers hold farming rights and the uncultivated land over which they hold hunting and other rights; but there is no precise term for it in the form of an abstract noun. Each such territory has its own proper nʊme: for example, Kitiak or Kumwatiak. The occupants also have what may be called a clan name. This clan name takes one of two forms. It may be a name given to the clan without reference to the district or it may be derived from the name of the district. The form Benangmam, the name of the people of Kitiak, means 'they eat meat', though no account is given of how or why they got the name. Or the clan name may be of the form Bemwatiak, that is, the people of Kumwatiak, possibly 'the people of the river place'. There is, however, no term which could be used in translating into Konkomba the sentence 'Kitiak is a district'. Equally, there is no term applied to and only to the group I call a clan. The term *onibaa*, literally, 'one man' and, by extension, 'the descendants of one man', is applied in its strictest usage to the members of one major lineage. The clan, however, may be composed of up to six major lineages and this group of lineages is also spoken of as *onibaa*, even though no genealogical demonstration of common descent between the lineages can be given. There is or remains only a belief in common descent from a now unknown ancestor.

Despite the absence of specialized terms in Konkomba for what I call 'district' and 'clan', I will seek to show that these two units are the most important ones in the Konkomba political system and that they do in fact operate in that system, the former as the largest precisely known territorial unit and the latter as the largest precisely known structural unit. In what follows, when I speak of a district, a precisely knowable group of real or putative agnatic kinsmen is implied as the occupants of the territory; when I speak of a clan, a precisely knowable stretch of territory occupied by that clan is implied.

Within each district there are stretches of farming land known by terms which denote the type of farm worked on them. The stretches of land which intervene between the cultivated areas are not suitable for cultivation because of laterite out-crops or wet season floods and swamps. A district therefore comprises both land suited to two major types of farm and also land which cannot be cultivated; it may include lakes and always includes water sources; it may include a stretch of river. From this land and the waters found on it the inhabitants of the district draw all their food supplies except salt and tobacco. Some raise small cash crops. From its trees they get wood for fires, dug-out canoes and building poles. The district is often all but self-supporting. That it is not wholly self-supporting is shown by the incidence of small markets, which are not reached by travelling traders and are attended by only a few and probably contiguous clans.

A district is occupied by a clan whose members live in one or more hamlets within its boundaries. The number of hamlets in a district varies from the one of Waju to the eight of Saboba. The number of compounds in a hamlet may be as few as one single compound; this arises when one man decides to build his house apart from his neighbours or by the removal of all inhabitants but one household. Such hamlets do not long remain in that stage of growth or disappearance. The largest hamlets encountered at present include some twenty to thirty compounds. In the recent past larger hamlets may have existed at Kedzabo, Saambwer and Saboba, all of which districts have suffered severe depopulation. At these places one sees the sites of many former compounds. In the bush, sites of whole hamlets may be found, while the hamlet name Tilengbene indicates that it was a site once abandoned and later reoccupied. The name is derived from a word which means 'deserted compounds'.

All hamlets are named and the name of one of the hamlets may be the district name—for example, Kitiak, Kpeo or Saangul. Of these only some are held to be meaningful; Kitiak is said to mean 'the place of the stones'. This is a reference to the fact that the hamlet stands on part of an ancient river terrace and there is a beach of rolled pebbles at the eastern extremity of the hamlet. Or the name of the hamlet may be of the form Udzado or Gbiedo. The suffix '-do' may be translated here by the word 'house' in its sense of a descent group. Of the examples given, Udzado is derived from the name of Udza, the present elder of a small hamlet, formerly much larger, while Gbiedo is occupied by a group of agnatic kin which claims descent from a common ancestor Gbir.

Whatever may be the distribution of hamlets and population within the district, there are three forms of district organization. There are first, districts in which all male inhabitants and all unmarried female inhabitants belong to one unitary agnatic kin-group which claims descent from one man; secondly, there are districts in which two or more such groups each claim descent from one man; thirdly, there are districts in which the two differently descended groups are assigned different political and ritual roles in the district organization. I call the first type of clan unitary, the second compound and the third, which is a special kind of compound clan, contrapuntal. The contraposition of major lineages of one clan is discussed at greater length later. At present contraposition of lineages may be said to be the division of roles between two major lineages of one clan.

There are two exceptional districts which do not fall into any of these three classes. The exceptions, Saangul and Kukwen, are discussed in the next section and are shown to be special variants of the compound type. I also show there that the three types are merely progressive stages in the development of a district and clan.

In order to illustrate and expound what I have said, I now describe a number of districts (Map, p. 37). The district of Waju is a small one containing but one hamlet of four compounds, the heads of which claim descent from one common great-grandfather. Because of this they say 'we are the sons (descendants) of one man' (*ti je onibaa*). The district contains its own shrines (*luwaa*, pl. *nguwaa*). There are several of these, of which the most important in this context is the Earth shrine, *Ntengbe*.[1] In the regions in which Konkomba have been settled since the Dagomba invasions, the Earth shrine is the *sine qua non* of a district; that is, in those regions included in the term *Kekpokpam*, Konkombaland. In the regions of northern Krachi and elsewhere, regions into which many Konkomba are now moving, the significance of this shrine disappears. To the possession of an Earth shrine other criteria will later be added, but in Konkombaland a district is invariably centred on an Earth shrine. It is at this shrine that the principal rites of the year are carried out when 'They pour to the Earth', *bi kper keteng*.

The elder (*onekpel*) of Waju also serves in the place of its Earth priest (*otindaa*). The term *onekpel* is applied to the senior man of the kin group which occupies a district or to the senior men of its subdivisions. Of the elder it is said, 'he holds the people', *o dzo benib*.

---

[1] Professor Fortes has pointed out to me that this word is of the same form as that for an Earth shrine in Talne. In Talne the word is *tengaan*, which is made up of *teng* = land and *gaan* = skin. Similarly with *ntengbe*. The word *ke-teng* (=*land*) is infixed into *m-be* (=*skin*).

The term *otindaa* has two applications: first, as the form of the word shows, he is the 'Owner of the Earth'; of him, it is said, 'he holds the people, he holds the Earth too', *o dzo benib, o dzo keteng mu*. In a contra-puntally organized clan and district the two kin groups are known as *onekpelanib* and *otindanib*, the Elder's people and the Owner of the Earth's people; the latter are said to be the earlier settlers in the district. In another sense *otindaa* means 'one who was sent by the Earth'. He or she is therefore one who stands in a special relation to the Earth, and may be called on to cut the throat of a fowl or animal sacrificed to the Earth shrine. At present (1951) there is no Owner of the Earth in Waju, and the elder therefore leads all the sacrifices himself.

Waju is also an exogamous unit. It has its own farm and bush lands which run down to the Oti river; it therefore contains a stretch of river in which it has fishing rights.

Another district of similar size and order to Waju is Kugar, to the west of Waju. Of Kugar nothing need be said except that it, like Waju, is an offshoot of the district of Nalog. Of these three districts the elders say 'we are children of one man', *ti je onibaa*. Since Nalog describes itself as *onibaa* and the other two are offshoots from it, it follows *a fortiori* that the later districts are descended from the apical ancestor of the earlier clan. This statement summarizes an historical process of settlement, of population increase, of the division of a larger group into three groups of like order. But the use of the term *onibaa* does not, as used in this inclusive sense, imply the reciprocal rights and duties which hold between members of one autonomous district. The implied relation of common descent cannot be established genealogically.

The district of Nalog contains two hamlets, one called Nalog and the other called Dzakpe. These lie one on either side of the Demon–Saboba road, separated by perhaps a mile of empty land unsuitable for cultivation. Again, the district has its own shrines which include its Earth shrine. Each hamlet has its own elder of whom the senior, at present the Nalog elder, is the elder of all Nalog and may be called the district elder. Again, Nalog district includes its own bush and farm lands and again these lands run down to the river. But it is not an exogamous unit. The two hamlets may intermarry though each hamlet is itself an exogamous unit. The hamlets assist each other ritually, for example, when a death occurs in either hamlet.

The three districts of Waju, Kugar and Nalog describe them-selves, not as Betshabob, a tribal designation, but as Benalog. This

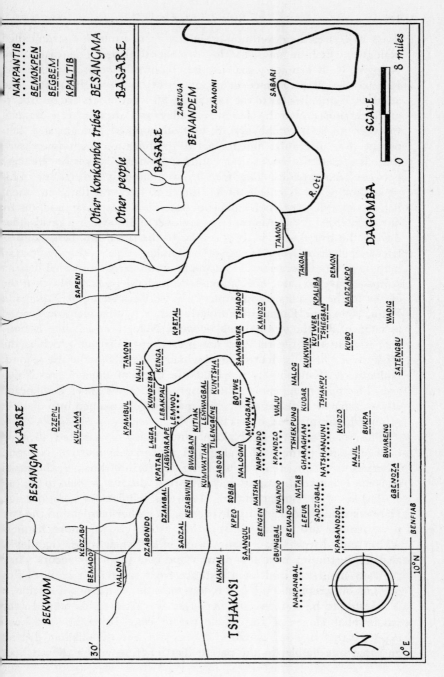

usage expresses their common derivation from a fourth district called Nalogni, which belongs to the Betshabob tribe. The district of Nalogni, itself a unitary district, has other offshoots of which one, Kutsha, lies at a distance of about twenty miles to its north, and another, Tama, lies far to the east of the Oti. Yet others are in process of formation down the Kulpene valley and in northern Krachi. Between the long established, distant offshoots of Nalogni and their parent clan all regular and formal communication has now ceased: there is merely the assertion of common descent. This is not the case between Nalogni and Nalog, for they are bound by a ritual link. This ritual link is an extension of a ritual link between the component hamlets of a district. Its formal expression is the sending of cloths by one linked district to the other to lay over the body of a dead elder during the burial service. It is similar to the ritual link between districts which are *mantotib* to each other, a linkage that involves reciprocal help on all ritual occasions. The link between parent and filial district seems to have no name in Konkomba though the persons who bear the cloths to the burial are sometimes referred to as *mantotib*. Nalog and Waju, Nalog and Kugar are similarly linked in this reciprocal ritual assistance. But the original link between Nalogni and Nalog is non-transitive in that the tie does not pass from a district which is the offshoot of a first district to a third which is the offshoot of the second. Nalogni and Kuntsha are not linked in the way Nalogni and Nalog are. The reason appears to be simply one of distance. Konkomba always offer in explanation of the separation of kinsmen into distinct groups the simple phrase 'it is far', *ni da*.

The relation between Nalogni and Nalog is asserted to hold between both hamlets of Nalog and all three hamlets of Nalogni. There is no inconsistency in applying this form of linkage; the ritual assistance between parent and offspring district seems to be an extension of a similar linking between hamlets of one district. Hamlets come into being by division of an earlier hamlet and the two new hamlets are ritually linked. But while two or more hamlets within one district have many ritual links, when a new hamlet is also the beginning of a new district and clan (and this occurs when the new hamlet is built at a distance from the parent hamlet) this one link only remains. While it is non-transitive in the one direction, it is asserted to be transitive in the other in that it holds between the whole filial clan and the whole parent clan. It might have been expected that this link would hold only between the offshoot district and that one hamlet in the parent district from which the offshoot came. The evidence from burials tends to show that the link is one between clans and not merely one between segments of clans. In Bwakwin district the link has been tested in a burial rite and the link did operate between the offshoot district and the subdivision of Bwakwin other than that from which the offshoot claims to have originated. In sum, the link seems to hold between all the subdivisions of the filial districts and all the subdivisions of the parent districts.

It must be emphasized that a new or filial clan and district has its own shrines distinct from those of the parental district. Of these the essential one is the Earth shrine (*Ntengbe*). When a man or group of men wish to go and settle in a stretch of unoccupied bush, they consult a diviner who discovers for them whether or not it is advisable to move and, if the answer be positive, the location of the shrines, commonly groves of trees, in the new area they propose to occupy. Thus a new relationship is established from the beginning between a group of kinsmen and the territory they occupy. Migration does not necessitate the cutting of all links with the shrines of the parental district, although the links die out in time; but it does imply the immediate carrying out of separate sowing rites and Earth rites. The first and major step to district autonomy has been taken, and a new clan and a new district have come into being.

Yet not all persons leaving their parental district move into unowned bush. It may be unoccupied in that no one lives and farms there. Konkomba, however, though they claim to be the original occupants of much land now held by Dagomba, do not regard it as their land. Consequently, when a Konkomba moves to the Kulpene river south of Saambu and in the Chiefdom of the Na of Miong, he does not consult a diviner, since 'the land is for the Dagomba', *keteng je Bedagbamja*. He does not seek an Earth shrine. It is only within Konkombaland proper that the question of new shrines arises. This land is, in general, 'land for Konkomba', but the particular Konkomba who intends to use empty land must discover and sacrifice to the shrines on it. When a man or group of kinsmen move into an area in Konkombaland already occupied by other Konkomba, then it is with, and only with, the agreement of the existing occupants who already have the necessary shrines. This may be the origin of contrapuntal clans, though only one instance of this kind of accretion was discovered.

To return to the organization of Nalongi district, Nalongi lies to the north-east of Waju around the junction of the two roads leading from Yendi to Saboba. The inhabitants of this district are sometimes referred to as the Benalog and sometimes as the Nalogtib. There seems to be no special significance in the form used, and I will use the first.

Nalogni contains three hamlets and a fourth is now appearing. The three principal hamlets are, from north to south, Bwarado, Kotiendo and Wadzado, while Ditshie is a subdivision of Wadzado. Bwara, Kotie and Wadza are eponymous ancestors of their respective hamlets, while the name Ditshie is topographical.

Nalogni is a large district whose farm and other lands stretch over an area of about thirty square miles. It too has river rights and its own Earth shrine. This and other shrines are in the charge of an *otindaa*, who was 'sent by the Earth' and holds his ritual office because he is the senior man of those in Nalogni who enjoy this ritual status.

He lives in Kotiendo and his seniority is that of status in a ritual category and not seniority in a kin group. Since he is not an elder of even his own division of Nalogni he performs the rites in the shrines when called on to do so by the elder; he is the guardian of the shrines but not the ritual head of his district.

Each hamlet has its own elder, who is the oldest man of the hamlet, and the senior of these is the elder of the district. At present the elder is Ungula of Wadzado.

Nalogni, has, then, the two criteria so far used to define a district: land and an Earth shrine. But unlike Nalog, Nalogni is asserted to be an exogamous unit. The reason for this lies in the structure of the lineages of these two districts. In short, Nalog has two major lineages, each in one hamlet; Nalogni has only one major lineage but its living members inhabit three hamlets. Nalog is a compound district; Nalogni is a unitary one despite its three hamlets.

In fact, a number of marriages have taken place between Kotiendo and Ditshie and one between Kotiendo and Wadzado proper. Of these marriages the Benalog say that they were not properly arranged marriages in that no bride corn or bride services were given for the women—'they were lovers and he took her', *bi bwa tab, o tshu u*. None the less, since the women can be inherited should the 'husband' die, it appears that they are accorded the status of wives.

This matter will be better discussed when the lineage system has been considered since it also bears on the fission of lineages. The point to be noted here is that, though Nalogni is asserted to be an exogamous unit, it is no longer one in fact.

Another example of the spreading of a clan is given in the offshoots from Kumwatiak. This district until recently had two hamlets, Kumwatiak proper and Kuwane; Kuwane is now deserted. The district was compound and is now unitary. The people of the district are called the Bemwatiak. Its principal offshoots are Kpeo, Lefur and Nimie. The last named lies far away to the east of the Oti. As in the case of Nalogni the ritual link of burial assistance is kept only with the nearer filial district of Kpeo. Kpeo, a district of two hamlets, has its own offshoot, Bewado. The link between Kumwatiak and Kpeo is not extended to Bewado, but a new link is formed between the two last named hamlets.

I have given an account of two kinds of district and new districts are formed by fission. There is no seniority, ritual or other, accorded to the first of a series of scattered, related clans. This follows from the non-transitivity of the ritual link between a parent clan and its offshoots and the autonomy of the new Earth shrine in each new district. It is a reciprocal link and involves neither clan in a similar link with other districts. But the burial assistance can only be given if the districts lie at no great distance from each other. A body must be buried on the day of death and as soon as possible on that day. Once, when the agnatic kin of a dead woman were a long time in coming, the interment was delayed and one man, growing impatient, demanded if they proposed to smoke and eat her. Since interment should not be carried out until the representatives of the linked district have arrived, the greater the distance the greater the likelihood of delay. The upper limit at which this link can be maintained appears to be about ten to twelve miles. It is an easy ten miles from Nalogni to Nalog and the link survives; it is a hard twelve miles from Kitiak to Ngangen and the link does not exist.

I have so far described unitary and compound districts. I now consider the contrapuntal district of Kitiak which comprises two hamlets.[1] The larger hamlet is Kitiak proper and the smaller is the single compound of Ngkwodo. The people of the district and its offshoots are known as the Benangmam, a term which is applied to each contraposed lineage. They describe themselves as 'the children of one man' even though each group traces its descent to a different apical ancestor. The term *onibaa* is thus extended and may here be translated by the phrase 'fellow members of a district'. The two contraposed groups are known as the *otindanib*, Owner of the Earth's people, and *onekpelanib*, or 'Elder's people'. Kitiak has five shrines

---

[1]Contrapuntal clans are rare. I know only of 6 out of about 100.

of which the relevant one is the Earth shrine. The clan is an exogamous unit.

The principal hamlet is a fairly compact one but is divided into four sections on principles of descent. These divisions are spoken of as Kotodo, Dzengendo, Jatshado and Ngkwodo. The two former divisions are the Owner of the Earth's people and the two latter are Elder's people. I will speak of the Elder's people as a whole as Ngmangeado and subdivide it into Natiedo and Kpambildo; I will speak of the Owner of the Earth's people as a whole as Kotodo, and of its two subdivisions as Fanindo and Dzangendo (Genealogy I at end of book). All these terms are derived from the names of ancestors, of whom Koto is the apical ancestor of the major lineage of the Owner of the Earth's people and Ngmangea is the apical ancestor of the contraposed major lineage, the Elder's people. The compounds of these divisions are to be distinguished by their territorial distribution, shown in the diagram of Kitiak with Genealogy I. These two divisions give each other ritual assistance in the principal rites of the district and at burials, but there are occasions on which they are ritually distinguished.

Kitiak is an example of a close-knit, compact hamlet since the compounds all lie near together with the exception of the one owned by Ngkwo. This last demonstrates the first step towards the formation of a second hamlet within the district. The district has farming lands of both kinds, bush lands and river rights. It also has three lakes.

Several offshoots of Kitiak have come into existence, though of these one has now disappeared. This was a hamlet within the boundaries of the district and was on ground on which is now built the hamlet of Tilengbene, occupied by a segment of the neighbouring Bekumbwam clan. No one knows where the former occupants now are.

A second offshoot is Ngangen district which lies a dozen miles away to the east of the Oti on the road to Kedzabo. Earlier occupants of Ngangen are said to have been people of the Bekujom though they have now gone elsewhere. Ngangen has its own Earth shrine but no other shrines. On occasion they use the shrines of Kitiak when directed to do so by a diviner. Yet it has the essential Earth shrine, its own lands, and is an exogamous unit.

The precise genealogical connexion with Kitiak has been lost; nor is there any certainty about which of the two contraposed groups they come from. As in the parallel case of the spread of the Nakpantib from Nakpando-Proper, the people of Ngangen tend to claim that they came from the Owner of the Earth's people of Kitiak.[1] This is perhaps because of the continuing connexion with the shrines of Kitiak rather than through some genealogical connexion. Ngangen has its own offshoot in the district of Napin.

Another offshoot of Kitiak is the new district of Banjuni and in this case the genealogical connexion is precisely known, since Waju, the first settler there, is still alive. Banjuni lies in the Kulpene valley to the south of Sambu in the Dagomba chiefdom of Miong. Banjuni has no Earth shrine, since the 'land is for the Dagomba' and Waju cannot sacrifice to it. He did not consult a diviner to discover new shrines. None the less Waju sees to it that the land receives its proper offerings and he calls in a Dagomba to cut the throats of fowls offered while he invokes his own forefathers.

Banjuni is an exogamous unit; the men who settled there to create it all came from one exogamous unit. The region is one still little populated, though in recent years settlers from Kitiak and Tilengbene of the Betshabob tribe, from Botwe of the Bemokpem tribe, and Tshegban of the Begbem tribe, have settled near to each other. Settlers from Nalogni lie to the north in the same valley.

Other settlers from Kitiak have recently gone to northern Krachi and to Kulepi, near Salaga. These settlements are like Banjuni in their organization. Yet other offshoots of Kitiak lie far to the east of the Oti and are but little remembered. They were mentioned once in a description of a rite to end a feud between two districts. Since one of the districts at feud was known to belong to the Benangmam and therefore was an offshoot of Kitiak, some of the young men of the Kitiak Benangmam went to see the rite. Of these men two are alive today and in their memories lies the connexion between these two districts.

A district closely similar to Kitiak in organization and order is Bwakwin. It consists of two hamlets, each a contraposed major lineage, which do not intermarry. There was at one time a third hamlet but it is now deserted. Bwakwin has one offshoot in the district of Namam which stands to Bwakwin as does Ngangen to Kitiak, or Nalog to Nalogni. Bwakwin is a closely built group of

---

[1]There is a district called Nakpando and the occupying clan is called the Nakpantib. But there is also a tribe known as the Nakpantib. Consequently, to refer to the clan and district of Nakpando a Konkomba uses the term *Nakpando-do* which I translate as Nakpando-Proper. The spread of the Nakpantib tribe is discussed later.

compounds in which the two hamlets are separated by about fifty to
sixty yards.

The division of a third contrapuntally organized district intro-
duces some new factors. There is no name which accurately describes
this district. It consists of two contraposed lineages, each, unlike
those of Kitiak and Bwakwin, separately named. The Owner of the
Earth's people are the Benasom, the Elder's people are the Bekumbwam. It is this district to which the term Saboba is applied by
Dagomba and by cartographers. The form is a corruption of the word
Tshabob or Betshabob. The region surrounding the present police
station was once much more thickly populated than it is now. An
entire district, occupied by the Bekujom clan, has disappeared. All
the surrounding districts, both to the west and to the east over the
river, are districts of the Betshabob tribe. Thus this district stands
nearly in the centre of the Betshabob. The market, which is controlled
by an elder of the Bekumbwam, is known as the market of the Betshabob to the Betshabob themselves and to non-Betshabob alike. The
Dagomba term 'Saboba' must be derived from a Konkomba usage.
When it is used here it will have the more limited application to the
one district of the Bekumbwam and the Benasom. And in referring
to the market I shall use the correct name, *Kakã*.

Saboba district consists at present of seven hamlets with an eighth
beginning. Of these, Kpalipa, Gbiedo, Tilengbene and Kakpene belong to the Bekumbwam, while Bwagban, Kpalib and Ntshaponi
belong to the Benasom. The point of earliest occupation was Bwagban
and from there the Benasom spread. It is said that the earliest point
of occupation of the Bekumbwam is the present site of the police
station which was built in 1944. Kpalipa is now the focus of the
Bekumbwam largely because it is readily got to, but also because the
late elder of the Bekumbwam lived there and the present chief, the
Dagomba-appointed Saboba Na, lives there.

Each hamlet of the Bekumbwam is an offshoot of the lost hamlet.
Each hamlet of the Benasom is an offshoot of Bwagban. All the
hamlets together form a district which has its own Earth shrine in
Bwagban; they share the farm and hunting lands of the territory and
the fishing rights in its waters.

It is not, however, an exogamous unit. Each kin group, the
Bekumbwam and the Benasom, is such a unit but the units may
intermarry. The two original foci of the contraposed groups were
separated by some two miles and the intervening land is much of it
flood plain, only to be crossed in the wet season by the built-up paths

called *ngkwo*. At the present time the hamlet of Kpalib of the Bena-som and that of the Bekumbwam called Kpalipa are almost contiguous and the distinction between them is not readily seen. On the southern side of Kpalipa lies the hamlet of Gbiedo, also a Bekumbwam group. But while Kpalipa and Kpalib may intermarry, Kpalipa and Gbiedo may not even take lovers from each other and they inherit each other's widows. Mere proximity has failed to break down the rule that the Bekumbwam and Benasom intermarry, as contrasted with the in-stances of Kitiak and Bwakwin, both contraposed districts, where the genealogically distinct groups living in close contiguity in one hamlet do not intermarry.

The Benasom have one offshoot, which is the district of Kpatab, and the relation of Bwagban to Kpatab is as Nalogni to Nalog. The Bekumbwam have similar offshoots in Kesabwini and Jabwarape. Both Bekumbwam and Benasom have recent offshoots both in the Kulpene valley and in Krachi.

An example of a contrapuntal district similar to Saboba is that of Kedzabo, in which the contraposed lineages each inhabit several hamlets and each has offshoots which have reached the status of dis-tricts. Kedzabo is also a region of very severe depopulation where the empty and ruined compounds outnumber the occupied ones.

A possible example of the coming into being of a contrapuntally organized district is found at Najil. Najil and Najil Setshedo are hamlets occupied by members of the Begbem tribe. Nejil Pa is occupied by people of the Nakpantib tribe. The Begbem are the Owners of the Earth. The two contraposed groups intermarry though they share a common territory with one Earth shrine.

To summarize so far: a district is a territorial unit occupied by one or more descent groups which together form a clan. Some of these districts are contrapuntally organized, in that they are occupied by two descent groups each claiming a single apical ancestor, that is, each is a major lineage, and there is a division of roles between the two groups. In some clans the contraposed major lineages may not intermarry. The majority of districts are occupied by either unitary or, more usually, compound clans. Such districts are occupied by one or more descent groups and each group claims to be of common descent from one single ancestor. When the district is occupied by one major lineage it is always an exogamous unit. When it is occupied by two or more major lineages then the district is only an exogamous unit in some cases where its major lineages are contraposed. The major lineage itself is invariably exogamous.

The district can be defined as a territorial unit containing an Earth shrine and inhabited by a clan. It is the largest defined territorial unit of Konkomba organization and the clan occupying it is the largest unit of Konkomba political structure. Clans and their component lineages will be analysed in a later section. It is sufficient to say here that a clan may consist of one to six major lineages which assert, though they do not demonstrate, descent from a common ancestor.

I have shown how new hamlets and districts can come into being. I have also said that hamlets may be deserted and later reoccupied and rebuilt. Districts may also disappear and Lemwagbal is in process of doing so. The people of Lemwagbal belong to the Nakpantib tribe and came originally from Mwagban. The district now contains but one hamlet, a place of two compounds called Udzado. Udza wished to join some of his kinsmen who have already left Lemwagbal and has offered his land to Ngagbi, the Owner of the Earth of Kitiak, a contiguous district. This offer took the form of suggesting to Ngagbi that they should together sacrifice to one of Udza's shrines. Not to the Earth shrine, since Ngagbi already has one, but to a shrine in a lake on Udza's land. Were Ngagbi to accept, then Udza would leave, the land of Lemwagbal would be absorbed into Kitiak and Lemwagbal would disappear as an autonomous unit.

I have said that there is no precise Konkomba term translatable by 'district' and no term only translatable by 'clan'. The reality of these two units of organization, the land unit and the social unit, is demonstrable in all activities. Their reality is also apparent in Konkomba myths and consequently in Konkomba thought about themselves.

There appear to be few migration myths in Konkomba. Most Konkomba songs and stories are ephemeral and for the greater part topical, dealing with recent events. Such migration myths as are found are also explanations of the totemic tabus of the clan that tells the myth. On the other hand, not all clans observe such tabus; I know of only five clans that do. The Benangmam tabu (*kwo*) the leopard, the Bwakwintib and the Kpaltib tabu the crocodile, the Sobibtib the cobra, and the Bekumbwam the hyena. Totemic avoidances are more generally found linked with the beliefs of those who 'hold spirits' and with those 'sent by' a shrine. They do not seem to occur at the tribal level.

These tabus may have tended to disappear with the destruction of the game formerly found in the region. On the other hand, clans are unstable and relatively short-lived units of organization and with the disappearance of a district its myths would also vanish.

Such myths as have been noted all refer to the period of the Dagomba invasion when some Konkomba were driven from their former territories. The retreating Kpaltib were, they say, taken over the Oti by a crocodile that swam with them on its back; when the pursuing Dagomba saw the Konkomba safely on the opposite bank, they plunged into the water only to drown. The leopard of Kitiak brushed with his tail the path along which the Benangmam fled and so obliterated their tracks to prevent the Dagomba from following. Such myths refer to the district and clan, constituting an expression of clan unity.

The autonomy of clan and district can be seen in all activities of Konkomba life. Indeed, it is sometimes difficult to discover the smaller segments because Konkomba tend to think in terms of the clan as a whole. Taking the outbreak of feud as an example, Konkomba always speak of this as though it concerned whole clans from the very beginning. Actual fights, however, begin between individuals or lineage segments and only gradually are other segments of a clan involved. Again, if one asks a man where his wife comes from, he will first give either the name of her clan or the name of her district, if she is of his tribe; if she is of another tribe he gives the tribal name. For it is only when other marriages are to be arranged that more precise genealogical connexions need to be traced.

Both these examples concern inter-clan and inter-district relations. Yet, even within the clan and district, the same tendency to think of the whole as indivisible is sometimes apparent. The senior elder of the lineage elders of a clan regards all clan members as his people, and it is only in contexts of particular activities that degrees of responsibility and privilege can be observed and recorded. In discussing affairs outside the actual context of work or rite, the senior elder of a clan asserts his undivided authority without contradiction.

In the following paragraphs I seek to do two things by describing farm, market, ritual and other activities. First, I try to demonstrate the autonomy of the clan and district as a unit of the Konkomba political system; secondly, I attempt to show that this autonomy is a function of the alignment of parts. It is this alignment of lineage segments into a clan by means of territorial, ritual, jural and agnatic ties which creates the political units of Konkomba.

All the activities and events now discussed, working on the farms, going to market, performing rites, and dealing with socially disapproved acts, take place within the territorial boundaries of the district and within the social framework of the clan.

Farm land is named in three different ways. First, it is named according to its location in relation to the compounds: these terms are *lenampar*, land around the compounds; *duu*, land lying beyond *lenampar* land, the home farm; and *timwoni*, bush lands, literally, in the grass. Secondly, it is named in accordance with the crops grown upon it; such names apply to particular plots. Thirdly, it is named according to the cycle of crop and fallow and again these terms relate to plots of land. It is the first class of names that is important now.

The names vary slightly almost from district to district, at least for the bush lands, though the term *lenampar* applied to the compound farms is widely in use. The term *timwoni* is applied to bush farm land, to distant land, to unoccupied land, and sometimes to any place other than one's natal hamlet. The bush farms are generally distant from the compounds by up to ten miles, much of which is made up of flood areas.

The general term for a farm in the bush is *kesaa* (pl. *tisar*) and a man returning from work there is greeted in the phrase *a saa*, your farm. There is no comparable term for a farm on *lenampar* or *duu* though the greeting *a di*, your corn, refers to the *idi* (guinea corn) commonly grown on this land.

The head of a household, which may be an elementary, a polygynous or an extended family, has his own lands in each of the three areas. When he marries, a man may continue to live in his father's compound, and as his own family grows, by the birth of children and by the addition of other wives, he acquires land of his own, first in the bush and, later, around the compound (*lenampar*). As an example, let me mention Sekwadzim, elder of the Bekumbwam, who died in 1950. Of his six sons, Kwadi and Satila were fully independent as regards all forms of land and each had a compound of his own. Dzimwa and Dzakpa had their own lands of all kinds as well as their own granaries, although they continued to live in Sekwadzim's compound. The former had two wives and the latter had three; each had three children. Dzager and Tigen had no farms of their own and farmed for Sekwadzim, even though Dzager had three wives and four children and Tigen one wife and two children. The order of age is as follows: Kwadi, Dzimwa, Dzakpa, Satila, Dzager and Tigen. Kwadi, Dzakpa, Satila and Dzager are the sons of one mother while Dzimwa and Tigen are sons of another. After Sekwadzim's Second Burial his food stores were divided as was his remaining land. Now bush land is not controlled and divided as is the compound land and there is unused and fallowing land there. A man may farm what he is able to work in the bush; even girls may get their lovers to work them a plot of groundnuts there. In dual and contrapuntal districts the only division of bush land lies in the separation of the lands of each major lineage. Over the years the elder sons of Sekwadzim had received areas of compound land from their father. What was left at his death was divided into two parts. That under cultivation in 1951 was kept by the new elder of Kpalipa, for Sekwadzim had been both elder of the Bekumbwam and of a division of them. That land which was fallow in 1951 was divided between Dzager and Tigen. The four brothers Dzimwa, Dzakpa, Dzager and Tigen continue to use the one compound.

My other example is from Kitiak, where Itsho, Nowu, Lati and Mewin are brothers who share a compound. The first three are sons of one mother; they are *naabo*, full maternal siblings, to each other, while Mewin is to the others *taabo*, literally *te a bo*, father's child. The elder three have each their own farms and granaries. Mewin, though recently married, has as yet no farms of his own but works for Itsho. The available compound land is insufficient to provide for all of them so that only Itsho and Nowu have compound land while their younger full brother Lati takes in extra bush land on which to grow his guinea corn.

These instances exemplify the principles of land holding within the district. They show the right of any man to farm on the bush lands; the right of sons to inherit compound land from the father should they be of age; and the principle of reversion of land to the elder of the kin group. It was the elder of the kin group who redistributed the land among the sons of Sekwadzim while retaining some of it for himself. In the second example, the elder of Kitiak did not enter into the assigning of land, since Itsho is considerably senior to the others and had previously stood as 'father' to them. However, in Kitiak again, when Gbandzar died and his two sons had left the region, the Owner of the Earth first gave some of Gbandzar's land to Dzager to farm and later the rest of it to Suba. After the deaths of their own fathers these two boys had been brought up in Gbandzar's household and were treated as his sons. The Elder of Kitiak at present holds a great deal of compound land that was left by men who moved out to Krachi; but as young men grow up, marry and build their own compounds, he will assign land to them. In the meantime they farm for him or one or other of the senior men of the Elder's people.

Since land is given over to sons as a father ages or to grown sons on the death of the father, particular pieces of land tend to pass from father to son. Even though a father may die when his sons are small they have a claim to that land when they are of age. Konkomba are not fully aware of how strictly land passes down a descent line and assert that it is the elder who always inherits from a dead person. Diviners condemn the modern practice of inheritance by a younger brother which, they claim, shows a decrease in the authority of the elder. However, the strong tendency of the territorial groupings of the compounds to show close agreement with subdivisions of the main kin group of a district demonstrates further the line of inheritance, at least as far as the recent past is concerned. This division of land is shown at its strictest between the Elder's people and the Earth priest's people. Each of these is a major lineage, each is itself segmented into two or three minor lineages. The minor lineages are the effective units within which land passes; Lati of Kitiak has no compound land and he belongs to the subdivision called Fanindo, a division in which all compound land is in use; but land was made available to a younger man who belongs to Dzangendo in which subdivision there was un-used land which could not pass to someone outside that subdivision.

Lineage growth and fission, and the appearance of new hamlets within a district, or of new hamlets which begin a new district, go together, but not *pari passu*. If compound land is sufficient to provide farms for all, then, though the lineage splits, the hamlet does not divide. This is the case in the Kitiak district. Conversely, in the Saboba district lineage fission and hamlet formation have kept more equal step and this is the case in many districts.

In reciprocal assistance in farming on the compound land, that is sorghum or guinea corn farming, the divisions, or minor lineages, of the district are seen at work. The reciprocal assistance is given when a man invites a work party (*o gba ngkpawin*), for which those who respond are rewarded in beer at the end of the day. The invita-tions are sent, not to individuals, but to the heads of compounds who assign members of their households to this or that work. This giving of assistance is reciprocal in that, should members of a household fail to co-operate, then when the head of that household in turn invites assistance few respond. The women of Okpa's household did not give assistance at any work party with the result that when Okpa called one, only five girls responded. Of these, three were daughters of the elder of the kin group who had overruled their objections, and the remaining two were small girls. No married woman went.

In Kitiak the elders of each contraposed division called work-parties and in each case representatives from the contraposed division attended. This did not happen when junior men of the Owner of the Earth's people called parties; these were attended only by men and women of their own major lineage and by women married into it. It sometimes happens that two parties are called on the same day and when this happens the minor lineage tie is clearly stronger than that of the major lineage.

The young men of Ngmangeado, one major lineage, turned out only for the elder of the contraposed lineage of Kotodo, though the young men of the minor lineage of Dzangendo turned out for several senior men of Ngmangeado. This was because the young men of this minor lineage outnumber not only those of the other segment of Kotodo but also those of the major lineage of Ngmangeado, and it is on the young men that the burden of hoeing falls. In this work reciprocity may not be taken to mean exact equivalence of return.

Women do not go to sow at work parties outside their own major lineage and married women do not sow for men in a minor lineage other than that into which they are married.

When a minor lineage is also a separate hamlet the position is simplified. In Nalogni, where each hamlet is a minor lineage, only men of the same hamlet give assistance to a junior man, though when Ungula, the elder of all Nalogni, called a work party, only representatives from the households of the elders of the other hamlets attended, and when Wanu of Kotiendo, a blind man, called one, only Ungula (outside Kotiendo) sent a worker. Again, when the Owner of the Earth of the Benasom, who lives in the hamlet of Bwagban, called a work party, only members of his minor lineage attended. However, in 1951 both the Benalog and the Bekumbwam, in the main, were fallowing compound land. Work parties on bush land are differently organized and do not call on the wider ranges of agnatic kinsmen or on members of a contraposed lineage.

Another example of the clan and its divisions at work is the late dry season hunt which follows the making of poison and arrows. This hunt may be referred to as *leluu*, from *bi nga leluu*, 'they make quiver'. It is carried out every two or three years and is done by each district separately. Among the Betshabob, only the Kitiak district carried it out in 1951.

The Kitiak hunt begins on Kakã, the day of the Saboba market, and ends on Sakpa; that is, it begins on a day on which there are some

limitations on farm work and ends on the holy day (*lekwobil*), a day
on which no farm work may be done, a day of rest. On the day of the
hunt none goes to market. The following tabus are observed: first,
sexual intercourse is prohibited on the night before and during the
hunt to those taking part; secondly, no member of the entire district
may wash during the four days; thirdly, a husband may not eat food
cooked by his wife.

The hunt was in the charge of an elderly, but still vigorous, man
who represented the Owner of the Earth, who is now too frail to
hunt. He took with him earth from a shrine to assist in the hunt.

On the first morning boughs of the dawa-dawa tree were cut; these
and mats were used to erect shelters in which the poison was prepared and near which the hunters slept, since they may not re-enter
the hamlets until the hunt is over. The shelters are built some two to
four hundred yards from the compounds, and food is brought there
to be eaten.

Six groups of hunters are formed as follows: two from Fanindo,
two from Dzangendo and two from Ngmangeado. The first four are
Owner of the Earth's people and the last two are the Elder's people.
The grouping follows the contrapuntal division of the district and
within each major lineage a further division takes place following
the segmentation of the minor lineages.

I had been assured beforehand that these hunts range outside the
boundaries of the hunters' own district. The only time that boundaries
were crossed was when the hunt entered land now farmed by the
people of the hamlet of Tilengbene, land which at one time belonged
to Kitiak and was given over by them to its present occupants. But
the river was not crossed and the hunt did not pass into territory of
the Lemwol district of the Nakpantib tribe, nor into Lagea district of
the Bemokpem tribe.

The hunt ends with a triumphal march round the hamlet to en-
circle the house of the elder three times before entering it to present
him with the bag. This he then divides among the compound heads
of his own people. The elder of each major lineage in Kitiak was presented with the game caught by his own people.

In this hunt the divisions of a clan come together in a common
activity. Throughout the hunt the divisions maintain their identity
and at the end they separate to present the game to the heads of the
major lineages involved. In this form of ritual hunt each of the major
and minor divisions of the district keeps to its own place in the line
of advancing hunters.

It was once suggested by an elder that districts linked together in the relation of parent district to offshoot district share their hunts, the game being given to the senior of two or more elders involved. No further evidence of this emerged. It is clear that in a district containing several hamlets the game would go to the senior or district elder. This elder was firm, however, in his assertion that the senior of three district elders, those of Kumwatiak, Lefur and Nimie, would get the game. I received no confirmation of his view although the point was put to many elders; but if it were correct, district autonomy would be less complete than I have suggested.

The autonomy of clan and district is indicated in the organization of Konkomba markets. In an earlier section I spoke of market space and market cycles. No market could exist solely for the use of members of one clan owing to the small size of Konkomba clans. Markets are therefore part of inter-clan, inter-tribal and international relations. But since markets are controlled by one clan, the clan in whose district the market is held, market control is a pointer towards clan and district organization.

The Yendi, Saboba and Galimata markets appear in most market cycles in eastern Dagomba and in some of those to the east of the Oti; Yendi certainly draws on sellers from as far east as Basare, though it disappears from the cycles of districts lying north of Saboba. In Eastern Dagomba there are six principal markets each one of which is the main market of a cycle of six markets. The seven-day Muslim week has not yet affected the market cycle.

Of these six principal markets, two Konkomba ones are Kakã, in Saboba, and Mange, better known as Galimata, in the district of Tshakpu. Kakã is the second largest market of Eastern Dagomba and is still growing rapidly, with the result that it has recently come under the control of the Native Authority in Yendi. All Konkomba markets have, of course, long been patrolled by police in both Togo and Ghanaian territory because they have a reputation for fighting. Their fights do not, and never did, take place in the market, for at no time was a man permitted to enter a market carrying his bow and arrows. The assumption of Native Authority control emphasizes the economic importance of Kakã market. Though it is regarded as the market of the Betshabob tribe, as Lamo is regarded as that of the Bemokpem, and Wapul as that of the Benafiab, Konkomba of many tribes attend it and, on occasions, Kabre and Tshakosi. Kakã, however, draws principally on the trans-Oti region, since there is no market of comparable importance within forty or fifty miles to the east, though there are larger markets at both Sansane Mango to the north-east and at Basare to the south-east.

The market falls into two distinct phases. In the late morning and early afternoon bulk trading is done in corn, yams, rice, millet, cotton and kapok in season, in sheep, goats and fowls; this is an export trade in that the goods are taken by traders to Yendi and farther afield. In the afternoon, after about 2.30 p.m., the market fills up with people from the nearby districts when purely local trade is carried on. Each transaction deals only with small quantities and many of the attenders are there merely to drink and amuse themselves.

Kakã, like all Konkomba markets, was once wholly under the control of the clan on whose land it takes place. It is still partly so. Each market has a shrine, bearing the same name as the market, to which sacrifices are regularly made every three years and as occasion may demand. Kaka stands on land of the Saboba district, and centres upon a group of kapoks and baobabs; amid the exposed roots of one ancient baobab lies a stone on which the sacrifices are offered.

The *onjandaa*, or market elder, is at present Jando, a lineage elder of the hamlet of Gbiedo of the Bekumbwam clan of Saboba. In contrapuntally organized clans there are always some shrines at which the senior man of the Elder's people carries out the sacrifices, not the Owner of the Earth. Thus, the market of Saboba is not controlled by the Owners of the Earth, but by their contraposed group, the Bekumbwam. As far as memory goes, the eldership has run in the lineage segment which occupies the hamlet of Gbiedo. The probable successor also comes from this lineage. He is very deaf and always accompanies Jando, who is blind. Together they gather market tax in the form of guinea corn, tobacco, rice, and so on. They collect only from the sellers of grain and vegetable products, not from sellers of livestock. In these days there is also the Native Authority market fee to be paid.

The sanction that Jando may invoke to control the market is his ritual control of the shrine. In the trees are swarms of bees and it is believed that an unconfessed thief would be stung to death by them. If a thief were to confess, he would buy a guinea fowl which Jando would sacrifice on the shrine Kakã. One market day the bees swarmed and caused a terrified rush into the open.

All Konkomba markets are organized in this way, from the large one of Lamo to the tiny one at Nalog. Kakã market is attended by approximately 500 persons excluding those from the hamlets within a two-mile radius of the market. These hamlets have a population of slightly over 1,000, of whom the vast majority attend the market. Of the 500, 70 per cent come from east of the Oti and from distances of up to thirty miles. Nalog market draws no more than fifty people at a time all of whom come from the immediate vicinity of Nalog. The figures given above do not include the traders who come in by lorry from Yendi; no outside traders visit Nalog.

Thus, though markets may now draw on people and goods from over a wide area, the organization of a market may still rest wholly in the hands of an elder of a kin group on whose land the market takes place; should the market be a large and growing one its organization still remains partly in the hands of such an elder. The market elder holds his office in virtue of his status in a lineage of the clan which holds the district.

In ritual activities the clan (and district) is also a unit, the largest ritual unit known to Konkomba. It is true that clans participate in each other's rites and that representatives of several clans will gather to sacrifice to the land of a clan carrying out the rite of 'they sacrifice to the Earth'. At such a rite, however, the sacrifices are made to the land of one clan at a time. There are no tribal rites. There is no wider conjunction of ritual segments than the segments of one clan; though these segments may be joined by representatives of other clans, such visitors come from clans which stand in special, dyadic ritual relations to the clan performing the rite.

As an example I may instance the assembling of the divisions of the district of Nalogni in a purificatory rite. A child died after a short illness. It was buried with little ceremony, in the presence of the elder of the clan and the elder of the father's minor lineage. Four days later a rite was performed to expel from the clan the sickness that killed the child. There were present Dzambil, the father of the child; Tamwin, the elder of Kotiendo, the subdivision of the district in which the child died; Wangma, another senior man of Kotiendo; and Ungula, the elder of Wadzado and of all Nalogni. None represented the third division of the district, Bwarado. A medicine called *Kaalku* (possibly, 'do not kill') was made by soaking the roots of five different trees and plants in water. This liquor was put into a pot and the roots were placed on a mat. Tamwin poured beer into a calabash while Wangma spoke first and addressed the ancestors generally, not calling on them each by name. He said that the ancestors knew this medicine and had given it to their descendants. If any root had been omitted, let the ancestors tell the living. Tamwin then spoke, pouring beer on to the ground at the name of each ancestor:

'You gave us this medicine; I take it and give that child. I do not know what it is; if it is water I give. My ancestor Bwara! take water and give to your forefathers. I do not know them; tell them how it is. My ancestor Kotie! take your water, give to your younger brothers, give to your older brothers, and give to your forefathers. They all ate of this medicine; you will reach them all. You know how to make this medicine to give and stay (? keep) inside the compound. You know how to do it; I do not know.'

'Udzwar! you too take; your water is there; give to my fathers, and give to my grandfathers who stand in the compound.'

Tamwin now killed a cock and dropped the blood on the roots. He again spoke:

'*Kaalku*! your red cock is here. I give it you now; take it and give to those you know. I do not know them; you will tell them for me.'

In these addresses both the medicine and the ancestors are addressed, but not the ancestor of each subdivision of Nalogni. Tamwin addressed the dead Bwara, who had no representative at the rite, but failed to address the dead Makpada whose descendant, Ungula, was present. It is typical of Konkomba rites that something or someone is omitted and therefore no significance need be read into the omission of Makpada.

The roots were put back into the liquor which was then taken into Dzambil's compound. In each room Dzambil dipped his finger into the pot and drew a ring round the wall of each room. This concluded the rite but for the drinking of beer.

The district of Nalogni is occupied by a major lineage of which the three subdivisions are minor lineages. Each of these emerges in the course of the rite. The same subdivisions of Nalogni are also seen at work in the rites performed after the guinea corn harvest has been gathered in. New food rites vary somewhat in form; on this occasion they were performed in the separate compounds. For example, Mada of Kotiendo gathered his wife and two small daughters together. First he killed two small chickens, one for each child, letting the blood drop on the wall of his wife's room. Into the blood he stuck some of the chickens' feathers. He then put a calabash on the ground. This calabash symbolizes his *ungwin*, a word which may be translated as 'spirit' since it is described as 'that which God gives a man'. While Mada poured water over his calabash he spoke as follows:

> 'My spirit! if you rest in a hole in a tree, take new food. Rise up and get it. If I go to the farm and hoe one furrow, let there be two furrows. If my wife hold a child it grows; when day breaks let me hear she is pregnant.'

He then killed a guinea fowl, letting the blood drop on to the base of the upturned calabash.

This rite was performed by seven people that morning. It was Dzambil, the senior man, who gave the word to begin and not Tamwin, the elder of Kotiendo. Tamwin had already completed these rites in his own house; nor were any rites carried out this day in either Wadzado or Bwarado.

Those who performed the rites were Mada, Wanu, Bofun, Opia, Nampa, Sukpe and Dzambil whose compounds, 7, 9, 10, 8, 5, 3, 12 respectively, are in the plan of the hamlet of Kotiendo at the end of the book. If there is a distinction between those of Kotiendo who did and did not perform the rite on this day, then it is a territorial one. Of the group of compounds lying to the northern end of Kotiendo, the head of only one failed to take part; this was Babie, a trypanoso-miasis case, who is frequently incapable of rational action. The two groups, those who performed the rites and those who did not, are not distinctive subgroups of a minor lineage since Dzambil and Tamwin are full brothers. In Kotiendo the elder first carried out the rite himself and thus indicated that it should now be performed. House-holders then carried it out in spatially distinguished groups, each led by a senior man.

Before the series of household rites just described are started, a diviner is consulted on behalf of the whole district to discover whether or not there is some ritual impediment to their performance. On this occasion the diviner found that a girl of Kotiendo was ritually unprepared and that certain purificatory rites should be carried out on her behalf. At the time of her birth her father had failed to kill the birth fowls for her. In fact, I know of no instance in which this was done, but fathers always say that some day they will do it. Now her 'spirit' wanted a fowl and a ring. Since she was pregnant at the time, the full rites could not be performed, and a provisional sacrifice was therefore made to enable the guinea corn rites to continue. The diviner had found that Tamwin, elder of Kotiendo, her minor lineage, had to provide the fowl, that Ungula, elder of all Nalogni, her clan, had to pour the water and beer during the rite, and that Madug of Bwarado, the third minor lineage, had to kill the fowl. Both Ungula and Madug sent a son to represent them. Thus, in the preliminary rite intended to clear the way for a major rite, all three divisions of Nalogni were represented. This enabled the people of Kotiendo, that is, members of one minor lineage, to perform their rite, which was done in the individual compounds.

The performance of the New Yam rites by the Ngmangeado division of Kitiak district was another instance of the subdivisions of a district working separately. While certain rites were carried out at Ngkwodo, an offshoot hamlet, the same ones were performed at the compound of Mamam, the elder of Ngmangeado. These are the two minor lineages of one major lineage. The rite began as one for Mamam's compound but afterwards other rites were carried on for those who 'hold spirits' in the major lineage. We are only concerned with the first rite here.

On the floor of the compound the following objects were laid: six 'spirit calabashes' (*titatwir*, s. *ketetug*) belonging to members of Mamam's household who 'hold spirits', containing feathers from fowls sacrificed to the spirits which they symbolize; a bowl which is filled with earth from the shrine *Luwaa Tshiag* in Nakpando, belonging to Minjendo, Mamam's wife, who was 'sent into the world' by its power; one diviner's staff owned by Bisa, Mamam's son; one *ntshejatu*, a calabash covered with netting, a woman's spirit symbol which is owned by Tawo, Mamam's second wife. Those ritual objects not belonging to 'spirit holders' belonged to members of the household; the 'spirit holders' came to Mamam's house for the rites since the oldest of them is Mamam's son, Bisa. Mamam mixed water and beer and poured it on the ground while he spoke the following invocation:

> 'My father! Ngmangea! Jatsha! Koko! Njopu! For you I do something. Arise and stand on the thing. New food comes, children come to the compound. A man holds his word; we keep it. Take new food. We want to eat. We want also to give you, my forefathers, new food, so that you too may eat.'

Mamam then killed a fowl and dropped blood on the spirit calabashes. The sacrifices to the spirits then began.

Again, the divisions of the district are seen carrying out a rite, not together, but simultaneously. On this occasion the rites were carried out by one of a pair of contraposed lineages of the district. The other lineage took no share in the rite. Indeed, the rites carried out by that lineage were extremely sketchy and performed on an earlier day, while its 'spirit holders' carried out their rites for their spirits during Namishie. Namishie is the Konkomba name for the fire festival widely known among the Mole-Dagbane speaking peoples as Bugum. So far very few Konkomba districts take note of Bugum; the Owner of the Earth's people of Kitiak used it to carry out rites for their spirits, while in Saboba district the children came out with blazing grass torches and held mock fights. As they run round they chant:

> *N kashie. Kokwo shie.*
> I will burn. All will burn.

That was the extent of the ceremony.

These outlines of rites show the contrapuntally and the unitarily organized districts in ritual contexts. Those carried out separately in the different compounds in Kotiendo together make up a whole which is a rite of a minor lineage and hamlet. Those carried out in the separate compounds of Ngmangeado together make up a whole which is a rite of a major lineage, though that lineage occupies only part of the hamlet of Kitiak. The rites described are therefore carried out by kin-groups and not by territorial units. Yet the two divisions of Kitiak often come together for ritual purposes, as a rite at the Earth shrine will show. The following people were present at the rite: Nadzo and Nagmaken of Fanindo, Ngagbi and Okpa of Dzangendo, Mamam and Nakwadzar of Ngmangeado. Thus the Owner of the Earth's people and the Elder's people were both represented but the second minor lineage of Ngmangeado were not; no very senior man is living there at present. Some time earlier the wife of a Kitiak man had gone on a visit with her child and during the course of this her child had died. A diviner found that the reason for the child's death was that the Earth wanted a white sheep. Gathered together, the elders and senior men of the district killed a white sheep at the Earth shrine. Ngagbi addressed the shrine, since he is the Owner of the Earth and had provided the sheep; Nadzo killed the sheep and Mamam spoke the parting invocation. Thus the three senior men of the principal divisions of the district had each a role in a rite which concerned their common land.

In the rites so far described the district acts as a ritual whole, but it also has parts which can, on occasion, work by themselves. The ritual autonomy of the parts is seen in the New Guinea Corn rites and New Yam rites which are carried out in the separate compounds of the minor or major lineage. The unity of the minor lineage is seen in the rite to expel a sickness from Kotiendo and in the rites for those who 'hold spirits' held at Ngkwodo and Jatshado. The unity of the major lineage is seen in the rite to purify the girl before the New Food rites could go on. And finally, the unity of the two contraposed lineages is seen in the Earth rites performed jointly by members of both the groups.

We now come to what is perhaps the most important aspect of district and clan autonomy, namely, the district and clan as an area and entity of social control respectively. It might indeed be assumed, *a priori*, that in a society such as this if the clan and district is the major ritual unit then it will also be the major unit of social control. It is in fact the case that these two concepts—ritual unity and jural unity—do in this society go *pari passu*. The more closely two men are united in ritual ties, and this closeness follows, in the main, from closeness of agnatic kinship, then the more surely will the sanctions on correct behaviour operate between them. Within the clan are the localized lineage segments and as structural distance between segments increases so does the force of the application of moral control diminish.

The principle stated by Fortes (1945), that the unit of moral control is the group of men that sacrifice together, is true also of Konkomba society. But it is here less firmly stated and I never saw it invoked; none the less, should one clansman offend against his fellow clansman, the offence can be expiated or eradicated by sacrificing together.[1]

The clan is a body bound by moral obligations. Within the bounds of the district there is a sense of moral obligation towards one's fellow clansmen that decreases with the increase in structural distance. But there is also a consciousness of moral obligation towards the clan and district as a whole. This is best seen in inter-clan disputes when whole clans may be involved in feud[2] or brawl. In feud a man may be obliged to aid any man of his clan; in a fight over fishing or hunting rights a man may be called on to defend any part of his clan's district against encroachment.

I do not here discuss 'law' because Konkomba have no legal

---

[1]This paragraph is quoted from p. 186 of the article 'Territorial and Lineage System of Konkomba' in *Tribes Without Rulers*. The reference is to Fortes' *The Dynamics of Clanship among the Tallensi*, 1945.

[2]In the article in *Tribes Without Rulers*, the term warfare has been substituted for feud. I have retained the original as a distinction is later made between fighting within the tribe ('feud') and fighting between tribes ('war') (ed.).

institutions, in that there are no patterns for formal legislation nor for judicial decisions nor are there law enforcement officers of any kind. Law, in the sense of 'social control through the systematic application of the force of politically organised society',[1] does not exist in Konkombaland. This assertion is no less true at the clan and district level than it is at the tribal level. Nowhere does there exist a Council of Elders in the sense of a coming together of a group of senior men to hear both sides of a case and to reach a decision on it. When Konkomba call upon elders in a dispute it is in order that the elder of one disputant can put his case to the elder of the other disputant. Each elder takes up and argues the case of his own follower and together they may reach agreement. But this is neither arbitration nor decision by a judicial body, nor can the original disputants be compelled by force to accept any agreement of their elders.

Evans-Pritchard[2] speaks of law as 'a moral obligation to settle disputes by conventional methods, and not in the sense of legal procedure or legal institutions. We speak only of civil law, for there do not seem to be any actions considered injurious to the whole community and punished by it.' In a similar sense the term 'law' could be applied to Konkomba practice, yet it seems appropriate and useful to reserve the term to the stricter usage of Radcliffe-Brown and Seagle[3] usages in which law is prescriptive as well as normative and is publicly sanctioned. Yet, as among the Nuer so among the Konkomba, there seem to be no public delicts and even witchcraft is, except for repeated offences, a private delict.

Wilson[4] speaks of law as 'that customary form of action in society which is kept in being by the inherent necessities of systematic co-operation among its members.' In this he seems to be expressing an idea similar to Evans-Pritchard's 'moral obligation'. Wilson goes on to say 'a breach of law is a course of action, on the part of some individual or minority group, which is inconsistent with the normal and accepted form of co-operative action and which would therefore, if unchecked, make continued relationship between law breakers and other members of their community impossible; it threatens to dissolve society into anarchy.' Among the Konkomba it would perhaps be too much to say that such actions threaten anarchy, but otherwise

[1] Roscoe Pound, quoted by A. R. Radcliffe-Brown, article 'Primitive Law' for *Encyclopaedia of the Social Sciences*, reprinted in *Structure and Function*, 1952, p. 212.
[2] E. E. Evans-Pritchard, *The Nuer*, 1940, p. 168.
[3] W. Seagle, *The Quest for Law*, Knopf, N.Y. 1941, p. 7.
[4] G. Wilson, *Land Rights of Individuals among the Nyakyusa*, R-L Papers, 1938, p. 22.

the point he makes goes near to the facts of their situation. Some acts by individuals and groups impede communication within the society and disrupt the steady running of the parts. When such acts occur, then countervailing action may be taken to restore communication. Or it may be left to God to intervene, for when Konkomba say 'God will not agree', they imply that a religious sanction operates to adjust imbalance.

What Evans-Pritchard emphasizes is a positive obligation to behave according to standards. What Wilson emphasizes in the second quotation is action taken by society after a breach of customary standards. The existence both of such standards and of sanctions on breach of them are, of course, found in Konkomba society. But the standards were at no time laid down by a legislature, are not interpreted by a judiciary and are not enforced by an executive. Therefore, if the term 'law' is to be used only in the strict sense of Radcliffe-Brown's definition, some new term should be found to cover the quasi-legal or para-legal methods of peoples like Konkomba. I will speak of jural activities. This is a term used by Fortes; he says that jural relations involve lineage segments: 'What we find . . . is that all jural relations involve a configuration of rights on the one side and a configuration of responsibilities on the other, both corresponding to the range of lineage segments involved. And no jural transaction is complete until the whole configuration of rights, and responsibilities, on both sides, is brought into action'.[1] By the term 'jural' I seek rather the quasi-legal executive activities: those acts of individuals, as in retaliation, or of groups, as in ostracism, which are a reaction on the part of those offended against an offender, acts of retribution which are approved by Konkomba society as a whole. An offender who calls out against him the anger of his society has failed to attain the required standards of behaviour, and in retributive acts or jural acts by individuals or groups against the offender the moral support of the society is always with the offended person. A jural act in this sense is a punitive act which has the moral backing of the society.

This definition must also include the action of the elder in situations of breach of custom. The elder's role is never punitive or retaliatory, as I see it, for he does no more than exert his ritual power and his moral authority to insist, for example in a case of theft, on restitution by the thief. In brawls he commands obedience because brawling is an offence against the Earth and the elder who stands in

[1] *The Dynamics of Clanship among the Tallensi*, 1945, p. 230.

ritual relations to the Earth is its guardian. The elder is the oldest man of the clan, the closest to the Earth as well as to the ancestors, and is the repository of custom. His authority is moral and ritual; he is most learned in the mores of his clan and his role is primarily to remind his people of their moral obligations to their clansfolk, to recall them to proper standards of behaviour. Though he has no power to punish by force, still, to run counter to his commands is itself sacrilege. It may be added that when sanctions are enforced against an offender they have always the backing of the elder.

Let us consider some examples of acts which impede communication and the jural activities which restore it. These acts include the attempted killing of a fellow-clansman, quarrels and brawls, wife-beating, destruction of crops and theft. In this place I consider these acts only within the bounds of one clan. Later, when I have more fully analysed the structure of a clan, I give some examples of similar acts between clans. But between clans or between members of different clans jural acts are wholly retaliatory and often lead to clan feud or an outbreak of tribal war. Up to the level of clan and district there is the authority of the senior elder of a clan and of the elders of lineages acting in concert to compose quarrels and brawls within the district. Up to this level there is a ritual authority which can, in virtue of the elder's relation to the Earth, command obedience because he may pronounce that the 'Earth will spoil' if certain acts are done. But there is no authority able to compose quarrels between men of different clans. There are special relations between neighbouring clans, which mitigate but do not obviate quarrels between neighbours. There is no tribal elder or other tribal ritual authority who can even arbitrate between men of different clans. Still less is there any supratribal authority; between tribes there is permanent hostility and war. To kill a fellow-clansman is an offence so awful that nothing can be done either to punish the killer or to save him from God's anger. To kill a man of a different clan 'does not matter'. It is the clan as a social unit within its district boundaries that is the autonomous unit of social control, within which jural acts are other than simple retaliation and within which there is a supreme ritual and moral authority.

No instance of homicide is known in which one man killed another man of his own clan. On two occasions there were quarrels which almost led to homicide. The first of these is readily dismissed since the would-be killer was Babie, the trypanosomiasis case, who fired arrows at and wounded one of his brothers. He was not held to be responsible for his actions: 'spirits hold him' it was said.

The second instance is much more complex. Ajila quarrelled with
Nnekwe; both are members of one minor lineage and live in the same
hamlet. A man brought his arrows with him to the market at Kakã
and Nnekwe stood by and said nothing, though arrows are forbidden
in the market-place by both Konkomba custom and British law.
Ajila arrived and said that he was the son of the market elder. He
then turned to Nnekwe and demanded to know why he had stood
there silently and had neither spoken to the market elder nor told
the man to take his arrows away. The point of this protest to Nnekwe
is that both men are members of the minor lineage in which the
market eldership runs. Nnekwe became angry; they fought and
Ajila threw Nnekwe. Then each went home shouting threats. Ajila
fetched his bow and arrows and came out announcing that *n ni
Nnekwe kuku tab*, 'I and Nnekwe will kill each other'. Dzakpa, a
kinsman of both the men, caught Ajila while the sergeant of police
stood by. These two calmed Ajila and took him off to drink beer.
Later in the day Nnekwe went to the police station and laid a formal
complaint against Ajila and so forced the sergeant to arrest him.
Ajila was later sentenced to three months' imprisonment.

The sympathies of the Bekumbwam, to whom both protagonists
belong, clearly lie with Ajila. When Nnekwe attended at a beer party
shortly after Ajila's committal he sat by himself and none spoke to
him. The time for co-operative farming was over and so no stronger
form of ostracism could then be applied.

On the other hand, had Ajila killed Nnekwe a supernatural sanction would inevitably have brought about his death; there is no rite
of purification for a man who kills his brother (*kper*). Both men are
quarrelsome, even for Konkomba. Ajila carries the long scar of a
previous fight across his shoulders. Nnekwe is both quarrelsome and
unpleasant, by turns loquacious and boastful or silent and surly. He
is generally believed to be a witch and a sodomite.

From one instance no conclusions can safely be drawn. Yet it
suggests that homicide of a close agnatic kinsman is all but impossible. The supernatural sanction is very strong and the necessary
conditions for murder do not occur. Ajila knew that his kinsmen would
not allow him to kill Nnekwe. For a brawl between kinsmen leads to
the intervention of other kinsmen to prevent bloodshed, whereas a
brawl between men of two different districts leads to a swift line-up
of opposed sides.

There is, I have said, no ritual purification for one who kills his
brother. Should any man do so the supernatural or religious sanction

would operate to eliminate the fratricide from the group and so restore communication within it.

The method of settling in a rite a quarrel between men who 'sacrifice together' appears to be seldom invoked. It was not invoked on this occasion, possibly because Nnekwe was held to be in the wrong and he was punished by ostracism. The quarrel was not composed ritually. I never, in fact, saw it done, though Konkomba say that disputes between agnates can be ended in a shared sacrifice to the land their quarrel polluted.[1]

Quarrels between clansmen, especially young ones, frequently occur. One day, for example, Taga came rushing through the guinea corn, his face contorted, his voice raised to an unintelligible scream of rage, while he brandished a sharp matchet. When he calmed a little, the cause of the quarrel came out. He had been walking about carrying the matchet when some of the young men asked him why he was so proud of it. The matchet, they said, was not his but belonged to Ngmaken, in whose household Taga has lived since his father's death. Taga denied that the matchet was Ngmaken's but said that it was bought for him. As he farmed for Ngmaken, why then shouldn't Ngmaken buy him a matchet? So the quarrel arose, but it died rapidly away because those around sought to calm and quieten the young men involved. It had occurred near to the compounds, although not in the presence of the elder. In the presence of the elder, and in lesser degree that of any senior man, voices may not be raised in anger.

Konkomba are aware of their reputation for aggressiveness and fighting. They are aware of and regret, in calm moments, the disruption caused by their sporadic fighting, in which lives may be lost. Various causes are given for these fights but commonly women are blamed. Women, Nadzo said, are not good. It was a woman who drove the Bekujom away from their old home near Saboba; women are always causing trouble.

Though many quarrels occur within a district none are over women, for the incest rules and the system of joking relationships operate to evade such frictions, since it is jealousy of husbands for wives and not jealousy of lovers for their mistresses that leads to fights. Further, within both the district and the hamlet, the presence and active intervention of kinsmen-neighbours operates to hold quarrels within bounds. Finally, the ritual and moral authority of

[1]This paragraph is quoted from pp. 189–90 of the article 'Territorial and Lineage System of Konkomba' in *Tribes Without Rulers*.

the elder demands that quarrels cease, that voices be not raised in his presence.

Women too quarrel in the compounds and in their anger reach out for branches of brushwood or the thicker stems of guinea corn as weapons. But I have never seen these weapons used and the quarrel usually dies away under the pressure of neighbours, of elderly women and, in the last resort, of the compound head.

Brawls between husband and wife also occur and sometimes a husband thrashes his wife, perhaps with the twelve-thonged whip called *lelalob*. Again, it is neighbours who intervene to prevent the woman from being seriously hurt. She has another recourse in that she may go off home to her father's house and what happens then is best discussed under relations between lineages. It is enough to say now that she may stay away for up to three months and if the husband has no other wife he is very hungry and uncomfortable until her return. Even if he has other wives they will not take on the work of the departed wife.

On one occasion, in the hamlet of Kpalipa, there was no intervention by neighbours to save a wife from a beating. One of the wives was seen to give beer to a Nalogni man in the market. Her husband took her home and beat her to make her confess her lover's name. On this afternoon all the young wives of Kpalipa were beaten and six confessed the names of their lovers. It is doubtful if, even in the old days, the men of Kpalipa would have set out to kill their wives' lovers; this would have involved them in feud with three separate districts. Among the wronged husbands was Kwadi, the Chief of Saboba. He laid a complaint before the Chief of Sunson who is the Dagomba divisional chief in this area. The Chief of Sunson summoned the adulterers to appear before him and he fined them in the Native Authority court. All the lovers were fined except that young man over whom the whole trouble started, for he, adhering to Konkomba custom, held that the Chief of Sunson had no judicial powers in such a matter and refused to go to the court. He has been neither fined nor punished in any other way.

This case illustrates several things; first, how slight is Dagomba influence in Konkombaland, for the adulterer held that what he had done was a private matter between himself and the husband and it seemed that he could not be touched unless he willingly appeared before the Chief of Sunson. The Government police in Saboba cannot be called in to deal with such a case. Secondly, it illustrates Konkomba practice in that adultery is primarily an affair between individuals and, in the last resort, between their kin groups, since, if the Kpalipa husband had killed his wife's lover, then he and his kin would have been involved in feud with the kin of the dead man. Even in these days when the police seek out a killer and he is imprisoned, and no Konkomba has as yet been hanged, Konkomba do not regard this as adequate redress: *bi mu kaku tie*, they too will kill theirs. Thirdly, it illustrates a basic cleavage in the hamlet, between the in-group of the agnatic kinsmen and the outgroup of the women married into the hamlet. When these two opposed sides are ranged against each other, the pressure of kinsmen neighbours on one single person is gone and the brawl is worked out to the end. This necessarily involves other districts and a wider range of action.

Destruction of crops is never deliberately done by one man against another, but a man's livestock can damage guinea corn since cows may wander from the paths or pigs may root among the farms. On one occasion in Kpalipa a man shot a kinsman's pig which he caught in his corn. The owner had no redress against the killer of his pig and could only cut his losses by selling the meat. Cardinall[1] noted that the killer of a domestic animal himself cut up and ate the flesh of the straying, destructive animal. This may have been a Bemokpem custom but has not happened in any case known to me.

The conjunction of cattle-keeping with corn growing on com-pound farms often leads to friction. The cattle are herded on open land by small boys and girls, though only in the growing season or when they have to be driven to water in the very dry season. The cattle have to be brought back to the compounds at night where they are stalled in the byre (*kenakwo*) near dung fires which protect them from mosquitoes. The boys drive the cattle at great speed along the paths which lead back through the corn to the compounds, but in the early growing season before the shoots are tall, cattle often stray from the path. One evening Banmeja severely beat the son of his neighbour, Nakwadzar, for letting a cow stray on to his corn; he chased the small boy through the corn, lashing him as they ran. The elder came along and called on Banmeja to stop, pointing out that if the boy had done wrong, it was the father who should punish him; no one else has the right to do so.

This instance shows the power of the elder to intervene in a dis-pute, not to impose a solution, but to insist that things be done in the proper way. It also shows him protecting a weaker person against a stronger. The elder did not decide the boy's punishment, but asserted

[1]A. W. Cardinall, District Book, Yendi, 1916.

that, if punishment were required, it should be given by the proper person, the boy's father.

Theft is exceedingly rare in Konkombaland. Money was little known until recently, though the coins of the British West African Currency Board and of French West Africa have now replaced cowries as media of exchange. Konkomba practice was to bury money for safer keeping if considerable sums were held, that is anything more than a few pence. Only elders and compound heads hold larger sums and they too bury the money on the farm. Though I say that theft is rare, the precautions taken would seem to suggest a feeling of considerable insecurity.

Not a year passes but that some long-forgotten hoard of cowries, sealed in a pot, is dug up on one or other farm. On one occasion when such a pot was dug up, the police sergeant sent word to Jando, the market elder, to come and take charge of it. Far from taking charge, Jando refused even to see the sergeant. The money, he said, must belong to the Bekujom for it was on land once occupied by them that the pot was found. Only one of the Bekujom, therefore, could safely touch it. 'If I take it,' he said, 'I will die.'

When Suba returned from Krachi where he had gone to earn some money by farm work, he could not discover the money he had buried before he went and thought it had been stolen. He accused the young men of his minor lineage in Kitiak of the theft and insisted that they all go to a diviner in Nakpando-Proper to discover which of them was the thief. Not all the young men went, only those of his own subdivision, Dzangendo, but even they, the diviner said, were too many and he refused to start until some of them had been eliminated. Suba came back to explain this to the elder. However, no one was very sympathetic or worried. The consensus of opinion was that Suba had just forgotten where he had buried it. No other instance of theft, actual or suspected, has come to my notice. It is noteworthy that Suba accused only men younger than himself even though many of them had been absent in Krachi with him when the money disappeared, if indeed, it really did disappear.

There is, in any case, very little private property among Konkomba. The young men of a hamlet, or rather of a lineage of major or minor span, sleep in a room in the compound of the elder, but they have with them only bows and arrows or other weapons and some clothing. No one would take another man's bow and arrows for these are sacred objects. Garments are by no means private property and a pair of shorts will pass round all those whom they approximately fit.

But the cotton cloths now sold by travelling Yoruba, or bought in the south by young men who go to work on the farms there, are very highly prized and do not seem to pass from hand to hand. These and other precious things, including money, are kept in the mother's room, or the room of the woman to whom as an orphan child he was assigned. Apart from the woman herself only her children will enter the room; not even her husband does so during her absence unless it be the room of his senior wife in which ritual objects are kept. Thus, only the woman and those men and women who stand to each other in the closest of all Konkomba relations, that of *naabo* (literally *na a bo*, 'mother's child' or uterine sibling, etc.) to each other may enter the room. Even then, many people now possess wooden boxes to which flimsy locks are fixed, in which they keep their most cherished possessions.

It may be urged from the precautions taken that theft is something to be guarded against. On the other hand there is no privacy in Konkomba life; one is hardly ever alone. These precautions may then be an expression of a desire to have a place of one's own, rather than to safeguard oneself against loss.

In this chapter, I have given an account of the three types of Konkomba clans, the unitary, the compound, and the special form of the compound, the contrapuntal. Though there are slight variations of custom, all clans may be classified as one or other of these three types.

A district comprises a territory with its associated shrines of which the most important is the Earth shrine. The unitary clan and district is one composed of one major lineage. The compound clan is one composed of two major lineages together occupying one district. The contrapuntal clan is one composed of two major lineages in one district to each of which are assigned different ritual roles. The major lineage is always an exogamous unit. The unitary clan is therefore also an exogamous unit.

The question of district and clan exogamy is better discussed later when the clans are more fully analysed. Yet it may now be said that the compound clan is not an exogamous unit while the contrapuntal clan often is. I try to show in a later section that contraposition and inter-marriage of major lineages of one clan are alternatives, one of which will be chosen according to the territorial distribution of major lineage members when that lineage splits to form two lineages of like order. Contraposition of major lineages occurs, I believe, when two newly formed major lineages lie so closely together on the ground as to form virtually one hamlet. In time, however, as these two lineages grow and are more fully established, marriages are gradually permitted between them though the early marriages are almost certainly runaway marriages. This, I think, is what has happened in the two districts of Saboba and Kedzabo, both of which are occupied by clans whose contraposed lineages may intermarry. Each of the contraposed major lineages of both clans is scattered in a number of hamlets at some distance from the point of original settlement. In neither case has this led to major lineage endogamy but perhaps gradually to the breakdown of clan exogamy.

The district is an economic unit in the sense that it can be all but self-supporting. It is a ritual unit, though districts also come together to share in each other's ceremonies. But it is a divisible ritual unit since subdivisions of the clan carry out separate rites.

It is an autonomous unit of social control in that there is no supra-elder authority to impose a solution on recalcitrants of a district. Within the district there is no organized force which can be employed to ensure acquiescence; there is no coercion other than the ritual and moral power of the elder and the diffuse sanctions of kinsmen's disapproval, though this latter may on occasion extend to physical restraint.

The organized clan and district with its ritual and moral head, the elder, is the political unit of Konkombaland. The district is the largest unit within which arbitration, other than the arbitrament of the club and the arrow, is the rule. Radcliffe-Brown[1], writing of political systems, says that 'In studying political organization, we have to deal with the maintenance or establishment of social order, within a territorial framework, by the organized exercise of coercive authority through the use, or the possibility of the use, of physical force. In well organized states the police and the army are the instruments by which coercion is exercised. . . . In dealing with political systems, therefore, we are dealing with law, on the one hand, and with war, on the other.'

I have already said that in Konkomba society there is nothing one may properly speak of as 'law'. Equally, there is nothing one may properly call 'war'. There is no regimental system, and even age-sets are only vaguely defined. Yet, just as there are disapproved actions and disputes within clans which have to be dealt with by jural activities, so between clans of one tribe there are disputes and offences which are dealt with by means of warlike activities which

[1] A. R. Radcliffe-Brown, Preface to *African Political Systems,* ed. M. Fortes, and E. E. Evans-Pritchard, 1940, p. xiv.

may be called 'feud'. I reserve the term 'war' for the permanent hostility and sporadic fighting between tribes.

The district is a territorial unit occupied by a clan. The association between the clan and the land is close and the highest values expressed in the rites of the clan are those of fertility of land and of the group. The clan and the land are a duality; both can be seen and delimited. But each has its unseen, its religious, aspect. For the living group of kin the unseen, dead ancestors are recalled in the ancestor cult and in their function of providing the points of reference about which the lineage structure is articulated. For the land, the unseen, the religious aspect is expressed in the Earth cult and the sacrifices at the Earth shrine. But the land is not only the provider of food, it is the patrimonial land since it was here that the ancestors walked and are buried. A householder invokes his dead father; but the elder invokes the more distant ancestors, who in turn are asked to invoke 'those they know'. Time stretches back to infinity in one direction and forward to infinity in the other. The dead are invoked to give help to those now alive by making the land fruitful and by sending children to the living, so are the dead and the unborn brought into relation with the living duality of clan and land within the district.

IV. The Clan and Lineage System

THE district, the largest territorial unit of Konkomba organization, is occupied by a clan, the largest unit of political
organization. The clan is a structure composed of lineages,
themselves genealogical structures, and between lineages of one clan
agnatic relationship is assumed, even though no ancestor common to
all lineages is known. The widest usage of the Konkomba phrase *Ti
je onibaa*, 'we are (the children of) one man', refers to the clan. A
man speaks of his clansmen as his *dejaa* (s. *dejoo*).[1] Each clan is a
system of lineages. That is, it is a segmentary system of long-enduring, though not permanent, unilineal descent groups which are
localized corporate units with political functions.

What I earlier called a unitary clan is composed of one segmented,
major lineage; a compound clan is one composed of two segmented,
major lineages; a contrapuntal clan is one composed of two major
lineages in contraposition.

A lineage is a genealogical structure and between any two members
of a lineage of any span and generation depth kinship can be stated in
precise terms. This is not to say that the relationships so stated are
statements of historically accurate descent. It is only within the units
of the lower orders of segmentation and narrowest span that actual
relations of descent are accurately known.

The major lineage is commonly divided into two or three minor
lineages and the minor lineage into a number of nuclear lineages.
Below that level we find the families of living compound heads. Each
lineage is an agnatic descent group and until the highest level of
segmentation is reached two or more lineages make up one lineage of
wider span and greater time depth in the genealogical structure.

Starting with the lower orders of segmentation, the nuclear lineage
may be defined as the group of agnatic kin descended from an apical

[1]See p. 133 where a number of kinship terms are given.

ancestor, who is the father or grandfather of living compound heads. The minor lineage is a group of agnatic kin descended from an apical ancestor two or three generations back from the living compound heads. The major lineage is a group of agnatic kin descended from an apical ancestor three or four generations back from the living compound heads. For two major lineages of one clan no common ancestor is known. In describing the lineage in this way one adopts the point of view of the mature men of the society, the men who have married and established their own compounds, who are heads of families and are of all ages over forty. For them, the lineage stretches back through time as a ladder of generations ascending to the remote, apical ancestor who is the founder of the major lineage.

Clans are localized descent groups containing localized genealogical structures. The localization of a clan is precise and is exactly known. One clan occupies one district which is focused on one Earth shrine. Less inclusive groups are less precisely localized than the clan and the major lineage. But one hamlet and its surrounding compound farms usually constitute a minor lineage and the compounds of men of one nuclear lineage are often contiguous.

Konkomba do not often speak at any length about their lineages. The clan seldom numbers more than about 500 souls and relations between members of one clan are face to face relations. Konkomba never come together in large numbers to discuss common problems. The largest meetings of people are found in the markets or at Second Burials, and at the latter they are not gathered closely together in one place but are moving in groups of a dozen or so between the compounds of the clan that is performing the ceremony. The largest gathering of elders is at the divination of the cause of death of an elder, when perhaps thirty elders and senior men meet. These are occasions of more discussion and argument than occur for any other reason. The rite to purify the land also draws together groups of ten to fifteen elders and senior men, and it is on this occasion that the names of the apical ancestors of major and minor lineages are called and these dead are invoked to aid the living. Even on these occasions names are not invoked in orderly sequence and sometimes names occur that cannot be fitted into any genealogy.

Over against the identity of status of men who are *onibaa* stand contrasted those men of whom it is said, *Bi je bibaba*, 'they are by themselves'. There are thus two categories into which men are classified: from the point of view of men of one minor lineage, men of another minor lineage of the same major lineage are *bibaba*; men of the same two minor lineages are *onibaa*, as against men of a second major lineage of the same clan who are *bibaba*. The term *bibaba* can, according to context, indicate men of a different minor lineage, major lineage, clan or tribe from that of the speaker. The term *benatshom* is one used by an elder when speaking of men of his segment and can be used by the elder of a minor lineage, a major lineage or a clan.

It is only in response to pressure that difference of descent is invoked. It is clear that between men of different clans there is no agnation, while between men of clans as small as those of the Konkomba difference of descent within the clan is easily known to every mature person. A major lineage elder distributing the game after a hunt is in no doubt about who should get a share, since there are only two or three men who are eligible. Moreover their portion is of such a size that, when all elders divide the meat amongst their compound heads, these will have a share proportionate to the size of their domestic families. That is to say that the elder divides the meat with full and detailed knowledge of the households of its final recipients. There are no relations between lineages such that a particular part of any animal must be given by one lineage to another. It is only when an individual distributes meat at the Second Burial of a dead father or brother that a particular part is given to particular persons: even this is not a relation between groups but one between categories of kin, for the *umwetib* (mother's patrikinsmen) of the dead man receive the neck of the slaughtered animal. On the other hand, if the elder distributing the bag of a hunt be asked why he gives meat to another to share, he will reply *O mu dzo wa nib*, 'he too holds his people.'

Sub-groups of agnatic kin are therefore recognized within the clan and major lineage. They are in fact differentiated by difference of descent but, since lineages do not spread widely in space, either structural or ecological, such differentiation does not reach far back through time.

There are no specialists in genealogies among Konkomba; no one learns genealogies by a deliberate effort of study. Children hear the names of the nearer ancestors, their grandfathers, invoked in the rites in the compound, but do not enter the shrines in which are performed the major rites of the annual cycle nor should they be near when the elders purify the Earth. Some post-adolescent men always attend a sacrifice in a shrine, for theirs is the work of leading the sacrificial animal, and of killing, skinning and cutting it up. Even in the shrines the invocation is not an orderly roll-call but a babble of voices, as now one man then another calls the name of an ancestor of his line omitted by the presiding elder. Not all young men attend these rites; only two or three are taken along to do their part and they are chosen at random. Yet here is one situation in which the names of remoter ancestors are learned. As men grow older they begin to attend occasional rites such as a sacrifice to the Earth done on the advice of a diviner, even though they have no special duties in the rite. An elder going to a rite usually takes someone along with him 'to help him' and his companion is generally his successor-designate in the office. It is in ritual contexts, then, that names of remoter ancestors are invoked and consequently may be learned by young and by mature men.

These names can also be learned from the names of hamlets. Many of these are known by the name of the apical ancestor of the segment that occupies it and all can be referred to by such an eponym. To the name of the ancestor the suffix -do, house, is appended; for example, the district of Kitiak is occupied by two major lineages whose apical ancestors are Koto and Ngmangea and both the lineages and the parts of the hamlet which each lineage occupies are known as Kotodo and Ngmangeado respectively. On the other hand, Konkomba are not consistent in their use of these forms. While Kotodo is the only form used for that lineage, that of Ngamangeado is sometimes known as Jatshado. Jatsha was the father of the present elder. In what follows I shall name the segments after co-ordinate lineage heads. I do so for clarity of exposition though it is not a consistent practice of Konkomba. Their practice is just one indication that genealogical differentiation of descent is a validation of existing relations between groups and that this validation keeps closely in step with an ever-changing situation.

Konkomba acquire their knowledge of the remoter ancestors haphazardly and not by the discipline of learning a genealogy. Children grow up in hamlets grouped together under their elder. The authority of the elder is an ever-present fact; their fathers consult the elder about their personal affairs, while the children are there to see and to hear all that goes on. No unit is so large that the elder cannot know every child and that every child does not know the elder. To any child the elder is 'my father' (n te); any child of the lineage is 'my child' (m bo) to the elder. From this it follows that no child is ever in doubt where he belongs in the groupings of his clan; conversely, there is no doubt about who is the elder responsible for any child or man.

The validation of inter-lineage relations in kinship terms is seldom invoked in other than ritual contexts. Yet it is there ready to be

invoked when occasion demands. The founding ancestor is recalled in
the simplest of myths and the time between him and the fathers and
grandfathers of living men is filled in with other named ancestors
whose names not only complete a time scale but also diversify the
groupings descended from the founding ancestor. Though seldom
invoked, the genealogy is always there ready to be invoked; it is a
mnemonic device by which present practice can be explained in
terms of descent.

Let me illustrate this by reference to some genealogies, the first of
which relates to the Benangmam clan of the district of Kitiak (Genealogy I), a clan of two contraposed major lineages. The Owner of
the Earth's people are those descended from Koto; the Elder's people
are those descended from Ngmangea. Koto is described as 'the man
who first came here' while Ngmangea is 'he who helped Koto'. The
Benangmam, in such a context as explaining their genealogies to me,
tend to regard Koto as the ancestor who first settled in their present
place after the Dagomba had invaded what is now Eastern Dagomba
and expelled many Konkomba. The Benangmam claim to have come
from the region that is now Yendi; other clans claim to have come
from farther west. At other times their accounts of their movements
seem to indicate that they came from east of the Oti to their present
site on the western bank. However this may be, in their thought
Koto settled in Kitiak a very long time ago and he is, however
vaguely, connected with their expulsion by the Dagomba. This
if accurate would place Koto in the early seventeenth or late sixteenth century.

To Koto are ascribed four 'sons'—Fanin, Pane, Kune, and
Dzange. In practice the major lineage is divided into two minor
segments, that of Fanindo and that of Dzangendo. The status of
Dzange is dubious. He was first described as a 'brother' to Koto.
When I pointed out that this meant that only one generation lay
between Ngagbi, the present Owner of the Earth, and the people who
originally came to Kitiak, it was first suggested that Dzange was a
small boy when Koto was old and secondly that he was Koto's son.
That is to say, by juggling the relationships between persons named
in a genealogy any doubtful point can be explained.

Fanin is ascribed three sons and the line descended from Pane is,
in practice, assimilated to that of Fanin. Pane has one living grandson, Njesin, who is spoken about and treated as a member of Fanindo.

Kune is ascribed no sons at all. There are two possible explanations of this; either his 'sons' have been assimilated to the line of

Fanin or Dzange, or his sons left their natal district to found a new one elsewhere. The former seems to be the more likely explanation, since his is a name recalled by elderly men and one which has to be fitted into the genealogy somewhere. The effective segmentation of the major lineage is into two minor segments, Dzangendo and Fanindo, each with its own elder, of whom the senior is the Owner of the Earth of the major lineage.

The minor segments are in turn segmented into nuclear lineages. Fanindo has four effective nuclear lineages: Dzenjido, Jandzirdo, Tawandzado and Ngmatiedo. The apical ancestors of these segments are either the fathers or the grandfathers of the living compound heads. Dzangendo had six segments of which one has died out without male issue and one has been lost by fission to found a new district elsewhere. The removal of a group of men, commonly brothers, from their natal hamlet to found a new hamlet in unoccupied land may take two forms. First, intra-district fission in which the brothers found a new hamlet within the bounds of their natal district; secondly, extra-district fission in which the men who move leave their natal districts to found new districts in unoccupied lands elsewhere. The term *dejoo* (pl. *dejaa*), clansman, is not extended to a son of a man who has moved from his natal district; such a man is himself *dejoo* but his son is *otsha*, a stranger. The first generation to be born outside their father's natal district are not eligible to inherit lands or wives within the original district.

The contraposed major lineage of the Elder's people has as its apical ancestor Ngmangea. To Ngmangea are ascribed two sons, Kugbe and Natie, each of whom is an apical ancestor for the minor lineage descended from him. The minor segment of Kugbedo has only one household, that of Ngkwo, to represent it at present but, perhaps aided by its territorial separation from the rest of Ngmangeado, it survives as a segment co-ordinate with that of Natie. Each minor lineage includes nuclear segments; Kugbedo has only one while Natiedo has four.

In terms of the definition of lineage that I gave above, what I now call a nuclear lineage is not, perhaps, strictly a lineage, though it is both a segment of a supraordinate minor lineage and a localized descent group. But they are short-lived segments and their functions are not primarily political.

The nuclear lineage is a short-lived segment interstitial between the enduring minor lineage and a structure that I call the extended house (Konkomba use the word *do* in this and other contexts). The extended house is a group descended from a common grandfather, counting through both males and females. This unit has, so to speak, an agnatic core that is localized in the hamlet of the founding grandfather. The nuclear lineage is an extension of this agnatic core and is a short-lived segment that is interstitial between the enduring minor lineage and the transient extended house.

From Plan I (see Genealogy I) it will be seen that the hamlet of Kitiak is a compact hamlet except for the compound of Ngkwo which is an example of intra-district fission. Both the major lineages are localized in one settlement and the minor lineages are also clearly localized units. The nuclear lineages are not so distinctly localized as are the supraordinate segments.

Both these genealogies are simple examples of the Konkomba system of segmentation. The clan is a contrapuntal one and the two contraposed major lineages are divided into two minor segments. The only problem in them is the difference in generation depth of some of the nuclear lineages. Yet this can be explained, at least in part, in the following way. It is impossible to collect genealogies except in the presence of an elder. Though the elder may not himself always speak, no other person will speak of the ancestors unless he is present. Thus, to give a genealogy the entire hamlet turns out to join in the game, so that where young or fairly young men do not recall their grandfather's names the old men do. The nuclear lineage tends to shorten when the living representatives are elderly and old men, though there is another factor which tends to lengthen the nuclear lineage which will be pointed out in another genealogy. The nuclear lineages and the extended houses operate in the system of proscribed marriages and the marriage rules may relate, *inter alia*, to the nuclear lineages of the father's mother and the mother's mother. This is the farthest extension back of proscribed marriages through the generations. Now a girl's marriage is fixed at her birth; there can then be no doubt about her mother's mother's or father's mother's kin. A man's first marriage is arranged when he is about twenty, a second when he is about thirty and a third some time later. These marriages are arranged for a man by his father or pater. It is the older men who must know the kinship relations of the young men to see that the rules are not broken. Apart from this, every man knows his mother's mother's and father's mother's kin (*umwetib*) since, though he has no specific duties towards them, he is sometimes sent to them to represent his mother or father on such a ritual occasion as a burial.

The second genealogy (Genealogy II) relates to the Bekumbwam, the Elder's people of the district of Saboba. The contraposed segment of the Owner of the Earth's people is known as the Benasom. I have a genealogy for the Benasom too, though, after three attempts, it is still not very satisfactory. The Owner of the Earth, for some reason, was reluctant to talk of genealogies or, indeed, of anything very important.

This major lineage is segmented into two minor lineages; Gurdo and Dardo together make up one and Uwenido a second. There are a number of doubtful points in this genealogy. First, Uweni is ascribed to Ngmatie as a 'son' on some occasions and on others he is said to be 'the one who came with Ngmatie'. In accordance with this doubt about his relation to the founding ancestor, the descent lines coming down from him tend to be extended beyond the usual length. From Ngmatie to Oja, inclusive of both, is five generations whereas the more usual number is four. Oja is the oldest man of the Bekumbwam and, since he has no married son, the total number of generations in the genealogy is seven, a number that is frequently found. In other words there is only a semblance of extension; in fact, the total number of generations found in the genealogy does not exceed that frequently found. Secondly, the nuclear lineage of Gbandzo in Dardo is of doubtful status. None the less, the group of senior men who discussed this genealogy ascribed Gbandzo as a 'son' of Dar. Betsha, the grandson of Dar, himself a man in the fifties, left it to Jando, the elder of the segment, to decide the status of Gbandzo and he decided that he was a brother of Gbir and therefore a son to Dar.

The three segments Gurdo, Dardo and Uwenido occupy separate hamlets (Plan II, Genealogy II). Those of Gurdo and Dardo lie close together and function as one minor lineage. That of Uwenido lies at a distance of about half a mile from the others and it also functions as one minor lineage.

The major lineage of Ngmatie is contraposed to that of Kwaku, the apical ancestor of the Benasom. Together they make up one clan. The two major lineages intermarry. The Benasom are one major lineage segmented into two minor lineages, each in a separate hamlet. They are the Owner of the Earth's people. The Earth shrine lies near the hamlet of Bwagban, regarded as the first point of settlement of the clan. The relation between Ngmatie and Kwaku is variously said to be that 'Ngmatie helped Kwaku' or that 'Ngmatie came later to join Kwaku'. The Owner of the Earth's people hold three shrines:

the Earth shrine, *Ntengbe*, a shrine in the river, and another for the fertility of women. The Elder's people hold one shrine, that of the Saboba market, Kakã, the control of which runs in the segment of Dardo.

In effect, the functioning of Dardo and Gurdo together as one minor lineage pulls down or extends the lower orders of segmentation. The higher levels of segmentation, the major and minor levels, are also inconsistently stated in comparison with such simple genealogies as that of the Benangmam. Throughout the entire clan of the Bekumbwam and the Benasom there is a high correlation between lineage segment and hamlet; each segment is a localized unit. It may be that the retention of both Gur and Dar as apical ancestors of what is one minor lineage is due to the territorial separation of the two segments. Had the lineage been a more compact group in one single hamlet then, perhaps, either Gur or Dar would have been lost.

The next genealogy is that of the Benalog of Nalogni (Genealogy III). This is a unitary district of one major lineage which has three minor lineages. The apical ancestor, 'the first man to settle there', was Tindeja. The major lineage is segmented into three minor segments descended from the apical ancestors Makpada, Kotie and Bwara. Each minor lineage is segmented into nuclear segments.

The only question in this genealogy is the apparently unusual depth of the nuclear lineage of Baluen of Bwarado. Yet, once again, if the number of generations be counted from the children of Mananji to Tindeja the total is six, a number that is sometimes exceeded.

Each minor lineage is localized; Bwarado and Kotiendo each occupy one hamlet while Makpadado occupies two hamlets, one known as Makpadado (or Wadzado) and the other as Ditshie. The division of compounds between Makpadado and Ditshie does not entirely follow the segmentation of the nuclear lineages, though there is a tendency for this to happen.

The economic, ritual and jural activities described in the previous section illustrate the relations between the localized segments of clans and lineages described in the present section. The territorial groupings are also kin groups and each local group is either a clan or a segment of a clan. There is no need to multiply examples now, since the inter-relations of segments will be further illustrated later when I come to the relations between clans and tribes. But in conclusion I will summarize the activities in which participation, or degree of participation, is determined by lineage membership:

1. Work parties on the farms: if two work parties fall on the same day a man goes to the party of the man who stands closest to him in the lineage system.

2. Hunting: especially in the large, ritual hunts lineage membership is important, for this decides a man's place in the line.

3. Ritual activities: participation in many rites, especially land rites, is fixed by seniority in the segmentary system; in burial rites, too, lineage status is important, but here matrilateral kinship also plays its part; the groups of men and women who 'hold spirits' are organized wholly within the framework of the segmentary system.

4. The ceremonies that mark the arrival of a bride at her husband's hamlet.

5. Payment of bride services: though a man tends to call on men of his age-set to assist him, he first calls on those of his age-mates who are nearest to him in the segmentary system for it is they who are likely to inherit the wife should he die.

6. The inheritance of widows and the assignment of orphaned children.

7. Fights and feuds.

THE RITUAL SYMBOLS OF THE MAJOR AND MINOR LINEAGES

I speak of *Dzambuna* as a ritual symbol since it can be defined only in description. It is a crocodile's head encased in the pulped root of the tree *Hymenocardia Acida*, which is used also in making the rain medicine and as a protective after eating a toad. The roots are pounded, soaked and allowed to dry hard round the head. The encased head is then bound with string and porcupine quills are inserted under the string. The whole lies on a turtle shell. Often found with *Dzambuna* is a horn, *igi* (from *nggi* a horn). The horn has feathers from an original sacrifice bound to it and contains charred roots of plants not known to me. The point of the horn is inserted into a hole in a specially prepared clay block from which it can easily be withdrawn.

Dzambuna is not generally spoken of as a *luwaa*, a shrine; it is sometimes specifically denied that it is a *luwaa*, yet I have also heard this sentence, *Dzambuna a waa lena* (*Dzambuna's* shrine is there). On the other hand it is not *njog*, a medicine. It is *Dzambuna* and I shall speak of it as a ritual symbol. The *igi* is sometimes said to be a *njog*, a protective medicine that is dangerous if misused.

The *igi* horn is placed outside the compound of a dead elder during the Second Burial rites when the diviner is at work finding out the cause of the death. It has two other important uses. First, should a man kill someone who is not a fellow clansman, he goes straight to the *igi* and lies beside it. He sleeps with it for three nights to protect him from the ghost (*kedzengdzo*, lit. shadow) of the man he has killed. Should he not dream of the dead man that night he is safe, though his bow and arrows must nevertheless be destroyed. Secondly, it is used as a protection against the ghost of a 'bad' animal (*onamu*, pl. *inamu*—a dangerous animal, an animal that is dangerous both alive and dead). The lion, leopard, bush cow, crocodile, and perhaps the hippopotamus are included in this category. The spirits of game animals killed in the hunt are addressed and perhaps placated, but no ritual protection is needed against their ghosts. When a bad animal is killed the killer seeks the ritual protection that a homicide uses.

The ritual protection of the *igi* is invoked during the mock hunt held during the Second Burial of an elder and in the burial of a leper. Dead elders are promised an enormous bag of game, and skulls of long-dead, game animals are placed on their graves. In the past the ritual hunt, the *leluu*, may well have been associated with Second Burials and today it closely precedes them. However that may be, during Second Burials a mock hunt is held in which posts painted with red and black spots are hammered into the ground and then stalked and shot with arrows. The first shots are taken by the grandsons and sons of the dead man who are followed by other men of the clan. The first man to hit the post rushes back to the dead elder's compound to crouch down outside the young men's room. He does nothing while there but waits until shouts tell him that the 'animal' has been shot by many young men, when he quietly rejoins them. Konkomba seem unable to offer any explanation of this but it seems to be a symbolic seeking of the *igi*'s powers to protect a killer.

Dzambuna has no such obvious uses, though it is sometimes said that a man who has killed another man sacrifices a fowl to it. When it is found it is always in the compound of the elder of a major lineage and an *igi* is always found along with it. The *igi* is generally, but not always, found not only in the compound of the elder of the major lineage, but in the compound of an elder of the minor lineage as well.

The Benangmam clan has two *Dzambuna* (I know no plural form), one in the compound of the elder of each major lineage. Each elder has an *igi* as well. But neither elder of the second minor lineage of each major lineage has an *igi*.

The Bekumbwam have no *Dzambuna* but each elder of a minor lineage has an *igi*. In Kpeo district each major lineage elder has both *Dzambuna* and *igi*. In Bwakwin district the Owner of the Earth has the *Dzambuna* and each major lineage has an *igi*. Among the Benalog each minor lineage has an *igi* and there is one *Dzambuna*.

These are typical examples of what one finds in many districts. One clan elder, that of the Sobibtib, has a *Dzambuna* and three *igi*, all of which he says he inherited from his predecessors.

What is happening is this: the *Dzambuna* is always found in the possession of the elder of a major lineage; the *igi* is always found in the compound of an elder of a minor lineage and a major lineage elder is, *a fortiori*, an elder of a minor lineage. But some major lineages have no *Dzambuna*. One elder explained that his predecessor had taken it off with him to Krachi and when that elder died the *Dzambuna* was not returned and the elder added—'If I like I will go there and fetch it'. Since Konkomba are incorrigibly negligent of ritual duties one need feel no surprise that many elders have never bothered to fetch back a *Dzambuna* that has been removed, or to acquire a new one. Again, not all minor lineages have their own *igi*. This occurs when, and only when, two minor lineages occupy one single hamlet. Then it is also the case that there is only one young men's room in the hamlet and the *igi* is a protection primarily for the young men.

We may say that *Dzambuna* is the symbol of the major lineage and that the *igi* is the ritual symbol of the minor lineage. These symbols are kept in the room used by the *Benatshipwam*, the young men, of a major (or minor) lineage. The protective function of the *igi* explains why it is kept there rather than in the room of the senior wife of the elder, in whose room most of the elder's medicines and ritual symbols are kept. It is most commonly the young men who fight and who are most likely to need the protection *igi* gives to the homicide; it is they who hunt and need protection from the ghosts of the *inamu*.

Dzambuna, on the other hand, has no protective powers. It is, unlike the *igi*, an object of sacrifice. It is sometimes offered new yams and new guinea corn as part of the New Food rites and sometimes a fowl is killed to it. The new food should be offered to *Dzambuna* before any member of the major lineage eats of it. The ceremony is simple, even by Konkomba standards. The elder goes by himself taking with him a part of a new yam and, laying it on *Dzambuna*, says: 'Dzambuna! you too get new food; today I want to eat and give you too.'

After this simple rite is carried out, the rites in individual compounds and those done by spirit-holders (*kebwabig*, pl. *mbwabim*) to
their spirits may be carried out. Simple as it is, it expresses the unity
of the major lineage.

Dzambuna and *Ntengbe* symbolize two different mystical orders.
Ntengbe symbolizes the mystical aspect of the Earth; *Dzambuna* symbolizes the mystical aspect of the people, the members of the major
lineage. The Earth shrine is relatively timeless. At one Earth shrine
the ancestors invoked their ancestors, the present elders invoke their
known forerunners and will in turn be invoked by their descendants.
Dzambuna is a temporary symbol of a present reality—the major
lineage as it stands at a given point in time. It is not a symbol of the
ancestors for the ancestors are not invoked through it; it is a present
possession of the living kin group and symbolizes it.

The segmentation of a clan and major lineage into smaller units
is clearly demonstrated in the relation of a wife to her husband's
clansmen. A woman speaks of her husband's clan as her *tshatijaa*.
A woman entering a clan as a wife stands in specified relations to the
lineage segments to which her husband belongs. A bride is known in
Konkomba as *otshakpe*.

First, Konkomba say that 'a woman does not marry one man'. Indeed, a girl is sometimes betrothed not to a specific husband but to an
elder who, when the girl is old enough to marry, will give her to whichever of his sons is old enough to marry. The practice shows that the
marriage relation is not conceived primarily as one between individuals
but as between a woman and a kin group. A man on the other hand
does not marry his wife's kin group; there is no sororate, no replacement of a betrothed wife who dies before reaching nubility nor return
of the bride corn already paid for a dead or runaway bride.

There is no ceremony that can properly be called a wedding.
When a woman goes to her husband she slips out of her native hamlet
accompanied only by a young man of her husband's kin to guard her
or a sister to cheer her on the way. On arrival at her husband's hamlet
she does not at once go to his compound but stays for up to six days
in the compound of the elder of the major lineage. At present the
elder does not lie with the bride but, since a man sleeps with one of
his wives from market day to market day, that is, for six days, the
retention of the bride in the elder's compound for that period may be
a symbolical wedding of the bride to the major lineage in the person
of its elder.

When the elder gives her word, the bride goes to her husband's compound where she meets some of the young men (*Benatshipwam*) among whom will be men of all the minor lineages of the major lineage. She is forced to kneel upon the ground in the compound of her husband when the 'young men' threaten to beat her with a *lelalob* (a twelve-thonged whip) should she refuse to reveal the name of her lover. Once she has confessed, nothing more is done. This ceremony marks her relation to the 'young men' of her husband's major lineage, the group on whom would fall the burden of fighting should her husband quarrel with her lover. The lover or, at least, the man named by the bride, avoids the hamlet and district of his former mistress's husband.

A third ceremony symbolizes the bride's relation to her husband's clan. Some months after her arrival in her husband's compound the bride brews beer for sale to her husband's clansmen. Members of both major lineages of her husband's clan buy and drink of this beer; even small boys contribute their pennies. The husband gives as much as ten shillings; elders of major lineages give five shillings; other men give sums which vary between one and four shillings. The larger sums are contributed by senior men in the major lineage of the husband and by men who stand closest in kinship to him and so are potential husbands to the bride. In effect, the brewing of beer and selling it to her husband's clansmen provides the wife with a fund of money with which to buy corn for further brewing and for trading in the market.

The final ceremony which demonstrates a bride's relation to her husband's clansmen is the *lesabwan*; the word is a verbal noun which means 'day of cooking'. On this day the bride, assisted by her sisters who visit her for the purpose, cooks for her husband's clansmen and their wives and children. Considerable quantities of food are distributed on two successive days, all provided by the bride's kin and especially by her mother. The quantity of food distributed to each person marks the closeness of her relation to him or her. I need only note the distribution to men. The elder of the major lineage of her husband gets the largest share of all. Of major lineages other than that of her husband, only the elder gets a share. Within her husband's major lineage the shares given are largest to men of her husband's nuclear lineage; the next largest shares go to men of other nuclear lineages of her husband's minor lineage; smaller shares go to men of minor lineages other than her husband's. Within these broad classifications there are variations which indicate relations of respect to senior men. There is even variation within her husband's nuclear lineage.

In general one may say that the largest shares go to the men most likely to inherit her should she be widowed.

A wife may joke with these potential husbands. She addresses them, jokingly, as *n tshar*, 'my husband', and they may address her as *m pu*, 'my wife'. Intercourse between a man and a wife of his clansman is strictly forbidden. The joking relation obtains only between a woman and man of her husband's minor lineage younger than the husband. Men older than her husband a woman addresses by a term of respect, but to all men of the minor lineage she may give beer to drink, either in public in the market or in private in the compound. Should she offer beer to a man outside this lineage span, other of course than to a joking partner of another category, she will do so through her husband.

This joking relationship is one between potential spouses between whom sexual relations are forbidden.

THE AGE SETS AND THE 'YOUNG MEN'

The Konkomba terms *onatshipwatotib* and *osapwatotib* are best translated as 'male age-mates' and 'female age-mates'. They are derived from *onatshipwa*, young man, and *osapwa*, young woman. A group of age-mates includes all the men and women born in a period of approximately four years. The groups so formed may conveniently be spoken of as age-sets, though they are not named sets.

The age-sets stratify Konkomba major lineages into fifteen sets, beginning with the children between four to eight years of age in the youngest set, up to the elders in the oldest set. For each set of males there is a correlated set of females.

The Konkomba definition of an age-set is a negative one; namely, that the male and female sets taken together should not contain two consecutive children borne by one mother in the major lineage. After the birth of a child sexual intercourse between the parents is forbidden until the child can walk. If the parents indulge in intercourse it is believed that the child already born will die. On the other hand extramarital intercourse on the part of the mother is not believed to lead to the death of the child, though a child conceived in adultery is believed to have a difficult birth.

It is not easy to say when Konkomba children can walk, but I believe them to do so much later than do European children. Children are carried by the mother in a cloth on her back probably until they are at least two years old and perhaps for longer. Indeed, children of more than three years of age are often carried about by older children; though well able to stand by themselves they seldom walk far un-aided. One child born on 29 October 1951 was still not crawling fourteen months later in mid-December 1952. When laid on a cloth after his bath he was making movements which indicated that he was about to begin crawling.

Children are continually suckled until the mother is again preg-nant. Indeed, a boy of six or seven was occasionally given the breast by his mother since she had no younger child. It was reported, though I did not see it, that a boy who must be at least fourteen was still occasionally given the breast by his mother. This latter instance aroused comment though the former did not.

It is likely that sexual intercourse is forbidden between the parents of a child for at least two and perhaps up to three years after the birth of that child. Should a child die in infancy, the prohibition lapses. It is very rare for a woman to have more than five surviving children and the highest number of pregnancies recorded, in a very small sample of thirty-two women now past childbearing, was nine pregnancies; this number occurred twice. By pregnancies I here mean children carried to full term or, at least, to seven months; pregnancies which led to a birth even though the child may have been still-born.

There is no formal closing of an age-set and opening of a new one. Young children under the age of about four are not regarded as hav-ing age-mates but, when a child is born to the mother of a child not yet in an age-set, then the age-set may be said to come into being. The formation is marked by no ceremony. It is true that it is after this time that the children have the tribal face mark cut, but the marks are not cut on all children on the same day nor is it done in any sort of rite. Again, there is a marked tendency for the girls of the oldest age-set of unmarried girls to have their body decorations cut together. Generally this is not done until the girls are almost old enough to marry, though younger girls not yet nubile will sometimes accompany the older ones to be decorated at the same time. Again, there is no ceremony. None the less, there is a rough correlation between the cutting of the face marks and entry into the first age-set and, for girls, between the cutting of the body decorations and entry into the oldest set of unmarried girls.

It does occasionally happen that a woman bears two consecutive children more quickly than she should. This is seen either when one small age-set is followed by a large one and the apparent anomaly is explained in this way, or when two children of one woman are put into one age-set, though, by definition, the set cannot include them.

It will be seen that the Konkomba age-sets are not precise and accurately known structures. The female sets are, of course, dispersed when the members of it marry. The male sets stratify the major lineage, not the clan. It is seldom possible to correlate, with certainty, the sets of one lineage with those of another. The principal difficulty is not the placing together of two sequences of age-sets when the whole sequence of fifteen is found in a major lineage. But since all Konkomba lineages lose population by extra-district fission, it often happens that one or more consecutive sets may be lost in this way. The gap is then simply closed. For example, in the Ngmangeado of the Benangmam, Mamam, the oldest man of the lineage, is the only man of his set still alive and his set is followed by one that contains, *inter alia*, Ngkwo, a man at least fifteen years junior to Mamam. The intervening sets are lost. An elder can, it is true, recount the sets of the children and adolescents accurately enough. But he is inaccurate about the sets two or three junior to his own. The only method of collecting sets of age-mates is to ask each individual for the names of his age-mates and laboriously check the whole sequence. Any man knows his own age-mates; he knows less accurately the set older and the set younger than his own.

The age-sets therefore give a birth order or order of seniority within the limits of the major lineage. A man knows his place in his own set exactly; he knows the members of senior and junior sets and can therefore place himself relative to individuals of his set and can place his set relative to other sets. The principal function of the age-set system is to define seniority within the major lineage and it is seniority that decides who shall hold political and ritual office. The elder of the major lineage is its oldest man; the leader of the 'spirit holders' is the oldest one among them; the Owner of the Earth, not in the sense of an elder of a particular lineage but in that of a category of persons 'sent by the land', is the oldest man of that category within the major lineage. In any situation it is the senior person who exercises authority.

The relations between age-mates are relations of juniority and seniority fixed in memory by the age-set system. It cannot be said of these age-sets, as it is said of age-sets and age-grades of some segmentary societies, that where the lineage divides the age-set unites. The Konkomba age-sets lay out all the male members of the major lineage in a strict order of seniority.

Yet lineage segmentation does divide lineage members and does confer diversity of status. The unifying role carried out by, say, the Dogon *Awa* society, is carried out in Konkomba structure by the association known as the *Benatshipwam*. The term means simply the 'young men', from *onatshipwa*, a young man. The association may be defined as one of all the post-adolescent unmarried men of a major lineage. The parallel term *Besapwam*, 'young women', is also used of the nubile, unmarried girls, but this is a group without corporate functions.

The 'young men', as a group, have two important corporate functions; first, they carry on feuds on behalf of the lineage and, secondly, they dance at burials.

Konkomba now say that the kin of a man who has been killed in a fight will kill any man of the clan of the killer. This assertion does not seem, *a priori*, to be very probable nor does it accord with the degrees of responsibility and privilege found to operate in other situations. In one fight, in which no one was hurt, men of two minor lineages of different clans were involved. Members of another minor lineage of the same major lineage as one of the groups of protagonists stood by not far off but did not intervene. Members of a major lineage contraposed to the major lineage of one group of combatants passed by and were in no way likely to be involved at that time. Clearly, there are degrees of involvement in a fight and perhaps in a feud. If a man be killed the duty of killing in revenge falls first on the brother of the dead man who, probably, should kill either the killer or a close agnatic kinsman of the killer's. Konkomba tend to think in terms of the larger units of segmentation, though in actual situations finer distinctions in terms of the smaller segments are in fact drawn; but in discussing the development of a feud they tend to jump from the initial killing to the final involvement of the whole major lineage and even clan. It is certain that, in the end, the whole clan may be involved in a feud but I was not able to watch the development of one.

In the fight referred to above, it was the young men who were involved in a brawl over a woman belonging to the minor lineage of one of the groups who fought and was married into the other. The woman's husband, a middle-aged man, did not take part in the fight. It began between two individuals and spread to include members of both minor lineages, while kinsmen of the same major lineage stood by ready to help their kinsmen. The 'young men' as a group fight together against the 'young men' of other lineages.

In addition to warlike activities, the 'young men' have an important ritual role, that of dancing at burials of elders. Elder in this context is defined as a man or woman who has a married daughter or a son who, had he been a girl, is old enough to be married. The dance of the 'young men', the *Kenatshu*, is danced for members of the clan or for women married into the clan. Women are therefore danced for twice, once by their husbands' clansfolk and once by their own.

Should a male elder die in the late afternoon, that evening the 'young women' dance in the open space outside the dead man's compound. At midnight the 'young men' begin to dance and dance without ceasing until nine or ten the following morning, perhaps on through the day until the elder is buried. They will be joined by the 'young men' of the clan's *mantotib*, that is, another clan that stands in a reciprocal ritual relation with the clan of the dead man; by 'young men' to whom the dead man was *umwidza*, mother's brother; by 'young men' from the *umwetib*, the patrikin of the dead man's mother; by 'young men' sent by elders of contiguous districts, and by others who come to enjoy the dance.

This dance is a solemn occasion, not a beer party. Though the dancers go on unremittingly for up to ten hours, the refreshment offered is millet crushed in water.

The same dances are also performed for dead women members of the clan on the day when a calabash (*lekpojig*) representing the spirit of the dead woman is sent by her husband's kin to her own paternal kin (*nindzatib*).

When a neighbouring elder dies, an elder sends several of his 'young men' to dance or drum for the dancers at the burial.

Membership in the association of the 'young men' therefore confers certain duties on a young man; first, the duties of defending clan lands or fishing rights against encroachment by other clans and of fighting and carrying on feuds on behalf of kinsmen. The association therefore has political roles. It has, secondly, a ritual role in burials and, since dancing at burials of neighbouring elders is one strand in inter-clan relations, this role, though primarily ritual, has also a political aspect.

The association has no initiation rites, no rites of entry or departure. Nor does a man grow old with a group of fellow members as he does with his age-mates of the age-set. While the age-sets segment the major lineage horizontally, the association of the 'young men' brings the young men of the lineage together and confers on its members equality of status as dancers and warriors. The age-sets are a mnemonic system defining seniority and juniority. The 'young

The young men dance at Kenatshu

A dead woman's co-wives dance at her funeral

men' is a loose association, entered during adolescence and left at marriage by all men. In so far as the Konkomba lineage system can be said to have a centrifugal effect, this association can equally be said to have a centripetal effect, binding together in a common status men of diverse lineage standing.

Membership of this association also confers certain rights on a young man. The elder of a major lineage must always provide a room in his compound which is known as the 'young men's room'. This is also the position for an elder of a minor lineage when his group forms a separate hamlet. In this room they keep their bows and arrows, their dancing headdress (*ipiedza*) and some clothing. They may, and generally do, sleep together in it.

It is in this room that *Dzambuna*, the ritual symbol of the major lineage, and the *igi*, the protective medicine and symbol of the minor lineage, are kept. Here the young men may sleep together, though each has a home in the compound of his pater to which he may go should he wish. In the dry season the young men often scatter, while in the wet season they sleep together. They may be seen in the evening gathering together in the house of the elder where food is prepared for them. The young men eat what is available for them there and they then scatter in twos and threes, taking with them the sons of the elder, to eat again at one or more of the other compounds of the lineage. They later return to sleep in their allotted room.

I have sought to give an account of the segmentary system of a Konkomba clan as it works at a point in time. The clan is the largest unit of political organization because it is the largest unit in the Konkomba system within which there can be arbitration between elders of the component segments, where ritual sanctions and the sanction of ostracism can be applied against a fellow-member. The clan also comprises the largest group of men who will come to the aid, in a fight, of a fellow-member. Moral obligation within the clan, but not beyond clan limits, and warlike relations or their possibility outside the clan, but not within its limits, make the clan the political unit of the Konkomba system. Elders have no power to punish by force or to impose such a penalty as a fine on an offending member of the clan. Their authority is ritual and moral. There are few rewards of office in this society, unless the plurality of wives enjoyed by the older half of the male population at the expense of the younger men be so regarded. There is no exaction of tribute or of services by the elder. The only material rewards of office are the right to distribute game after hunts, and perhaps to reserve a large share for himself, and the advantage elder status gives in farm work, for when an elder calls a work party there is always a good turn-out. The elder is also the owner of the dawa-dawa trees, which are valued for their food.

The clan is a segmentary system of enduring, agnatic lineages which on the levels of the major and minor lineage are localized corporate units with political functions. The clan, a territorial and ritual unit, is segmented into major lineages and the major lineages are segmented into minor lineages. The groups of agnatic kin, which result from this segmentary system of three orders of segmentation, are in turn territorial, jural and ritual units. Since, in this society, the maintenance of order within the clan is kept by ritual and moral sanctions and not by the application of organized force, then ritual and jural units are also political units.

But the segmentary units are not permanent groups though they may be, and often are, long enduring. The groups are as they are because of common descent at the highest levels of segmentation and diversity of descent on the lower levels of segmentation of their genealogical structures. This diversity of status within the segmentary system is held in memory by the genealogies given above. These genealogies are not statements of actual relations of descent; they are rather a mnemonic system with a depth proportionate to the variety of observable groups of living agnates. The genealogical structure of the lineage is no more than a validation, in terms of descent, of relations between groups of living kinsmen and some variability must be expected in it.

V. Marriage and the Extended House

KONKOMBA practise the betrothal of infant girls to young men in their early twenties who thereafter give bride service and pay bride corn to their parents-in-law, until the girl is of an age to marry. The infant girl is known to the man as his 'wife' (*pu*); there is no distinction in Konkomba between a 'betrothed girl' and a 'wife'. By 'wife' I shall mean a girl who has joined her husband in his compound and when I use the verb 'to marry' it is as the translation of the Konkomba phrase which means 'to go to the husband'.

When a girl child is born, her parents are approached and given presents of pots of beer and fowls by the parents of a young man of between twenty and twenty-four. Often the parents of the girl receive several offers amongst which to choose. Sometimes the first step is taken by the young man himself who sends a gift of firewood to the mother of the child, who is confined to the room in which the child was born for a week after the birth.

The approach to the parents of the girl is made as soon as the sex of the infant is known. There is often competition between those seeking wives who try, by making large gifts, to persuade the parents to betroth the child to them. There is also competition to send the gifts to the parents as quickly as possible; to this end a young man's sister, herself married into another clan, will not only send speedy word of a female birth to her brother but will even warn him of expected births, so that he can have firewood ready to send to the mother should the child turn out to be a girl.

If the first gifts be accepted then the sender knows that he is being considered as a prospective son-in-law. The gifts should not otherwise be accepted. Some weeks later, in effect when it is clear that the child is likely to live, another pot of beer is sent. When the child is several months old the decision should be made and a son-in-law chosen from among the contestants. An elderly man with children does not always specify the son on whose behalf he is asking for the girl but has the child betrothed to himself even though, when the time comes for her to marry, he will pass her on to whichever of his sons is ready to marry and has no wife.

The father of the newly born infant does not always accept offers for his daughter but announces that he is holding her in the hope of making an exchange. Once the decision is made nothing more is done until either the mother of the betrothed girl bears another child, or until the betrothed child is four or five years old, when the payments of bride corn and services begin.

The ideal scheme of payments of bride corn is as follows: once the betrothed girl has reached the age of five the payments begin. There are three forms of paying the guinea corn called respectively 'They beat corn', 'They send corn' and 'They tie corn'. The first payment, 'They beat corn', should be of two baskets of guinea corn in grain, paid when the girl has passed infancy; two to three years later the second payment is made, 'They send corn', a payment of two or three baskets of corn. The year after, the series of payments known as 'They tie corn' begin; these are tied bundles of heads of corn, in the first year one bundle, in the second year two bundles and so on up to ten bundles in the tenth year. The girl is now ready to marry and is about eighteen years of age.

The total value of these payments is about £20 at the current rates in the Saboba market. A basket contains the same amount of corn as does a 4-gallon paraffin tin; a bundle of corn is half a paraffin tin; a tin of corn sells at 17s. The opening gifts of beer and fowls of *Bi twi opi*, 'They negotiate for a woman', costs at market prices between 16s and 20s.

Once the girl's father has agreed that she shall join her husband, that is *tsha ta tshar*, marry, the husband makes two final payments, the bride's cloth and the bride's money. A cloth costs between 12s and 20s, and the money present, which goes in fact to the father-in-law, is 3s 6d.

The total cost of the bride corn and other gifts is therefore about £22. To this must be added the value of the work that a son-in-law puts in on his father-in-law's farm. In this work he is commonly assisted by his age-mates. The highest number of days' work given to a father-in-law was sixty days in four years. This young man has had two previous girls promised to him, both of whom died before reaching nubility. On the other hand when the father-in-law is distant from the home of the son-in-law, the latter may give no services for many years but, after that time, may go to his father-in-law's place for several months to work special plots of yams and corn for him. Setting aside fathers-in-law who live far off, a small sample count suggested that the average number of days' work given in any one year is 2.7. That is to say that in ten years a young man gives a month's work to his father-in-law which, at the present rates of pay on the Krachi farms, can be estimated at £10.

The total value of the bride corn, gifts and service may be estimated, at present, at £32. Yet the payments are seldom made in the ideal form. In the past, if the corn had not been handed over, the two presentations, 'They beat corn' and 'They send corn', could be met with a payment in cowries, and the third known as 'They tie corn' could take the form of a second and equal payment of cowries.

These payments are at present known as *ungkwob* and the value of each in cash is £2 10s. Konkomba count money in half-pennies and sixpences. *Ungkwob* means 100, that is 100 sixpences or 50s. I am not certain of the former meaning of the term but it may have meant 1,000 cowries. Thus £32 worth of corn and work may be commuted, at present, into two cash payments of £2 10s each, added to which is the bride cloth and bride money, making a total of £6 in all.

I have no useful figures on the annual cash income of a compound head but, even including the cash young men bring back from the Krachi farms, the average cash income of compound heads cannot exceed £10 a year. None the less, Konkomba are very well aware of changing prices in their own markets and it is possible that the young men are consciously avoiding expensive payments of corn and troublesome services by making a cash settlement that they can earn by a fortnight of wage labour. It may also be convenient to the parents-in-law to receive a cash payment.

Exchange marriages come about when two men exchange girls; the girls exchanged may be either 'sisters' or 'daughters', actual or classificatory, to the men. The girls need not be of the same age, but, since there is no repayment of bride corn should a betrothed girl die nor replacement of the dead girl with another one, if they are of the same age, the risk of loss through death is the same for both men. If the girls to be exchanged are infants, they are commonly promised to youths who, though exempt from paying bride corn, still owe some service to their fathers-in-law. Girls who have reached puberty and are to be exchanged are more likely to be given to older men. An older man with few or no sons is especially likely to seek to exchange one of his daughters for a wife for himself. These exchange marriages are a normal but infrequent form of marriage, numbering less than 5 per cent of all marriages.

The age of marriage for men is delayed until the age of forty, but from adolescence onwards they carry on love affairs. From puberty onwards, girls are allowed full sexual freedom by their parents until they marry. Both unmarried men and unmarried women often have three or four lovers in different major lineages at the same time. Some men claim to have as many as six lovers, all of whom they visit from time to time, though such a man visits one or two of them more frequently than the others.

The man has to visit the girl's home, unlike the Dagomba among whom the girl goes to her lover's house. The Konkomba lover visits his girl and sleeps with her in her mother's room. Thus, though he may visit her frequently he cannot always sleep with her, since he cannot go into that room if the girl's father is there with her mother. This and other circumstances, such as the presence in the hamlet of a kinsman of his mistress's betrothed husband, greatly reduce the number of occasions on which a pair of lovers may sleep together. Sometimes they may have to wait up to three months.

I said that girls are allowed full sexual freedom as far as parental control is concerned. Within the limits of the rules of incest this is true, but it is said that in the past all Konkomba husbands were jealous of their prospective wives' lovers and sought to discover and kill them. I find the assertion difficult to accept. It is true that a man who carries on an affair with a married woman is likely, if caught, to be killed by the husband. Many young married women, however, easily carry on love affairs simply by visiting their father's home from time to time. It has even been pointed out to me that guinea corn grows tall and thick. None the less, such affairs are very risky and do lead to killings and thence to feud.

As far as the girls who are not yet married are concerned, precautions are taken to prevent their future husbands from discovering who their lovers are. No joking references to lovers are made when a future husband pays a visit to his father-in-law's house; girls do not speak to their lovers outside their own paternal hamlets and especially do they avoid speaking to them in the market. A girl sends messages to her lover through his sister or through her own brother.

Yet husbands do sometimes watch their future wives. I called one night on Kwadi, the Dagomba-appointed Chief of Saboba, and found him away from home. He later explained that he had gone to greet his father-in-law. His son, during my call, had been much franker;

he said that his father had gone to hide in the guinea corn near his future wife's home in order to find out who her lover was. If spying of this sort was common in the past it is rare today.

From the relationship between lovers, marriages sometimes arise. If, as occasionally happens, the girl is not betrothed, a marriage can easily be arranged by the payment of £5 and the marriage gifts. This is a fully approved and acceptable form of marriage. Or an unbetrothed girl may run away from home to join her lover in his home. This union can be regularized. The husband sends a kinsman to the girl's father *ke te gba njopu*, to apologize, and later he may pay the money and gifts. The girl may even insist, before she runs away, that the bride cloth be sent to her.

Should a girl elope who is already betrothed to another man, the situation is much more difficult. The husband still sends a kinsman to the girl's father to apologize on his behalf and later he pays the bride price of £5 and so establishes himself as a husband *vis-à-vis* the girl's clansfolk. But such marriages are not fully approved by the man's own kinsmen, even though such wives are, in fact, inherited as widows. The kinsmen, the men of a major lineage of a man who has enticed a betrothed girl, are subject to reprisals by the men of the major lineage that has lost a wife. Members of that lineage will in turn seek to entice to them either a daughter or a fiancée of the other lineage. If the former happens then the lineage that first illegally gained a wife now has to explain to a fourth lineage that they cannot meet their bargains; or, in the latter case, they will have gained one wife but lost a betrothed wife and, though the man who has lost a fiancée is aggrieved against his own kinsman, the matter is closed as between the two major lineages.

The position of a woman who runs away to join a lover is less secure than that of a woman properly married with bride corn and service. Her lover-become-husband fulfills the duties of a son-in-law, but she has not the full status of a wife within his lineage. For example, a woman who joined her lover in this way died a year or two later and the diviner found that she was killed by a witch. The witch was also found but the husband could take no action against him since, had it come to fighting, his kinsmen would not have supported him for a woman not properly married with bride corn.

Konkomba sometimes 'buy' women from the Kabre, a people who live some forty miles to the east of the Oti river and north of the Kotokoli Hills. Occasionally Gurma are 'bought'. It is said that in the past the payment was made in cowries; the present payment is four cows, worth between £40 and £50 at Saboba market prices. Of the 800 marriages recorded for the two clans discussed below, only six such marriages are included. Five were Kabre women and one was a Gurma. It is not only as wives that Konkomba 'buy' Kabre. Men without sons, who have not been able to borrow or inherit a 'son' from a kinsman, sometimes buy a twelve-year-old Kabre boy. A man usually resorts to 'buying' a Kabre woman only after he has married two or more women who have all died childless or leaving him with small children. And he will only do this on the advice of a diviner.

There is no deliberate avoiding of these Kabre women by their co-wives nor can any difference in status be noted between the child of a Konkomba mother and the child of a Kabre mother. But the women themselves must often feel lonely since the two languages belong to very different language groups and the women do not appear to become very fluent in Konkomba.

When a Konkomba dies, his wives have to observe a year of mourning during which time they wear a white cord round the neck as a sign. It is believed that any man who lies with a woman wearing this white cord will die. Widows, then, necessarily observe a tabu on sexual relations until after their husband's Final Funeral Ceremony. After the Second Burial the widows are inherited within the husband's minor lineage and most frequently within the husband's nuclear lineage. Only two modes of inheritance of widows seem to be proscribed. A man may not inherit his own mother; nor does a man inherit his son's wife. But sons inherit widows from their fathers, elder brothers inherit from younger brothers, and inheritance ranges as wide as an agnatic third cousin or his son. Preference is given to the nearer relatives of the dead man—first, his brothers, then men of his nuclear lineage and finally men of the minor lineage.

There is no levirate among Konkomba. On the death of her husband a woman goes to a second husband within the same minor lineage and her children by the second husband belong to him, not to the first husband. There is, indeed, a tendency to ascribe all a woman's children to her living husband rather than to their begetter. In any case, in many situations it is of little importance which of a group of kinsmen begot a child since 'a woman does not marry one man'. It is only when marriages are to be arranged that the begetter should be known, though even then it is not essential. This knowledge is not always accurate. A considerable number of women are pregnant when they go to their husbands as brides; this is understandable as they appear to practise no form of contraception. In this case, the genitor of their child is a lover, not the husband. However the distinction between the genitor and pater is not maintained, for a child belongs to the woman's husband and he is the child's *te*, father. There is a word, *obombo*, which means 'a child who does not know its father'. I have never heard the term in use and can only suppose it to refer to a child growing up in the compound of its mother's father; there is no provision for a child except in the compound of a husband.

Husbands show not the slightest sign of displeasure at the pregnancy of a bride. Indeed, it was pointed out to me that if a girl becomes pregnant by her lover the husband will get his wife all the sooner, together with a child, a situation which pleases most men. The recollection that the bride was pregnant when she came to the husband seems rapidly to pass away. With the passage of time, the pater of a child is thought of as having begotten the children of which he is the social father.

There are no prohibitions on marriages between members of different tribes or clans. The ritual relation of *mantotib* between clans or major lineages does not prohibit marriage. I give some figures for the clans of the Benalog and the Benangmam showing their marriages arranged by tribe; both these clans are of the Betshabob tribe.

TABLE I

| | Benalog | | Benangmam | |
	Men %	Women %	Men %	Women %
Betshabob	68.4	75.2	82.4	86.3
Nakpantib	20.8	19.3	6.2	4.8
Bemokpem	1.8	1.3	8.5	6.2
Benafiab	0.3	1.3	—	—
Besangma	0.6	0.4	1.8	2.7
Bekwom	0.6	—	—	—
Kabre and Gurma	1.2	—	0.6	—
Dagomba	0.3	—	—	—
Not ascertained	6.0	2.5	0.5	—

The Benalog are contiguous with two large clans of the Nakpantib and they have a high percentage of marriages with them; the Benangmam have nearer neighbours of Bemokpem tribe than have the

Benalog and show a higher percentage of Bemokpem marriages. It would appear that distance is an important factor.

Table II shows the marriages of these same two clans arranged by distance.

TABLE II

	Benalog		Benangmam	
	Men %	Women %	Men %	Women %
Under 3 miles	45.0	48.0	42.7	54.5
3–12 miles	25.4	19.5	28.0	27.6
12–20 miles	9.5	14.0	14.0	8.3
Over 20 miles	1.5	6.8	6.1	2.8
Not ascertained	18.6	11.7	9.2	6.8

There is no system of prohibited marriages between clans nor does there seem to be any system of preferred marriages between clans. Apart from the rules prohibiting marriages between categories of kin the choice of a spouse appears to be random. Contiguity appears to be important and it is easy to see that near neighbours are likely to hear quickly of births in a clan. Yet women of the same clan whose sons are seeking wives and who meet in the market tell each other of births in their husband's clans. Thus marriages may come about between quite widely separated clans.

The prohibitions on marriage between categories of kin are expressed by Konkomba in terms of a unit they call the *do*. This term has two usages. First, it can be used in a sense close to that of the noun *lenampar* and the verb *kwi* in their sense of 'home'. In reply to the query 'Where are you going?' a man may reply '*Lenampar*', 'the house', or he may reply '*N ka kwi la*', 'I go home', or he may reply '*Ti do*', 'Our house'. The primary reference of the term *do* appears to be the household occupying one compound. It has an extended use, namely the group descended from a common grandfather to which are added the women married into the group. The agnatic line that is the core of this group is itself a descent group that may, and sometimes does coincide with the nuclear lineage; but the extended house itself is not a lineage.

When speaking of the group of compound inhabitants I shall speak of a household, *do*, and when speaking of the extended use of *do* I shall speak of an extended house.

Though Konkomba think of the extended house in terms of the agnatic core plus the females added to it, it might be looked at as a descent group counting through both males and females. The *do* might be thought to be the group descended from a common grandfather counting through both males and females, a group often spoken of as a kindred. For example, among the rules prohibiting certain marriages there is the following one: a man or a woman may not marry into the mother's extended house. A second rule states that a man or woman may not marry into the extended house of the father's sister's husband (Fig. 4).

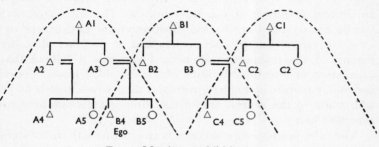

FIG. 4. Marriage prohibitions

According to the rule above B4 may not marry A5 or C5 and B5 may not marry A4 or C4. Were the rules applied in this simple manner the prohibitions could be discussed as prohibitions on marriages between kindreds. This is not possible because the rules are extended. B4 is prohibited from marrying not only his father's sister's daughter but any woman so classified. B5 is prohibited from marrying not only her mother's brother's son but may not marry a man of the same major lineage as her mother. The Konkomba think of marriages in terms of exchanges between extended houses not as exchanges between kindreds.

The unit of the exchanges is the unit I call an extended house. It is not a lineage because it shifts in each generation and it functions only in the marriage system. This is seen from the extended house shown in Genealogy V. From the point of view of Ngagbi his extended house is the group descended from Dzange who may or may not be his grandfather in fact. From the point of view of Bela, Ngagbi's son, the extended house is the group descended from Dongwi who died more than fifty years ago; while from the point of view of Bela's son the extended house is the group descended from Ngagbi. The extended house is a temporary unit which comes into being in every generation and endures only until the birth of a new generation in the male line. Ngagbi and Pela belong to one extended house; their sons Bela and Kakudza belong to different extended houses. It has to be borne in mind that a girl is betrothed at birth while her brother's first marriages are not arranged until twenty years later. From this it follows that the inter-relations of their extended house and those extended houses with which it is connected by marriage are in continuous change, as girls are born and betrothed and boys pass adolescence and are betrothed. The prohibitions on marriage relate to individuals not only as members of a category of kin but as members of extended houses. The marriages of Konkomba are arranged not by the prospective spouses, except in runaway marriages, but by their elders and, if they are alive, by the parents of the prospective spouses. From this it follows that the calculation of inter-relationships of the extended houses concerned is done by mature and elderly men and their wives, that is by people who stand in the central one of the three generations found in an extended house.

The rules prohibiting marriages between kin, with their extensions to other members of the extended house, can be set out as follows:

A man may not marry—

(1) Women of his major lineage.

(2) Women of the extended house of his mother.

(2b) Women of the extended house of the mother of any man of his extended house.

(3) Women of his father's mother's extended house, though he may marry into the extended house of his mother's mother.

(4) Women of the extended house of his father's sister's husband or of his sister's husband.

(4b) Women of the extended house of the father's sister or sister of any man of his extended house.

(5) Women of the extended house of his wife.

(5b) Women of the extended house of the wife of any member of his extended house.

A woman may not marry—

(1) Men of her major lineage.

(2) Men of the major lineage of her mother.

(2b) Men of the extended house of the mother of a member of her extended house.

(3) Men of her father's mother's extended house.

(4) Men of the extended house of her mother's mother, though marriage to another extended house of the mother's mother's minor lineage is a 'good' marriage.

(5) Men of her father's sister's husband's extended house and men of her sister's husband's extended house.

(5b) Men of the extended house of the husband of a member of her extended house.

(6) Men of the extended house of women married into her extended house except in an exchange marriage.

Some of these rules have been stated with perhaps excessive simplicity, for they may be modified in their application. For example, a man may not marry into his mother's extended house, yet should a man fail to get a wife elsewhere his mother will approach her own people on her son's behalf. One man was betrothed to his mother's father's brother's son's daughter. This betrothal is not strictly an infringement of the rule though some elders felt it needed to be explained. The point they made is that there is a difference of mother at the point where the agnatic line of the wife meets the husband's mother's agnatic line in a common ancestor three generations back from the husband and wife. In other words they are descended from different wives of a common great grand-father. This is a form of explanation often offered where it may seem that the rules are being infringed. It is expressed in Konkomba as being a difference of 'room', *kedig*; the 'room' indicates a woman or mother. A man, when speaking of his wife, will point to her room to indicate the wife of whom he speaks and in discussing descent lines the 'room' indicates the mother from which the line started.

In another case, a woman married her father's brother's daughter's son; her husband therefore married his mother's father's brother's daughter. That is, he married a person he addressed as *nawa*, mother's younger sister, while the wife married her *umwidza*, mother's brother (Figure 5). The rule as stated above was broken.

But again, the wife's agnatic line and the husband's mother's agnatic line descend from different wives of an ancestor common to both spouses and the distance between them is thereby held to be increased. In similar cases, where difference of mothers at some point is not known, it is assumed. As one elder always urged, 'If they don't come from one room it doesn't matter.' The instance quoted here is the closest marriage of kin that I found and I do not think that such marriages are frequent.

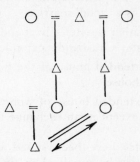

FIG. 5. Relationship between a husband and wife

The rules stated above fit together in a coherent system. They may, taken severally, be said to result from certain principles of organization. The first rule for men and women emphasizes and follows from the solidarity of the major lineage. It is to be noted that intermarriage of members of different major lineages of one clan is not always found to be possible for contraposed lineages. Intermarriage of major lineages of one clan and contraposition of major lineages of one clan appear to be alternatives. In any case, if the marriage system is one of exchange of rights over women against goods there can be no exchange within one solidary group.

The rules (2) and (3) for men, and (2) (3) and (4) for women seem to arise from the closeness of the maternal tie. There is no closer link for Konkomba than that between persons who are *naabo* to each other. This word is literally *na a bo*, 'mother's child' [i.e. uterine siblings, ed.]; also through the mother is created the widely ranging tie of friendship between persons who are *nabo* to each other, literally *na bo*, 'mother child'. Any two persons whose mothers come from the same major lineage are *nabo* to each other [i.e. fellow 'sisters' sons', ed.]. In consequence of this *nabo* relation links are created between individuals which range as widely in space as do the marriages of the women of any one major lineage and which endure through the life of each individual. The relation carries with it no ritual, economic or other duties. It is simply a relation of friendship.

Rule (4) for men and rule (5) for women are corollaries of rules (2) for both men and women.

The rules relate primarily to individual men and women but they are extended in various ways to include not only the extended house of one's own mother but, for example, the extended houses of the mothers of men of one's own extended house. Konkomba explain this and similar extensions in the following way: if a man were to marry a woman of the same extended house as a man of his own extended house and should later die, then the second man might find himself forced to marry his mother's sister, real or classificatory, his *nawa*. And this would be impossible.

Rule (5*a*) for men and rule (5) for women follow from the absence of the sororate. The extension of rule (5) found in rule (5*b*) for men follows from the danger that a man might be forced to inherit his wife's sister. There is, in fact, one instance known to me in which men of the same extended house married sisters by different mothers. It came about through the death of the first husband of one of the women, who was inherited by a man of the same minor lineage as her husband and whose brother had married her sister. Though they admitted this to be unusual, the elders concerned urged that it only happened because the first husband died and that should either of the present husbands die the survivor could not inherit the sister of his wife and that, finally, though the girls have the same father they come from 'different rooms'. One result of such a marriage is that the children of these women are both members of one extended house and *nabo*, 'mother child' (fellow 'sisters' sons'), to each other; that is, they are 'brother' or 'sister' and *nabo* to each other at the same time.

The rules may be thought to arise from two principles of organization; first, the closeness of the uterine tie and, secondly, the unity of the extended house. Such an explanation does not, however, account for the different extension of the rules for males and for females. If a girl may not marry into the extended house of her mother's mother, why may a boy do so since the tie between grandson and grand-daughter to the agnatic kin of the mother's mother is equally close? An explanation of the rules in terms of these two principles is therefore inadequate.

The rules of marriage can be seen as a system of exchange of goods against rights over women. In any marriage a girl is betrothed and bride corn and bride service is given for her over a period of a dozen years. This is an exchange of goods and services against rights over women. The rules given above can be expressed in the following diagrams. I take the primary statement of the prohibitions as applying between individuals for simplicity in the diagrams.

Starting with a male and counting back through the generations in the agnatic line we get the following result. The horizontal lines represent generations and the vertical lines represent extended houses.

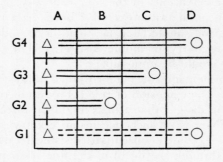

FIG. 6. Illustrations of marriages between extended houses (i)

A man may not marry into his mother's extended house nor that of his father's mother (Fig. 6). He may marry into the extended house of his father's father's mother if it be known. Put inversely, a woman's descendants in the lineage of her husband cannot marry back into her own extended house until the third generation (son's son's son). Fig. 7 demonstrates that the same result is obtained in the case of a girl.

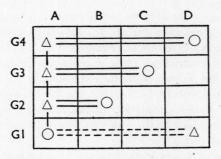

FIG. 7. Illustrations of marriages between extended houses (ii)

With the marriage prohibitions traced in the uterine line a different result is achieved (Fig. 8). A man may not marry into his mother's extended house but he may marry into the extended house of his mother's mother.

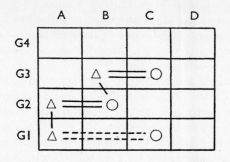

Fig. 8. Illustrations of marriages between extended houses (iii)

The prohibitions for a girl in the uterine line may be set out in Fig. 9. A girl may not marry into the major lineage of her mother and, *a fortiori*, the extended house of her mother: nor may she marry into the extended house of her mother's mother.

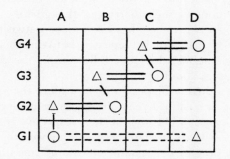

Fig. 9. Illustrations of marriages between extended houses (iv)

It may be seen from these diagrams that in the agnatic line the prohibitions on marriage are identical for a man and a woman but that they differ in the uterine line. This difference has nothing to do with the incest regulations, as exemplified in the prohibitions on taking a lover, for these regulations are identical for both men and women. A man or woman may not take a lover in his or her own minor lineage nor in the minor lineage of his or her mother. None should have two lovers in any one major lineage; though this rule is frequently broken when two men of one major lineage are lovers of the same girl, I know no instance in which two girls of one major lineage share one lover. No prohibition attaches to the taking of lovers in the mother's mother's or father's mother's lineage or extended house. If the extension of the marriage prohibitions for a girl are not connected with incest regulations or the exchange of goods in marriage, it may be connected with the difference in age of betrothal and marriage for girls as against their brothers.

Figs. 6 and 7 suggest that marriages are an exchange, a *prestation totale* in Mauss's term, of goods against rights over women. These exchanges are unrepeatable and irreversible through two succeeding generations because the extensions of the rules proscribe repetition of marriages between two extended houses. If we work back in the agnatic line we get exchanges between one extended house and two others (Figs. 6 and 7). If we count in the uterine line the exchange passes from one pair of units to one unit of the first pair and a third unit. In Fig. 9 a woman of D married C; her daughter marries B and her daughter's daughter marries A. Goods pass from C to D, B to C and A to B and it is not until the third generation, the daughter's daughter's daughter of the first woman, that a marriage back into extended house D is possible.

The prohibitions of such marriages, though they do not infringe the rule that once a marriage has been made between two extended houses marriage may not be repeated between them through two succeeding generations, does not follow from the principle. Their proscription comes about in another way.

A girl is betrothed at birth to a man of more than twenty years of age. Therefore the affinal relations of their extended houses are different for a sister and brother at their respective times of betrothal for there is twenty years, at least, between the two events.

If we count time in the agnatic and the uterine lines, the generations are of very different duration (Fig. 10). From the birth of a man to the birth of his son's son is at least eighty years. From the birth of a girl to the birth of her daughter's daughter need not be more than forty years. Konkomba count their generations through males in the extended house which has an agnatic core. This unit re-forms in each agnatic generation, though to one agnatic generation there are two uterine generations. Now a girl is betrothed at birth and her brother is betrothed twenty years later. That is, the brother is betrothed when the prohibitions brought into force by the marriage of his sisters close a number of extended houses to him.

We may therefore suppose that either the prohibitions on marriage for girls are widened and extended against those of their brothers or, conversely, that the proscribed unions for men are narrowed and

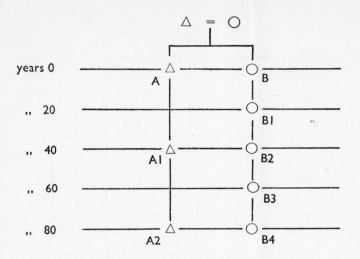

FIG. 10. Births in agnatic and uterine generations

contracted against those of their sisters so that the total number of possible proscriptions will be more nearly equal at the time of betrothal.

I take first the prohibition of marriage between a girl and her mother's mother's extended house, one which does not exist for a man. The changing extended house completes its cycle of change in about forty years or one agnatic generation, in which time two uterine generations have come into being. In Figure 10, A and B are brother and sister. A's son A1 is born when A is at least forty years of age, but B's daughter B1 is born when her mother is twenty years old and her grand-daughter B2 is born when B is forty and when A1 is an infant. B2 may not marry into her mother's mother's extended house and at her birth that extended house, in terms of agnatic generations, is just on the point of change, while on the birth of the next girl B3 the extended house descended from the father of A and B is safely past the point of change.

Or we may count time in betrothal periods (Fig. 11). Starting at nought for the birth of both A and B as brother and sister, A's son will be betrothed sixty years later, while B's daughter's daughter's daughter will be betrothed at about the same time. In other words it is not until the daughter's daughter's daughter of a woman married

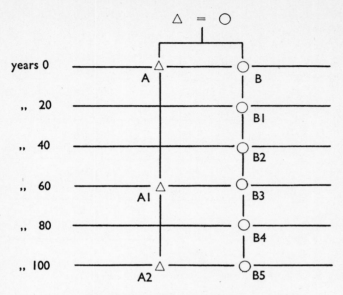

FIG. 11. Betrothals in agnatic and uterine generations

out of her own extended house is reached that her extended house is finally changed by the betrothal of her brother's son A1.

It seems likely, therefore, that the further extension of the prohibition on marriage with the matrilateral kin for a girl follows from the different age of marriage for men and women. The extended house changes with the appearance of male generations and, since there are approximately two uterine to one agnatic generation, the prohibition on marriage with the mother's kin extends one further generation for a girl than for her brother.

But this does not account for the wider prohibition for a girl who may not marry anyone of her mother's whole major lineage, though she may have a lover in a minor lineage other than her mother's of that major lineage. A man may not marry into the extended house of his mother and may not take a lover in her minor lineage.

Men and women begin to take lovers at nearly the same age, though boys tend to be a little later than girls. The difference is not comparable to the difference in their betrothal and marriage ages and consequently the range of their prohibitions is the same.

In a sample of sixteen extended houses of two major lineages the following result is obtained:

Average number of living descendants of the head of the extended house	14
Average number of wives of the head	2.14
Average number of betrothable males	3.1
Average number of betrothed females	2.28
Average number of brides betrothed to the extended house	1.4
Wives in the extended house	3.3
Average number of women married out of the extended house	4.0

From these figures, the total number of extended houses into which a girl newly born into this average extended house may not be betrothed can be estimated.

		No. of extended houses
Rule 1	excludes her own major lineage	—
Rule 2	excludes her mother's major lineage	16
Rule 2a	excludes extended houses of the mothers of members of her extended house	5.4
Rule 3	excludes her father's mother's extended house	1
Rule 4	excludes her mother's mother's extended house	1
Rule 5	excludes extended houses of the husbands of women of her extended house	6.8
	Total	30.2

The total number of prohibited extended houses for a male of twenty years of age in this average extended house are:

Rule 2a	excludes his mother's extended house	1
Rule 2b	excludes the extended houses of mothers of members of his extended house	5.4
Rule 3	excludes his father's mother's extended house	1
	Total	7.4

Now a man in his lifetime may marry several times and most men marry at least twice. The marriages frequencies by age-set for two major lineages are as follows:

Under 44	45–48	49–52	53–56	57–60	over 60
0.8	1.2	1.3	1.9	1.9	3.05

The average number of marriages for each man may be put at 2. Thus if the average extended house has 3.1 betrothable males each of whom marries twice then the excluded extended houses are:

$$2 \times 3.1 \times 7.4 = 45.9 \text{ extended houses}$$

Thus, for a girl at birth 30.24 extended houses are excluded from giving her a spouse, and for a man throughout life 45.9 extended houses are excluded from giving him a spouse. That is to say that in fact the prohibitions extend more widely for men than for women as a result of plural marriages. Were the men monogamous, then the prohibitions would be more nearly equal for men and women.

The Konkomba system of marriage may be said to be a system of exchange of rights over women against goods between units centred on an agnatic core which is a descent group. The exchanges are unrepeatable and irreversible through the two generations succeeding an exchange.

The rules prohibiting marriages may be re-stated as follows to emphasize their group character:

Rule 1. A man or a woman may not marry a member of his or her own major lineage. The major lineage is a solidary group between members of which this form of exchange is impossible because the rights over women to be exchanged against goods and services are rights over members of the group.

Rule 2. A man may not marry into the extended house of the mother of a member of his extended house; this rule in its application to women is widened to exclude any man of a woman's own mother's major lineage and a man of her mother's mother's extended house.

Rule 3. A man may not marry into the extended house of the husband of a woman of his extended house nor into the extended house of a woman married into his own extended house, except a woman married by exchange; a woman may not marry into the extended house of the wife of a man of her extended house except by an exchange marriage, nor into the extended house of the husband of a woman of her extended house.

Exchange marriages are a normal but not very frequent form of marriage. They do not contravene the principle of exchange involved in Konkomba marriage; they are a flat exchange of the rights over a woman against similar rights in place of the more normal exchange of rights over a woman against goods and services.

The effect of this system of proscribing marriages between units is to spread widely in time and space the range of matrilateral kinship ties. Matrilateral kinship is the principal link between individuals which serves to diminish the exclusiveness and isolation of the small agnatic kin-groups of the lineage and clan system. The secondary ties between those who are *nabo* (fellow 'sisters' sons') to each other, which arise from matrilateral kinship, serve to mitigate the inveterate aggressiveness of Konkomba. To a discussion of these effects I return later.

VI. The Lineage Over Time

THE extended house is a unit of three generations' depth, the descendants of a common grandfather through both males and females. Each generation that is born brings into being a new extended house. The boys grow up, marry and in turn beget the generation that creates a new series of extended houses in which these men are the central generation. In turn these extended houses endure only until their son's sons are born when they themselves become heads of extended houses. The progression of a generation from being the latest born to being the ancestral one takes at least 120 years and as laid out in a genealogy the extended houses are, of course, of uneven growth. This is necessarily so because a man's children are begotten in the years between his fortieth year and his seventieth. In a polygynous society such as Konkomba there is a wide range in the ages of the children of one man.

The extended house has a localized agnatic core which, in terms of generation depth, may coincide with the nuclear lineage or may be shorter. It depends upon the point of view of the individual man or woman. Referring once again to Genealogy V, the putative grandfather of Ngagbi is Dzange who is the apical ancestor of the minor lineage named after him. Bela, son of Ngagbi, looks to Dongwi, his grandfather, as the head of his extended house, while Bela's son, if he had one, would look to Ngagbi. A man is betrothed for the first time at about twenty years of age, for the second time at about thirty years of age, and for a third time, perhaps, at about forty years of age. These marriages are arranged by his father, either pater or genitor, a man of the older age-sets and one who is familiar with those marriages of the older generation which are relevant to the betrothals of the young man. Thus, when a man of the generation of Bela comes to arrange marriages for his sons and daughters all he needs to know are the marriages of Ngagbi and Ngagbi's sons and daughters, since, from the point of view of Bela's children, Ngagbi is the head of the extended house. The extended house is therefore best looked at from the point of view of the central generation, men and women, who are literally the children of one man.

If we look at the version in Genealogy I the nuclear lineage descended from Dongwi coincides with the extended house in which Ngagbi is in the central generation; but, though Nanga is dead and his son Suba is a householder, the extended house in which Suba is the central generation is still held to the nuclear lineage of Dongwi. The nuclear lineage of Kpa does not coincide with the extended house of which Kakudza is the central generation, because, despite the irrelevance of Kpa to the marriages of Kakudza's children, older men recall the relation of son to father between Pela and Kpa, and the line from Kpa to Kakudza is kept in being. It is in this way that the nuclear lineage comes into being. It is not a structure with important functions, it is an outgrowth of the extended house and one of a series of nuclei which go to make up a minor lineage.

In the previous discussion of the segmentary system I considered it synchronically. Now that the minimal levels of segmentation have been discussed, I can consider the relationship of these to the lineage system as a whole, a question which leads to an examination of the processes of lineage variability and growth. That is, I now consider the segmentary system diachronically.

Extended houses continually appear with each succeeding generation and they are the unit of population growth in a structural sense though in the biological sense the centre of growth is the elementary family. By population growth I here mean the birth of children and the appearance of new generations; I do not mean overall increase of numbers of persons; that I refer to as population increase. From the extended house, by extension of the agnatic line, which forms the core of the extended house, there appear the nuclear lineages. These nuclear lineages are all but without use; they are structures interstitial between the extended house and the minor lineages.

The growth of the nuclear lineage from the extended house presents no problem. The relation of the nuclear lineage to the minor lineage is more difficult. The question to be answered is: Are the major and minor lineages fleeting structures which endure only for a generation or are they long-enduring structures? If we suppose the major and minor lineages to be in continual change, we have to suppose that a process of lineage growth is always in operation at all levels of segmentation. In this process heads of extended houses, or some of them, become apical ancestors of nuclear lineages in the next generation; some of these become ancestors of minor lineages and one of them becomes in time the apical ancestor of the major lineage, only to disappear in turn. Such a process demands continual change, perhaps in every generation. Though no Konkomba structure is permanent, this hypothesis would mean that the name of the apical ancestor of the major lineage who 'first came here' would also be frequently changed. It demands an excessive transience of structure. Konkomba themselves regard the structure of the major lineage as a permanent one, as something that grew from the first man who settled there, as something that will endure through time to come.

The view that the major and minor lineages are long-enduring structures raises these questions. What is the process of lineage growth? What are the effects of the fission of hamlets, both within and without the district on lineage growth and increase? What is the effect of an increase in numbers of the population?

Two possible structural processes may be postulated to explain lineage variation. First, it may be that the major lineage in time grows in numbers and complexity to divide and form two structures of like order. Secondly, it may be that the form of the major lineages endures and that growth of nuclear lineages is counterbalanced by their fusion within the framework of the minor lineage.

These two processes may be known as lineage increase and fission and lineage growth and fusion. The former process affects all levels of segmentation and is connected with an overall increase in the population of the district; the latter process affects only the two lower orders of segmentation, the nuclear and minor lineages, and is connected with stability of numbers in the district. I first consider the process of lineage increase and fission.

The genealogy of any given major lineage may be looked at as a growing genealogical structure caught at a point in time. In another generation it may be wholly changed at all levels of segmentation. On this view the entire structure is unstable and in continuous change and the fission of the major lineage is a continuous process. That is to say that the present living group, which claims descent from one man placed three to four generations back from the living compound heads, makes its claim with some probability, though with loss of ancestors in the intervening generations. Lineage fission is to be observed at the level of the major lineage which splits to form two lineages of like order with new apical ancestors who appear at the major level in each succeeding generation.

I first take the genealogy of the Benangmam of Kitiak (Genealogy I). In effect Kotodo, the Owner of the Earth's lineage, is segmented into two minor lineages, that of Fanindo and that of Dzangendo. Though there is a line of descent from an ancestor co-ordinate with Fanin and Dzange, his descendant Njesin is in fact assimilated to Fanindo. The minor lineages severally describe themselves as *onibaa*, the 'children of one man', and together, as one major lineage descended from Koto, they also describe themselves as *onibaa*. Fanindo has four nuclear lineages as has Dzangendo.

The major lineage of Ngmangeado, the Elder's people, is similarly segmented into two minor lineages of which Kugbedo has only one nuclear lineage while Natiedo has four.

This clan exemplifies the working of the segmentary system at its simplest. They inhabit a fairly compact hamlet. No infringements of the rules of marriage between segments or of taking lovers in prohibited segments, no inheritances of widows outside the permissible segments are known. The segmentary system is here in equilibrium.

Let us now turn to the genealogy of the Bekumbwam of Saboba (Genealogy II), a genealogy which has some inconsistencies in it. Though Gurdo and Dardo work as one minor lineage they have as their common ancestor only the apical ancestor Ngmatie. In terms of generation depth from the living compound heads, Gurdo would be one minor lineage and Dardo another. No doubt the two ancestors appear on this level because their descendants occupy two distinct though nearby hamlets. The same is true of the third segment, Uwenido; in terms of generation depth this could be a separate major lineage.

The third genealogy, that of the Benalog of Nalogni (Genealogy III), is a simple example of the Konkomba segmentary system. But the rules of behaviour between members of the same segment are no longer strictly observed. Twelve marriages have taken place between members of Makpadado and Kotiendo. They were all runaway marriages but have been accepted by both sides and the women are now inherited as widows. Secondly, it is rumoured, though there is no certain evidence, that men and women of Kotiendo are having love affairs with each other. The major lineage is no longer an exogamous unit and it is possible that Kotiendo may no longer be a unit within which a love affair between two members is regarded as incestuous.

The variations in behaviour and structure are slight but from them the process of lineage increase and fission may be postulated; when a major lineage increases in numbers and complexity, it splits to form two lineages of the same order.

The population of the three districts quoted above is as follows:

TABLE III

| KITIAK DISTRICT | Clan members | | Wives | Total | Compounds |
	Male	Female			
Dzangendo	20	14	14	48	6
Fanindo	35	26	21	82	8
KOTODO total	55	40	35	130	14
Ngkwodo	5	1	4	10	1
Natiedo	24	4	11	39	6
NGMANGEADO total	29	5	15	49	7
BENANGMAM total	84	45	50	179	21
SABOBA DISTRICT					
Gurdo	26	17	17	60	8
Dardo	35	14	14	63	9
Uwenido	38	19	27	84	9
BEKUMBWAM total	99	50	58	207	26
NALONGI DISTRICT					
Makpadado	34	15	20	69	9
Kotiendo	58	23	34	115	13
Bwarado	53	50	80	91	11
BENALOG total	145	88	134	275	33

The figures in this table seem to suggest that a principle of limitations holds in the Konkomba structure and that once the major lineage includes more than about 250 souls it begins to split to form two major lineages.

I now take a fifth lineage for consideration, that of the Bwakwintib of Bwakwin (Genealogy IV). This clan, like that of the Benangmam, is now segmented into two major lineages in contraposition. A clan of two contraposed lineages may originate when segments of different clans and even of different tribes settle together in a new district. For example, the district of Najil is occupied by two segments, one of the Begbem tribe and the other of the Nakpantib. Yet there is another possible explanation of the way in which contraposed lineages may arise, namely, that it is inherent in the process of fission.

The Bwakwintib has two principal segments, one known as the Owner of the Earth's people and the other as the Elder's people, as have all clans when two lineages are contraposed. The apical ancestor of the Owner of the Earth's people is Bwambwam; that of the Elder's people is Kpolkpil. Now Mpa, the elder of the Kpolkpil's lineage, though he at first said that Kpolkpil's father was unknown, once remarked that the father was Bwambwam. By treating the two genealogies as one we get an even balance in generation depth between the apical ancestor and the two elders. These two segments together form an exogamous unit, though a member of one segment may have a lover in the other. The segments inhabit barely distinguishable hamlets. What we now have is one major lineage with a division of ritual roles between the segments.

The two major segments of the Benangmam also can be placed together in this way to produce the same result. Looking at Mpa's version of the Bwakwintib genealogy and that of the Benangmam, we may suppose each of these clans to have been one major lineage at some time in the recent past, a lineage which divided to form two lineages of the same order.

The inconsistencies of the Bekumbwam genealogy may be indicative of fission to come, while among the Benalog changing behaviour between segments may be another indication of the same process. There may even be an indication in the structure itself, for the nuclear lineages of Kotiendo and Bwarado are tending to lengthen.

It is in the process of lineage fission that contraposition of lineages arises. In both Bwakwin and Kitiak the two lineages live in grouped compounds spatially distinguishable but so little distant as virtually to form one hamlet. Many other clans have two major lineages that are not in contraposition. When this occurs the two segments are always widely separated within their common district. There are many examples of this—Kpeo, Sobib, Nalog, Tshegban and Gbendza. It may be suggested then that marriage of two inhabitants of one hamlet is never permitted, no matter what may be the structural relation between the segments to which possible spouses belong. When fission of a major lineage takes place, then, if the two segments are spatially close, marriage between them is not permitted and the segments are ritually distinguished as the Owner of the Earth's people and the Elder's people; but if the two segments are distant, then they may intermarry and do not go into contraposition.

It is in fact the case that most Konkomba clans are composed of two major lineages. Many have only one but few have more than two.

The Kukwintib have four and the Saangultib have three. I suggest that Saangul recently had two and that one divided and that Kukwin had two and that both divided.

The process of major lineage increase and fission may now be set out in seven stages:

Stage 1: A segment from an old established district settles to form a new district. The apical ancestor of this new settlement is a common ancestor of the new settlers. The segment is of the order of a nuclear or a minor lineage. The district of Banjuni and other districts down the Kulpene valley are of this stage.

Stage 2: The lineage of stage 1 grows to become a major lineage settled about one Earth shrine, an exogamous unit segmented into two or more minor lineages. There is a marked tendency, to put it no more strongly, for a major lineage to be segmented into two and only two minor lineages and this is invariably the case when the major lineage occupies one single hamlet.

Stage 3: The major lineage of stage 2 increases and splits to form two major lineages. This stage has two forms:

(*a*)   the new segments are ascribed separate roles, the contraposition of Elder's people and Owner of the Earth's people appears and the segments do not intermarry;

(*b*)   the segments are spatially distant from each other, do not go into contraposition nor do they at first intermarry.

Examples of stage 3*a* are the Benangmam and the Bwakwintib; of 3*b* the Kpeotib and perhaps the Bemwatiak.

Stage 4a: The lineages of stage 3*a* grow to become two differently named, intermarrying and contraposed segments. Examples of this stage are the Benasom and Bekumbwam of the Saboba district and the two major lineages of the district of Nakpando-Proper.

Stage 4b: The lineages of stage 3*b* grow to form two intermarrying segments that are not contraposed. Examples are the districts of Sobib, Tshegban and Gbendza.

Stage 5a: One or other of the two lineages of stage 4*a* grows and splits in turn. I suggest that the Saboba district is about to reach this stage which is also exemplified in the district of Kedzabo.

.   *Stage 5b:* Either or both of the lineages of stage 4*b* grows and splits: in the case of Saangul one major lineage only has split and in the case of Kukwin both major lineages have done so.

This series of stages of development can be regarded as a system of classification, within which every Konkomba clan known to me can be placed. The limitations on continued growth and fission within the district are limitations of land and space. The process of lineage increase and fission postulated above seems to be borne out by the data. The structure of any given clan at a point in time can be explained as being the product of the process.

Yet this cannot be the sole process at work in the Konkomba system for it demands a constantly increasing population; it demands a reorganization of the major lineage, and therefore of the lower segments, perhaps in every generation. It takes no account of extra-district fission. Even though for every Konkomba generation we have to allow forty years at least, one generation is too short a time for the cycle of major lineage increase and fission.[1]

Consequently it seems unlikely that major lineage increase and fission can be a continuous process though there are conditions in which it may take place. These conditions are given by the fission of hamlets and population increase within the district. Before considering the effects of hamlet fission on lineage growth I first consider the second postulated process, that of lineage growth and fusion.

In doing so one must assume that the apical ancestor of the major lineage is a fixed point of reference; between that fixed point and the accurately known extended houses structural adjustment will take place.

In the following table I show the number of the lineages in the three clans already discussed, the number of the fathers of the present compound owners (founders of extended houses) and the number of the present heads themselves.

TABLE IV

	No. of Major Lineages	No. of Minor Lineages	No. of Nuclear Lineages	No. of founders of Ext. Hses.	No. of Compound Owners
Kotodo	1	2	9	10	15
Ngmangeado	1	2	7	5	7
Ngmatiedo	1	2	8	13	29
Tindejado	1	3	11	16	41
Total	4	9	35	44	92
Average	1	2.25	8.8	11	23

[1] Fission within the district or lineage on the one hand and outside the district on the other are examples of what I have called partial and definitive fission. See 'The Fission of Domestic Groups among the LoDagaba' in *The Developmental Cycle in Domestic Groups*, Cambridge Papers in Social Anthropology, No. 1, 1958 (ed.).

The heads of extended houses represent 47.8 per cent of the number of compound heads, the apical ancestors of the nuclear lineages 38 per cent, the apical ancestors of the minor lineages 9.8 per cent, and the apical ancestors of the major lineages 4.3 per cent. That is to say that between the nuclear and the minor lineage levels there is greater loss of ancestors than one would expect if the loss were due solely to the method of counting descent in a single line. I do not know any way of estimating what the number of ancestors ought to be when we get back to the level of the minor lineage counting only through the male line, but I think it probable that lineage fusion and genealogical telescoping are going on between the level of the nuclear lineage and that of the minor lineage.

How does telescoping take place? Because of the very late age at which men marry very few men can recall their grandfathers and many do not recall their fathers, that is, their genitors. Of the elders of six major lineages only two have married sons and sons' sons. It is not unknown for a man to confuse his genitor with the man who reared him. Ngagbi, the elder of Kotodo, gave no fewer than three men as his father on different occasions; these men were Dongwi, who begot him, Dokwin, perhaps a confusion of sound, and Pela, who reared him. Ngagbi has no recollection of Dongwi. Similarly, Kakudza, son of Pela, has no recollection of Pela but thinks of Ngagbi as his genitor and pater since he was reared in Ngagbi's house. Again, in the same minor lineage, Dzager and Suba have no recollection of their fathers. They work land once held by Gbandzar, who reared them. Younger men know them as sons of Gbandzar; only the elder knows that they are the sons of Ngmwateng and Gongwa and further knows that he gave them Gbandzar's land because Gbandzar's own sons went away. This example is typical of Konkomba practice. The confusion which arises over who is the son of whom can arise only within the minor lineage, for it is within that span that children are changed from house to house and that widows are inherited. Yet a woman of child-bearing age is generally inherited within the extended house or nuclear lineage of her husband; only if there is no suitable husband there is she inherited by a more distant kinsman of her dead husband. Within the extended house it does not matter which of two brothers begot a particular child since the marriage prohibitions refer to the extended house of which brothers are always members.

It is noteworthy that while the wives of men who are heads of extended houses are exactly known and while the wives of men who

are apical ancestors of nuclear lineages are known, though perhaps
not accurately, the wives of the apical ancestors of the minor lineages
are quite unknown. This is a very pronounced difference between two
supposedly successive generations.

It appears that stability of lineage organization may be different in
degree at the three levels of segmentation. The nuclear lineages may
be taken to be fairly accurate statements of kinship relations. Further
back in the structure the distinctions of matrilateral kinship are irrelevant. If then the nuclear lineages are fairly accurate statements of
kinship relationships and the apical ancestor of the major lineage
is a fixed point of reference, then telescoping can only take place
about the level of the minor lineage.

By the fission of hamlets within the district the gross population
is not thereby diminished. A new segment appears within the district
boundaries of the clan and major lineage. Intra-district fission of
hamlets is part of a population increase within the structure of the
major lineage. The total population of the major lineage is likely in
time to increase and to pass the threshold of fission. Conversely, in
extra-district fission the gross population of district and major
lineage is reduced and may remain below this threshold.

The process of lineage growth and telescoping may perhaps be
regarded as an ideal, a theoretical process which could only take place
within a stable population living on adequate lands. Variation from
the ideal process occurs when the population increases. The increased
population is organized within the lineage structure by the partial
fission of the group. Or the increase in population is reduced and
neutralized by extra-district fission and the ideal process continues.
The reorganization of the original structure can itself come about
in two ways: first, if the increased population is in one hamlet the
fission of the major lineage results in two new and contraposed
lineages: second, if the increased population is distributed in new
hamlets within the district it does not lead to contraposition.

Hamlet fission in any form does not take place in a void. The conditions in which it occurs may be stated generally as follows. Pressure
on the available compound farm land, that is grain land, round the
hamlet is such that a serious number of men are forced to seek grain
lands in the bush. This in turn takes away land that should be used
for yams, rice or groundnuts and, further, it means that when the
time comes to use bush lands to fallow the compound land there is
none to be used. The lands of the departed Bekujom clan show what
happens when compound farms are not fallowed, for it is now little

better than gravel. Once all possible land in the district is taken up, one or two things must happen. Firstly, contiguous districts may give up land to their neighbours or some people must move out of their natal district; in the case of the founding of the hamlet of Tilengbene the Bekumbwam spread at the expense of the Benangmam. Secondly, there may be contiguous lands deserted by the people who had exhausted them. The Bekumbwam have also taken over some of the land deserted by the Bekujom; the Makpadado of Benalog has taken over deserted land in Ditshie; the Benangmam may one day move into the lands of Lemwagbal.

A clan's land boundaries are therefore not fixed for all time; they may advance or recede. Along with expansion of clan boundaries goes lineage increase and fission. But a point is reached when there is no means whereby a clan's land may be extended and then the only answer is extra-district fission. So it came about that the Konkomba, who in the early days of the Dagomba advance first retreated to the east of the Oti river, spread back to the western banks to occupy wide stretches of territory there. Today, with the exhaustion of that land, many Konkomba are settling down the Kulpene valley, around Salaga, south of the Volta around Yeji and in northern Krachi.

Konkomba do not lightly move from their native districts. The separation of kinsmen is a source of deep grief both to those who go and to those who stay behind. To every major rite this plea is added—'and bring the people back from Krachi'. A man considers long and earnestly before he makes the move; he anxiously consults a diviner to make sure that it is right for him to go. Yet the pressure of diminishing returns from exhausted soil is inexorable.

There is, on the other hand, no strong ritual or religious pull to counteract the centrifugal effects of lineage fission and land exhaustion. The age-set system provides no centripetal force to counteract lineage divisions even within the framework of the major lineage.

There is no strong ancestor cult stretching back through past time nor a strong Earth cult binding a man and his son to the land through future time. Nothing beside remains which could bind him to the soil on which he was born. A Konkomba can sometimes say where his father's house stood; none can say with certainty where his father lies buried. There are no sacred houses and though the land in which the ancestors lie buried is, *ipso facto*, sanctified, there are no points of reference for the ancestor cult such as the 'graves of the ancestors'. All a man needs in order to invoke the most remote of unremembered dead is a dead father and a compound door at which to sacrifice to him.

Lineage variation may be conceived of as happening in two ways, as the result of two processes which, perhaps, do not usually operate at the same time. If the increase in the population of a district is negligible or diminished or held in check by extra-district fission, the total numbers of people to be organized within the framework of a major lineage vary but slightly. If there is no population increase then the growth of extended houses is a simple sequence of generations, not an expansion of numbers. From the extended house the nuclear lineage appears. The heads of these interstitial structures are ascribed to the apical ancestor of the minor segment as his 'sons'. It does not matter what is the exact relation of kinship between this ancestor and the apical ancestors of the nuclear lineages. The example of Kotodo of the Benangmam, where Fane survives as an ancestor on the level of segmentation of the minor lineage despite the assimilation of his descendant into another line, suggests that at the level of the minor lineage some names must be given to validate, in terms of kinship, the division into different descent groups. Who the named ancestors actually were is no matter. But doubtless, as the nuclear lineages telescope together, the smaller are drawn to one of the larger ones and subsumed under the name of the ancestor who is the apical ancestor of the minor lineage. In the absence of population increase, the segmentary system is a simple one in which a clan is segmented into two major lineages, each of which is segmented into minor lineages (and usually into two minor lineages) which are themselves segmented into nuclear lineages, the interstitial structures between the enduring minor lineage and the ceaselessly shifting, changing extended house. This is the process of lineage growth and telescoping.

The form of the major lineage is constant. The apical ancestor has two 'sons' who are the apical ancestors of the segments of the major lineage. Their form is changeless though their content changes; the names of the ancestors of the minor lineages change with the fusion of the nuclear lineages but the form itself endures.

We are therefore justified in speaking of the Konkomba system as a segmentary system of long-enduring, unilineal descent groups which are localized, corporate units with political functions.

The equilibrium of a major lineage or clan may be disturbed by population increase and this may result in intra-district fission. In time a new segment, soon itself to become a minor lineage, appears. As the numbers increase one of the minor lineages is, as it were, torn off from the major lineage to form a new major lineage within the same clan and district. Or population increase may occur in one compact hamlet and in this case the segments of the original lineage go into contraposition. These are alternative forms of the process of lineage increase and fission. Whichever takes place, the changes involved are the result of but temporary imbalances and eventually the newly formed major lineages themselves achieve an equilibrium where genealogical telescoping occurs within the two minor segments of one major lineage.

VII. Links between Clans

I N the Konkomba system each clan emerges as a political unit.
But they do not stand in isolation, since a network of ritual relations between major groups and of affinal and kinship relations
between individuals and minor groups serves to link clan with
clan.

The two major links between clans are first, the reciprocal relation
of being ritual partners (*mantotib*, s. *manto*) to each other and
secondly, the relation between clans that are parent and filial clan
to each other. It is of the nature of Konkomba organization that these
links are not permanent; they are limited by distance and endure
only as long as the linked clans are near to each other. For example,
the Benangmam and the Bekujom clans were once ritual partners
when they were contiguous clans. Gradually the Bekujom moved
away and are now settled round about Kedzabo on lands for the great
part abandoned by former holders. Though these clans still assert
themselves to be ritual partners, in fact the relation no longer
operates. The Benangmam are unusual in asserting themselves to
have two clans as ritual partners and this I believe to be the result of
the shifting of the relation from the Bekujom to the Bekumbwam
while the memory of the link with the Bekujom yet remains.

To be *mantotib* to each other means that assistance must be given
by either clan to its linked clan on ritual occasions. At important rites,
representatives of a number of clans are usually present but it is
essential for a ritual partner to attend. Even at important special rites
for an individual, for example a rite to redeem a vow to a shrine,
ritual partners of the clan of the performer are usually the only out-
siders present.

Furthermore, when a clan is segmented into two major lineages,
each major lineage regards the other as ritual partner. There is a third
use of the word *mantotib* in reference to women. Clans that are ritual

partners are often contiguous and always near to each other; consequently the giving of assistance in burial ceremonies is an easy matter. A woman's own clan may be distant from her husband's, yet she must have the ritual assistance of female *mantotib* at her burial. Women of her own clan who have married into the clan of the husband of the dead woman or into clans close by, come to give assistance at the burial of their clan sister. These women are, on this occasion, known as her *mantotib*. Thus, clansmen and clanswomen who give assistance at the burial of a clansfellow are *mantotib*.

Fig. 12 shows the network of inter-relations between clans and major lineages. With only two exceptions each clan stands in one relation of ritual partnership and only one. The two exceptions are the clans of Bwakwin and Nakpando-Proper. Bwakwin are said to be the ritual partners of both Kpatab and of one segment of the Saboba district, the Benasom. Kpatab is itself an offshoot of the Benasom. Now it is only the Benasom elders who say that their ritual partners are the people of Bwakwin; in Bwakwin they say that these are the people of Kpatab and this link has been seen in operation on several occasions. The link between the Benasom and the people of Bwakwin has been seen at work in one rather doubtful case; this was the occasion of a rite to purify the Earth. But the Benasom were not represented at either of the two important burials in Bwakwin so that the claim of the Benasom elders is not borne out in practice. There were no important burials among the Benasom during my stay there. On the other hand, the lineage contraposed to that of the Benasom, that of the Bekumbwam, now certainly stands in ritual partnership to the Benangmam of Kitiak, though this may well have come about since the removal of the Bekujom, who were perhaps formerly the ritual partners of the Benangmam. It can only be said that the ritual partnership of the Benasom appears to be in change at present. Similarly, the contraposed segments of the people of Nakpando-Proper have different ritual partners. I do not know how this came about. Though they and the contraposed lineages of the Benasom and the Bekumbwam of Saboba district are alike in this, I know of no other instances of it. Perhaps it happens when a clan grows very numerous, as both these clans once were, though both have suffered severe depopulation in recent times.

The chart also shows a second abnormality. The Saambwertib are ritual partners to the Kpaltib of Kpaliba. This is the only exception known to me of clans of different tribes standing in this relation. The people of Saambwer and Kpaliba offer no explanation; were one to

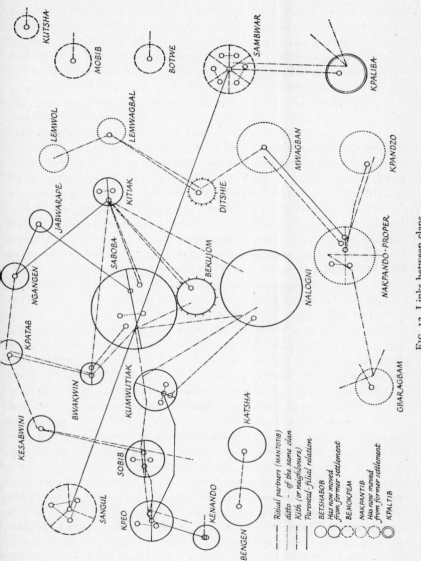

FIG. 12. Links between clans

ask the people of Nalogni, for example, why they are not ritual partners to those of Nakpando-Proper, they would say *Bi je bibaba*, 'they are by themselves'. In this context this means that they are of a different tribe. There is no doubt that the people of Saambwer and those of Kpaliba believe themselves to be of different origin; their migration stories indicate that they came from quite different regions.

An example of how the ritual partnership can shift is seen in a recent burial in the district of Lemwagbal. The ritual partners of the people of Lemwagbal were those of Ditshie, all of whom have now gone elsewhere. The people of Nalogni are now moving into the vacated lands of Ditshie. When an elder of Lemwagbal died his kinsmen told those Nalogni people who have moved into Ditshie and they also told the elder of the Owner of the Earth's people of Kitiak. Kitiak men and men from Ditshie went to dance for the dead elder. Someone must be present to help the dead man's kin in the burial and, since their ritual partners had left, the elder of Lemwagbal sought the help of neighbours even though they were of a different tribe. The death occurred when flood water was high and it was all but impossible to reach fellow-tribesmen in Mwagban across the river. This instance suggests how a relation of ritual help between clans of different tribe could come into being.

We may say that ritual partnerships hold between two clans and usually but not invariably between all the segments of each clan. It is a relation of reciprocal ritual assistance.

Akin to this relation is an unnamed relation between two clans who are parent and offshoot clans to each other. This too is a ritual relationship but it carries fewer duties than does that between *mantotib*. The clan that is an offshoot of an older clan retains a connexion with the shrines, other than the Earth shrine, of the parental district from whence their forefathers moved. For example, shrines in the parental district may 'send a child' to a man in an offshoot district, or a man in the offshoot district may vow 'something', for definite promises of a sheep or a goat are not made, to the shrine should it 'send him a child'. This tenuous ritual link endures long after any genealogical connexion between the districts has been forgotten. It is not a reciprocal link since the members of the parent clan have no share in the shrines of the offshoot clan. The relation is asymmetrical. There is also a link of reciprocal burial assistance between the clans if they are near to each other. The form this takes is that cloths are sent to cover the dead person while he is being carried to the grave; if the clans are too distant from each other for them to give each other help on the day of death but not so distant that the connexion between them is nothing but a memory, then word is sent some time later to tell the elders of the linked clan that a death has taken place. As was pointed out earlier this link is non-transitive since it does not hold between one clan and a third clan that is an offshoot of a second clan, itself the offshoot of the first.

Fig. 12 shows that in only one instance—that between Nakpando-Proper and Mwagban—does the ritual partnership relation and the relation of parental to filial clan overlap. There is no other instance of similar overlap of the two systems of linkage known to me. It is not therefore to be supposed that ritual partnerships arise from descent, though they are clearly of a very similar kind.

The hypothesis that clans linked as ritual partners are parental and filial clans is tempting. When applied to women the term *manto* does in fact refer to fellow-clanswomen in a ritual context. One might suppose that when used between clans the term also means 'men of common descent' in a ritual context. For the ritual partnership relation does not hold between clans of different tribes and it is by extra-district fission from a centre in which a population spreads gradually over a compact area that new tribes come into being. It looks as though the ritual partnership is in origin a tie between clans that are parental/filial clans to each other. But, since we know that the link can shift if one clan moves away leaving its linked partner without *mantotib*, to say today that clans are ritual partners does not imply a relationship of descent between them. The new tribe of the Nakpantib came into being by dispersion of population from the centre at Nakpando-Proper and from the primary offshoots of Nakpando-Proper. Since this was also part of the westward movement of Konkomba, after their original retreat to the east of the Oti, the Nakpantib were able to spread over a compact area. The double linkage between Nak-pando-Proper and Mwagban is perhaps an instance of a normal but infrequent linkage. None the less, this instance of the coincidence of the ritual partnership and the parental-filial clanship is the only one known with certainty.

There is a third kind of linkage between neighbouring settlements. It is best seen in the rites of *Bi kper keteng*, 'They purify the land'. We might perhaps speak here of 'kith'. When a clan proposes to carry out the rite they let the neighbouring elders know the date on which it will take place and those elders come along to drink beer. This is a distinction made by Konkomba themselves; the ritual partners must be present at such a rite, the others come for beer. But

the link of reciprocal visiting on ritual occasions is one of many
tenuous and undefined ties, usually quasi-ritual, between clans
which are neighbours.

There is no Konkomba noun equivalent to the term 'kith', but the
idea is expressed in the Konkomba phrase *Ti nji bi*, 'We know them'.
This phrase would not be applied, for example, to a group of Mossi
traders settled near a Konkomba market, since if Mossi are known
they are known with some hostility. The clans that 'know' each other
are neighbours; there are many ties of matrilateral kinship between
them, their members attend each other's first and final funeral
ceremonies, their young men and women carry on love affairs with
each other. Kithship is not a defined relation but is a relation between
structures. It imposes no formal duties on clan members but it works
in other than merely ritual contexts. For example, one does not seek
to drive so hard a bargain with someone one 'knows'; a man working
a ferry over the river takes 'one he knows' over for nothing, he takes
any other Konkomba for 3*d* and a Mossi for 1*s*. Between clans who
are kith a feud can be averted after a homicide.

Though the ritual partnership may arise in agnatic kinship, I am
more inclined to regard it as a relation between a clan and the closest
of its kith.

These links of different nature, each having its own field of operation, together form a network of ritual ties between clans. Long enduring through time, they are of but narrow extension in space. The
reciprocal tie of the ritual partners is one between contiguous clans
and is the strongest and closest of the three ritual links. The asymmetrical link between parental/filial clans extends more widely in
space but is of lesser intensity than that between ritual partners. The
tie of friendship between clans who are kith is a summation of many
individual ties of kinship and friendship. The three ties hold, with one
known exception, only between clans of the same tribe. They will
therefore be part of the definition of the tribal relationship.

The tie of kithship does not hold between members of different
tribes. In some places Mossi who have settled alongside a Konkomba
clan are invited to certain rites as kith. Down the Kulpene valley the
Konkomba who have settled there invite a Dagomba to do the killing
of sacrificial animals and other Dagomba come to drink beer. But in
the areas of long settlement which I call Konkombaland, the tie of
kithship does not hold between clans of different tribe. The only
exception I know is the instance quoted earlier of the burial in
Lemwagbal at which men of the Betshabob tribe assisted a clan of the

Nakpantib tribe. As was pointed out then, the conditions were abnormal. We may say that, in general, kithship too holds only between clans of the same tribe.

Though I am concerned with relations between long-enduring structures having political functions, some kinship relations are not unrelated to the political system. Matrilateral kinship creates relations between lineages which, though short-lived, can have political consequences during their short existence. Of the many ties of matrilateral kinship, two have political consequences. Of these the first can create a quasi-group relation and the second is purely a relation between individuals.

Though the extended house is the unit within which marriage prohibitions operate, the relation of mother's brother to sister's son and vice versa is a personal one. A man stands in much less close relation to the mother's brother of his half-brother by a different mother. The term *umwidza* is a reciprocal one used by mother's brother to sister's son and by sister's son to mother's brother. The plural form *umwetib* is used as a collective term for the kinsmen of the mother but not as a collective term for the kinsmen of the sister's husband for whom there is no collective term. The sister's husband is called *tshin*, as is the father's sister's husband. The term *tshuor* is applied to the wife's father, wife's mother and the daughter's husband. The plural form *tshuortib* most frequently refers to the sons-in-law, the daughter's husbands, and there is also the usage which means the wife's kin. Which usage is meant can only be gathered from the context; an elderly man speaking of his *tshuortib* refers to his sons-in-law, a young man using the word to his parents-in-law.

There are a number of collectives among the Konkomba kinship terms. A man speaks of his clansmen as his *dejaa* (s. *dejoo*) and a woman speaks of her clansmen as her *nindzatib* (s. *nindza*). A dead woman's clanswomen present at her burial are her *mantotib*. Both men and women speak of their mother's kin as their *umwetib*. The collective terms indicate fields of interest and the most important of kinship relations have each their collective which is used by a single speaker of descent groups to which he or she belongs. Women have another collective term for the descent group into which they are married; the husband's clansmen are a woman's *tshatijaa* (no singular), a term derived from *tshar*, husband, plus the possessive suffix *-jaa*.

The terms *dejaa* and *nindzatib* are those used by men and women respectively for their agnatic descent group; *umwetib* is the term used by both men and women for the group from which they are descended through the mother. These three terms are extended through the generations. The term *tshatijaa* also expresses an enduring relation, a relation of a woman to the *dejaa* of her husband. The term *tshuortib*, though it has a lateral expansion to persons of the same clan and generation as the wife's father and the wife's mother, is not extended through the generations to the wife's mother and the wife's sister. It does not appear to be extended in time (Figs. 13, 14, 15).

It is clear that kinship terms are extended through the generations only in the lineage of Ego's mother. The mother's kin form a group to which an individual and his *naabim*, 'mother's children', are related. This relationship is extended by the marriage regulations to prohibit marriages between any two extended houses that have the same woman in both. Yet, since a woman does not marry one man but a minor lineage, there is a relation between that lineage and the lineage of each wife in it. There is, further, a relation between all the children of a lineage and the lineages of all the women married into it. Each

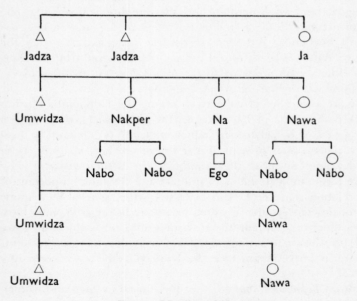

FIG. 13. Matrilateral kinship terms

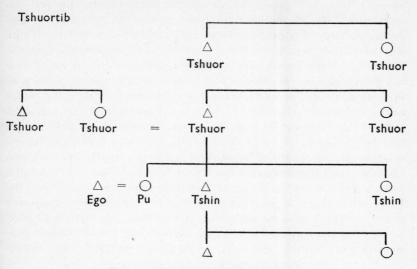

FIG. 14. Affinal kinship terms (male ego)

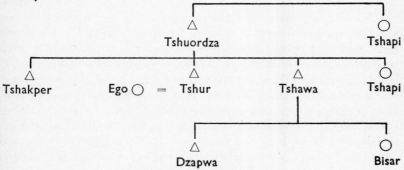

FIG. 15. Affinal kinship terms (female ego)

mother is a potential step-mother to any child of her husband's minor lineage. From this, in certain contexts, a quasi-group relationship develops. This is not to say that long enduring links between lineages are so formed, but through its elder the major lineage is linked to the mother's kin of that elder. It is when a death occurs in the elder's mother's kin group that the link operates. A man owes ritual assistance to his mother's kin when one of them dies. Between elders of major lineages this ritual assistance extends beyond the nuclear lineage of the mother and is given on the death of any senior person of her major lineage. It may take the form of a visit by the sister's son himself or he may send any of his young men to dance and drum at the burial. The primary relation of an individual to a kin group is thus extended. What would, in the case of persons of little prominence, be a purely kinship relation involving ritual duties is now extended from both actors in the relationship. The service is given to any important member of the mother's brother's major lineage by any member of the sister's son's major lineage. Such a relation can have political consequences and is a quasi-group relation involving two lineage structures during the short period of its life. For example, Tamwin, Elder of Kotiendo-Nalogni, sent beer to the Elder of Bwakwin when a senior man died there because Tamwin's mother came from Bwakwin; Ngagbi of Kitiak sent his young men to dance at the burial, for his mother also came from Bwakwin. On the death of Tamwin, if Tamwin is succeeded by Bewa, the relation will shift to Ipwasweni, whence came Bewa's mother, and on the death of Ngagbi the relation will shift from Bwakwin-Kitiak to Nabu-Kitiak, for the mother of Okpa, the likely successor to Ngagbi, came from Nabu.

The second important matrilateral kinship tie is that between *nabo*, children of women of the same major lineage. This is a purely individual relationship between persons and is in no way a relation between structures. With the exception of relations of hostility, it ranges more widely in the social space of a Konkomba than any other relationship; like all matrilateral kinship ties it may cut across the relations of permanent hostility between tribes. For this reason, the tie between *nabim* has its political consequences, since it serves to mitigate the severity of quarrels and consequently diminishes the homicides which lead to feud. It is a relation of obligatory friendliness between persons and carries no ritual or economic duties.

The three enduring inter-group relations together with the short-lived, quasi-group relations between the lineage of an elder and his mother's major lineage, the personal link between mother's agnates and sister's children, and that between those who are 'mother children' (*nabo*), all play a part in mitigating the exclusiveness of the small agnatic clan. Each in its field forges wider and ever wider links in the total social space from the dyadic relation of *mantotib* to the manifold relation of the *nabo* which transcends the boundaries of clan, tribe and people.

Some examples of ritual activities will illustrate the inter-relations of clans and major lineages. The first concerns the burial of a male elder. I do not attempt to describe the rites in detail but give a general account of how an elder should be buried rather than one of any particular burial. On the death of an elder or senior man, word is sent to the ritual partners of the dead man's clan, to the elder of his mother's lineage, to the elders of his wives' lineages, and to his married daughters and sons-in-law. The last are told on the day of death only if they live near at hand. If known, and if they are not distant, the filial and parental clans of the dead man's clan are also informed. Drums and gun-shots announce a death to neighbouring clans. Should it be market day the death is announced in the market.

While the body is being prepared for interment the widows remain in the room of the senior wife singing mourning songs. The body is shaved by the ritual partners, and is washed and dressed by them together with the 'daughters' of the dead man. In this context his 'daughters' are the unmarried girls of his clan and, especially, of his major lineage. The body is dressed by the ritual partners and covered with cloths sent by the ritual partners, by filial or parental clans, and by other major lineages of the dead man's clan, and is then placed in the open compound. The grave has meanwhile been dug by ritual partners and by fellow-clansmen who must be given assistance in this task by any stranger who happens to pass. The body is carried to the grave by the 'daughters' and 'sisters', that is, clanswomen of the dead man, assisted by the ritual partners. He is held at the graveside by these clanswomen while the addresses to the dead are made by elders of his clan or their representatives. The body is then interred and the grave is filled in by ritual partners and by his fellow-clansmen. Then the calabash which symbolizes his spirit is broken and the pieces pressed into the mound of the grave. During this time the young men of the clan of the dead man dance outside his compound. They are joined by young men of the clan's ritual partners, by young men sent by neighbouring elders, and by young men of the maternal clan of the dead man. A man is buried naked, though among the Benagbib the body is said to be buried in a goatskin. The clothing is removed from the body at the graveside before the addresses to the dead, during which the body is held with the hands over the genitals. For three days after the burial of a man, no farm work is done by the men of his major lineage, though this abstention is strictly observed only by men of his minor lineage.

Some days later the eldest son of the dead man makes clay and builds what may be called a tombstone. A circular plaque of clay about five feet across, with runnels for rain-water and mounded in the centre, is built over the grave and then decorated with cowries. The son sacrifices a fowl to his father on the grave saying, 'Take your fowl and give God and give your fathers. We too are well.'

In a burial the roles of the matrilateral and affinal kin are not sharply defined. Commonly young men are sent by the former, especially if the two districts are distant from each other.

On the day after the interment, beer is made by the clansmen of the dead man and all who assisted at the burial come to drink. Only close kin who have come any distance are fed. Daughters of the dead man bring back grain given by their husbands for this occasion.

In burial rites the groups who come to the assistance of the major lineage carrying out the burial are the other major lineages of the same clan, the ritual partners, filial clans and neighbouring clans. The affinal kin of the dead man are represented, sometimes by persons who themselves stand in no known relation of kinship to the dead man or to members of his major lineage. Unless they live near by, the sons-in-law are not present on the day of burial but they come to the beer party to which they have contributed. This is the last service they give to their father-in-law.

The actual persons who assist at a burial do so, for the most part, not as individuals in a kinship category but as representatives of groups which stand in long-enduring relations to the group of the dead man, since the ritual partnership, parental/filial and kith relations are relations between structures. The only purely individual relations expressed by the presence of members of clans other than that of the dead man is that between him and his sons-in-law.

The burial rites for a woman differ from those of a man in the following ways. Those who are told of her death are her husband's ritual partners, her own paternal clan, the clans neighbouring on her husband's, and, if near enough, her mother's clan. From her husband's and from neighbouring clans come women of her own clan married there to assist in the washing, shaving and dressing of the body; her clanswoman are her own *mantotib*. People to whom she is mother's sister come from neighbouring clans. Cloths are brought by her own clansmen to add to those of her husband's clan when the body is covered to await interment. The body is carried to the grave by her *mantotib* and her 'daughters', that is, girls of her husband's clan who also hold her at the graveside. Once the body is interred, the calabash symbolizing her spirit is broken into the grave-mound and the mound

is covered with clay mixed on the spot. No further graveside ceremony is done for her by her husband's kin. The women of her
husband's clan and the women married into that clan now dance
round a new calabash called the *lekpojig*, the calabash of the dead.
Sooner or later one of the dancing women begins to tremble and
eventually she bursts into tears and takes the calabash to dance with
it on her head. It is believed that the spirit of the dead woman has
entered her and she now leads the dance round the compounds of the
hamlet. The dancers dance briefly in each compound. The spirit of
the dead woman is bidding farewell to the women among whom she
lived. Eventually, the spirit of the dead woman leaves the woman she
first entered to enter now into one of the young men of her own
paternal clan, who seizes the calabash and makes off with it as hard as
he can go along the path leading to his own home with everyone else
in pursuit. Once out of the hamlet he slows down and, overtaken by
his clansmen, sets out for home, taking the calabash with him. On
arrival he gives it to the elder of the nuclear lineage of the dead
woman, who should sacrifice a fowl for her. The young women dance
for her, and sometimes the young men as well. The spirit of the dead
woman again enters one of the dancing women and again the dance
goes round the compounds, this time of her minor lineage. When the
dance is over the calabash is placed in the room of the senior wife of
the elder of the nuclear lineage of the dead woman until the time of
the final funeral ceremony.

Men must be buried in their own hamlets, not necessarily that of
their birth, but that in which they permanently reside. Should a man
die elsewhere the body is tied to a pole and carried to his own home
for burial. This is still done today. A woman should be buried in her
husband's hamlet; it is only her spirit that goes back to her own
clan. Should a woman die away from her husband's place she should
be carried back for burial. In one instance a woman died while visiting
her own clan. It was the flooded season and travelling was so difficult
that there was no time to send word to her husband's kinsmen to ask
bearers to come and fetch her. A dead woman is carried by her 'sons'.
She was buried by her paternal kin and two or three days later one of
her 'sons' was sent to fetch her. He brought back to her husband's
clansmen some earth from her grave and a kapok pod wrapped in her
cloth. The pod was buried with abbreviated rites. It was washed and
shaved and addressed by the elders; the young men danced. The
grave was of the usual form in miniature.

A man's death and a woman's death call into operation different ranges of ritual relations between clans. The ritual partners of the clan in which the death occurs assist in the burial of men and women of the clan and of women married into it. The neighbouring clans also take part in the burial of any adult. But on the death of a woman, the filial or parental clans of her husband's own clan are not told. Only two of the three ritual relations of her husband's clan are invoked. The attendance of persons to whom she was mother's sister is a personal choice. Sons-in-law have no role at a woman's burial but they do, as for a father-in-law, send corn or beer. Finally, a woman's own paternal kin must be present to take her spirit back to her own clan.

The operation of the ritual ties between clans that are ritual partners or kith to each other are seen at their simplest in the rite of *Bi kper keteng*, 'They pour (a libation) to the land'. A number of elders may come, since several clans are informed a few days in advance that the rite will be done. A Konkomba elder does not speak of telling an individual about the forthcoming rite; he does not say 'I told Tawam and Gbun', he says, 'I told Nalogni and Bwakwin'. In the rite as performed by the Benangmam of Kitiak, two neighbouring clans and the ritual partners were told, though only the latter came. The eight elders present were the elders of each minor lineage of the clan, one from each major lineage, in each case the probable successor to the present elders of the major lineages. The ritual partners, the major lineage of the Bekumbwam, were represented by their elder and one other man. The rite is a simple invocation of the ancestors with the killing of fowls, one fowl being contributed by each person present. The ancestors are asked to send rain, to make the crops grow. On the following day the Owner of the Earth and the Elder of the Benangmam visited the shrine in their district and sacrificed a fowl in each. The shrines themselves are now invoked:

'We sacrifice so that when we hoe rain will fall, food grow. Men too will grow. That is why we sacrifice thus.'

The rite as performed by the people of Saboba district differed only in that not only were fowls sacrificed but two sheep as well. The ritual partners of both major lineages were present and a representative of the elder of a fourth district. The elder of a fifth and neighbouring district was invited but did not come. As he was very old, he neither attended nor carried out any major rite that I know of. In all twenty people were present, the largest gathering of elders that I ever saw.

In the first of these rites, only the representatives of the clan whose lands were to be purified, together with their ritual partners, were present. In the second, members of the contraposed lineages of the sacrificing clan attended; their ritual partners and the representatives of neighbours were also present.

In this account of burial and Earth rites the fields of operation of the three principal inter-lineage and especially inter-clan relations have been exemplified. In this they are seen at work as positive, enduring links between long enduring structures. In other contexts they also work negatively. In ritual matters, clans linked by these ties work together to achieve a common end. In quarrels and fights the links operate to mitigate conflicts and to prevent bloodshed and homicide.

I therefore turn to inter-clan jural activities. I earlier defined these as the actions taken to restore communication within a clan after some act by an individual has disrupted the smooth running of daily life. There is nothing properly to be called 'law' among Konkomba; equally, there is no concept among them of 'crime' as an act punishable by law. I therefore speak of 'jural activities'. Jural activities within a lineage are acts performed by a lineage elder or the fellow-clansmen of the offender. The elder has the power to issue commands to an offender in virtue of the moral authority of his seniority and the ritual authority of his office. Fellow-clansmen may go so far as to restrain their clansman by force. But there is no punishment by force; neither they nor the elder can apply penal sanctions stronger than ostracism to an offender. In inter-clan relations there is no ritual and moral authority superordinate to that of the lineage elders involved in a dispute. Nor is there any tie between men superordinate to that of common membership of a lineage and clan which would enable observers to exercise restraint on an offender. Consequently, the only sanctions on disapproved behaviour between clans and between individual members of different clans are the threat of retaliation and the threat of force.

In some disputes, such as those that may arise over a runaway wife, there is something not far removed from negotiation between clans. Should a husband beat or neglect a wife she has one recourse open to her; she may run off to her father's house. Once there she may stay for as long as three months. By this act she puts the dispute with her husband on a different plane, since it is now a matter for discussion between representatives of the lineages of husband and wife. The husband, accompanied by his elder, goes to the elder of the wife's lineage to put his case. It is not a question of an appeal to an independent judge or arbitrator; it is a negotiation, often heated, between the two lineages. It may be carried on, to the disadvantage of the husband, before an audience of the men of the wife's lineage. It is not infrequently the case that the runaway wife is anxious to prolong her absence from her husband to be with her lover, though this is not a point mentioned by either side. The elders of the wife's lineage commonly tell her to go back to her husband since sometime in the future a wife will run away from their own lineage and, should she come from the lineage of the present complainants, will not quickly be returned.

A wife may refuse to return to her husband when told to do so by her elders. She can only do this by running away to live with a lover. But this leaves the lover's clan open to retaliation. For example, should either the husband's or the wife's lineage, in the first instance the minor lineages, have betrothed a girl to the lover's lineage, she may be withheld until the wife is returned. Or, as I mentioned earlier, a woman may be enticed by a member of the husband's clan, a woman who either belongs to the lineage of the lover or is betrothed to that lineage. These manoeuvres are no more than different forms of retaliation. The situation is a dangerous one that could easily lead to fighting between the husband's and the lover's lineages.

There are other forms of negotiation. For example, a man of the Bekumbwam lent a cow to Kunde of Bwakwin and later died. The dead man's son claimed the cow from Kunde who had sold it. The claimant made things more difficult by claiming two cows from Kunde who at once appealed to the elders of the Bekumbwam. They persuaded Kunde, who is a notoriously silly man, to pay up one of his own cows. This is the only case of cattle stealing that came to my notice. In it the defendant appealed to the elders of the claimant to intervene on his behalf with their man.

Cattle are never closely guarded and are only herded in the wet season to keep them from straying on to the farms. No fighting breaks out over cattle. Konkomba are much more concerned about hunting and, more especially, fishing rights. If men go out to hunt in twos and threes they either hunt over their own lands or over empty bush. Far more important are the communal hunts in the late dry season. A clan does not own exclusive hunting rights over its own lands; what it does hold are the rights to burn the grass on certain lands.

The technique of hunting is fairly simple. Fires are lighted to drive the game towards open spaces where they can be shot with arrows or caught with dogs; or they can be driven by the fires into the undergrowth fringing a river and there shot. All animals shot with arrows go to the elder of the major lineage of the killer; all game caught by a dog goes to the owner of the dog. Elders always own a number of dogs and the hunters must take these dogs on the hunt as well as their own. There are two methods of evading the handing over of game to the elder. When an animal is driven to cover, a hunter may seize his dog and throw it on to the animal instead of shooting it; and, in the evening as they make their way home, the hunters may divide a share of the bag before handing over what remains to the elder.

Not only the clan which holds the land hunted over may take part. Ritual partners and kith share the right to hunt each other's bush lands but may not burn the grass except on their own lands. Clans do not always insist upon this right to hunt each other's lands and this may be because the quantity of game involved is not very great. In any case it goes to the elder who does not always share it but may smoke it, often for sale in the market.

In 1951 there was a quarrel which might have led to fighting between Lemwol and Jabwarape. A hunting party from Lemwol found the Jabwarape people burning their grass. Quarrels during hunts are particularly dangerous because the hunters are armed with bows and arrows, knives and axes. On this occasion an elder took away the arrows and broke them and so prevented serious fighting. Though fighting was averted on this occasion by the action of the elder many fights have taken place in the past because of an infringement of hunting rights.

Fishing rights are of two kinds, river fishing rights and lake fishing rights. Only clans bordering on rivers have the former rights. These I take first. There seem to be no fights over river fishing rights. Rivers are fished with lines, traps and nets. Lines and traps are set by clans in their own areas. Net fishing is done communally when the rivers are low. This communal fishing expedition is undertaken by large numbers of men of neighbouring clans and the whole expedition works down stream fishing the waters of each of the participating clans. Only men are in this expedition and they fish with hand nets. It may be that the large numbers involved are a protection against crocodiles.

The catch of fish is the property of the men who catch it; it is not handed over to the elder. Much of the catch is eaten; the rest is smoked and sold in the market. It may be for this reason that the quarrels over fishing rights appear to be more severe than those over hunting rights. There is, in any case, little game left in Konkombaland. Or it may be the presence of women at lake fishing expeditions that makes quarrels on those occasions very severe ones. Be that as it may, quarrels over lake fishing have often led to severe fighting.

Not all clans have lakes but those who have one are obliged to share the fishing rights with neighbouring clans. The people of Lemwagbal sought to avoid having many people present when they fished their lake in 1951. They told only the elder of the Benangmam about the proposed day but women married into that clan told their kinsmen who also came along. The fishing could not begin until the elder of Lemwagbal arrived and he put off his coming until mid-afternoon in the hope that some people would leave. Eventually he came and the fishing began. At the time of year when the lakes are fished the water is no more than two feet deep. The participants rush into the water churning up the mud, the men armed with spears, knives and clubs, the women with basket nets which they plunge down into the water over a fish. There is very little system about the fishing. The crowd first works across the lake from south to north and then from west to east; this is repeated once and thereafter people wander about in the water wholly at random. Each person present got at least one fish and many had several. Some of the Niger pike were up to six feet in length.

The tactics used by the elder of Lemwagbal aroused some feeling in the waiting crowd. In 1948 similar tactics led to fighting between the people of Botwe and those of Saambwer in which the fight began with clubs and later both sides fetched their arrows. Eleven persons, one of them a woman, were killed. Such a fight, in which men are killed on both sides, does not necessarily lead to feud. Dispropor-tionate loss on either side is usually avenged later, but if the losses are equal on either side the flare-up may end on the day on which it began. No rite to 'end the fight' was done on this occasion. That is not to say that it is now forgotten; on the contrary, it makes further fighting likely should either clan again infringe its neighbour's rights or should a quarrel break out between them over some other matter.

In these communal hunting and fishing expeditions in which clans which are kith take part, the sanctions that can be applied should one clan act improperly are either retaliation or the force of combat.

The majority of fights between clans begin in a quarrel between two men over a woman. A husband who catches a man *in flagrante delicto* with his wife strikes out with the first weapon to hand. The lover, if he is fortunate, may get away with only a severe wound, though not infrequently he will be killed on the spot. Yet men are not always caught so obviously and indefensibly culpable, and then the quarrel develops more slowly.

I referred earlier to the progression of a quarrel between members of two clans to show how the different minor and major lineages of the clans were involved. In all quarrels I could observe, and in some described to me, the same gradation of involvement is to be noted. Such a quarrel may rapidly become a fight involving men of the two clans concerned. This particular brawl began when one man accused a man of another clan of aiding his sister, the wife of the 'father' of the accuser, in her love affairs. It was a market day and it was suspected that the woman had met her lover at her father's house. The man accused of aiding his sister had certainly concealed her whereabouts from inquirers.

There are two starting points for considering how quarrels may develop into feud and the mechanisms by which feuds may be averted. I take first the instance in which a man is killed in the heat of the moment and secondly one in which there is a brawl which may lead to homicide and thence to feud.

If the killer and the killed be of one clan, nothing more is done. The killer, it is believed, will sicken and die. If the clans of the killer and the killed be neighbours, kith to each other as earlier defined, then a fight between the Young Men, continuing into feud, can be avoided. When the news of the death reaches the clan of the dead man, horns and whistles are blown and drums beaten and, armed with bows and arrows, the young men set out to the clan of the dead man. If the elders are there, and if they are willing to prevail upon their young men, the battle may still be avoided. In the words of one elder, 'They (the elders) say their word is not good; they come in order to tell them (young men) that their word spoils, they should go.' That is, the elder tells them that their action will spoil the land. The elders of the two clans take a goat and fowls and beer provided by the killer's clan and sacrifice to the Earth. I was told that the sacrifices are made at the Earth shrine. There is some discrepancy here since the Earth shrine forbids goat. When the Earth 'wants a goat', the sacrifice is carried out in the elder's compound. Once this sacrifice has been performed nothing further is done.

If the elders are not there to prevent the fight then nothing can prevent the brothers of the dead man from killing in revenge. The elder continued, 'If he too kills, they will say that the one he killed must also be avenged. If no elder is there the fight will be terrible.' In short, a general fight is likely to break out.

I have never seen serious fighting. Cardinall wrote in the Yendi District Book in 1916:

'No prisoners are taken. The wounded of the defeated party, if left behind, are slain where they lie and babies of whatever age are either smashed on the ground or stoned. But no female is slain—an accident alone can kill them—although they take an active part in the affray bringing water to their men and urging them on with their cries and insults to fugitives. The dead of the defeated are left on the field of battle and if the victory proves a rout women and cattle are carried off to be ransomed later or to be held in captivity.'

Concerning the taking and ransoming of captives, and the taking of women and cattle, I have no evidence. In the main, the fights that Cardinall speaks of were some of many struggles between Saambwer and Kandzo in which, perhaps, unusual ferocity was shown. This long feud is widely recalled in Konkomba country today. There is no evidence for the slaughter of children nor for the taking of captives among the Betshabob in the past, nor among any other Konkomba at the present time. I do not believe that children were ever killed in Konkomba fights. Nor do I see how it would be possible to kill them, except, as Cardinall suggests for women, by accident. The fights tend to be running fights. For example, that between the Bemokpem of Lagea district and the Betshabob clan of the Benangmam is said to have ranged as far as Basare in a running and stalking battle. This may be vainglory on the part of the sons of the Betshabob who fought in it, but more recent fights also suggest that a good deal of territory is covered.

Once a fight has taken place between two clans, any occasion of friction is likely to lead to more fighting, especially if the side last defeated sees an opportunity for revenge. The Konkomba phrase *Bi mu kaku lebwan*, 'they too will kill in revenge', expresses the attitude of a clan which has lost men in a fight. Such intermittent fighting may go on for many years.

If a quarrel does not lead to immediate killing then an outbreak of fighting may be prevented. The presence of an elder or, better, of the elders of both sides, can prevent the fight from going too far. If the two clans engaged are on the lands of either and the fight is likely to spread on to the lands of both, then the ritual authority of the elders is such that they may forbid fighting there on the grounds that the Earth will be 'spoiled', that is, made unfruitful. In this way quarrels may be stopped very early and before any serious harm is done. Once a homicide has occurred, however, the development of the feud is likely to follow the course already described. Indeed, once a life has been taken the elder of the dead man's clan is himself likely to demand revenge.

Fights sometimes break out after markets when both sides involved are not on their own land, are outside the actual market (itself a shrine) and are unaccompanied by their elders whose moral authority could hold them in check. Since arrows may not be taken into the market, these fights are not often very serious even though men are armed with axes and knives.

It is said that, in the past, if a man found out the name of the lover of his betrothed wife he would kill him. Today, only the lover of a woman who has gone to live in her husband's compound is killed if caught. The method was to ambush him in the early morning on his way home from his mistress's house. The brother of the dead man was then obliged to avenge his death. The second death was likely to lead to general fighting and to a state of feud in which intermittent fighting took place over a good many years.

A feud between two clans of the same tribe can be ended in a rite. The condition for peace-making is weariness of endless fighting on both sides and the willingness of the elders on one or other side to make the first overtures. It is not a dictation of terms by one side to the other but an agreement between them to end the fighting. The rite is called either *Bi sub kedza*, 'They bury the fight', or *Bi sub tibwar*, 'They bury the words', that is, the quarrel. In this ceremony the elders of the clans at feud meet in the presence of the elders of a third and neutral clan. I cannot be certain of the relationship of this neutral clan to the others but I think it to be a clan that is kith to both. The elders bear with them some of the arrows of their 'young men'. A hole 18 in. deep by 1 ft. across is dug and lined with ashes and the arrows are laid beside it. Beer supplied by both clans is mixed and poured in small driblets on to the arrows while the elders of the opposing sides address the arrows. Fowls, one for each man killed, are sacrificed and the blood is dropped on to the arrows. The elder of the neutral clan carries out the killing of the fowls. The arrows are then placed in the hole and the elder of the third clan withdraws. The elders of the feuding clans then together cover up the arrows with earth. The beer is now drunk and the rite ends with a sacrifice to the Earth shrine of the district in which the rite is performed. The rite is clearly a burial rite. Unfortunately, I was unable to gather texts of the addresses to the arrows nor can I be certain about the district in which the rite is carried out; I incline to think that it is that of the neutral clan. This rite, it must be emphasized, can only be carried out between clans of the same tribe.

From quarrels over women, over hunting and fishing rights, feuds between clans may develop. At all stages of development there is the possibility of preventing the quarrel from going any further; even feud can be formally ended. The ritual and semi-ritual relations between clans discussed earlier operate to diminish the chances of feud and to mitigate the effects of fights that have broken out. This they do in various ways.

It is said that ritual partners may not kill one another. There is no record of ritual partners actually feuding with each other, but I have heard a man who was not only *manto* but also father's sister's son to the men he addressed, say in a quarrel 'What happened at Dzagberi will happen here'. The Dzagberi affair was the rising of some Benafiab Konkomba against a Dagomba chief in which they killed the chief, his wives and his elders. The threat was therefore a very strong one; yet, two days later, the same man greeted the men he had so addressed with every sign of amiability. His greeting was not re-returned. A quarrel once took place between a man of the Bekujom and a man of the Benangmam in which the Benangmam man was the lover of the other's wife, caught *in flagrante delicto*. The lover was not killed on the spot and the two clans were then ritual partners.

Clans that have a parental/filial tie do not resort to feud. They are not, on the other hand, *dejaa*, clansmen, to each other; the ritual sanction on killing a fellow-clansman does not operate if the killing should be between clans so related. Equally, they do not aid each other in feuds. The Benangmam of Kitiak did not aid their filial clan to the east of the Oti against the Bekujom nor were they aided by them in return. Against this, however, there is the long feud referred to above between the Saambwertib and the Kandzotib. These two clans are of common origin. That is, while they are not parent clan to offshoot clan they have a common parental clan.

Clans that are kith do occasionally come to blows and though I know of no recent killings, severe wounds have been inflicted. It is principally in quarrels between kith that the ritual and moral power of the elders operates most strongly. Further, it is in such quarrels that the elders are most likely to exercise that authority if only because the fighting would take place on the lands they are responsible for. In addition, between contiguous clans there are numerous ties of matrilateral kinship and a man may not quarrel with his mother's kin (*umwetib*). Thus, in a general fight between two neighbouring clans there are many men on either side unable to take part.

These three ritual relations were earlier shown as positive enduring links between enduring structures. They are now seen to have a negative, or reverse side. In the case of ritual partners and parental/filial clans, they exclude the use of force in settling disputes; between clans that are kith the likelihood of the resort to force is greatly diminished and, by use of the rite after a killing between two clans of one tribe, the fight can be kept within bounds and a feud averted. There are three degrees of ritual relation between clans. That between ritual partners is the closest link both positively, in binding the clans to reciprocal ritual services, and negatively, in the prohibition on killing a ritual partner. Secondly, there is the tie between parental/filial clans which positively links the clans in reciprocal burial services and, negatively, proscribes homicide between them. Thirdly comes the tie between kith which is undefined positively in that no specific duties are prescribed between them though they are present at each other's ritual occasions; nor is it defined negatively since, though it is possible, even permissible, to kill a neighbour, yet there are the means available to limit the effects of this killing and avert feud. A clan has only one clan of ritual partners; it may have one or more filial clans and one parent clan; and, finally, the number of its kith clans does not exceed three or four. There are no wider ranging positive links between lineages and clans than the common acceptance of the rite of *Bi sub tibwar* through which a feud between clans of the same tribe may be brought to a close.

The ties of matrilateral kinship that relate a man to his mother's clan, and through her to the children of all women married out of his mother's clan, his *nabo* or fellow 'sisters' sons', are also related to feud. Feud is a political institution and is carried on between groups. Yet it may begin on the level of a fight between two individuals, one of whom is killed. A man may not fight with his mother's agnatic kinsmen. This prohibition extends in diminishing intensity to the agnatic kin of the mother of a man of his extended house and in still lesser intensity to those of any man of his minor lineage. The two primary prohibitions are these: a man may not kill his *dejoo*, fellow-clansman, or his *umwidza*, his 'mother's brother'. Of the killing of men of other clans Konkomba are inclined to say *Na aje neba*, 'it is nothing'. In fact, there are the other group prohibitions I have already described.

The relation between *nabo* is not one of reciprocal duties but of obligatory friendship. That is, should they meet, and no matter where they may meet, they are friends. The *nabo*, 'mother child', and the *naabo*, 'mother's child', may be contrasted. Should a man be involved in a quarrel his male *naabo* will come unquestioningly to his assistance, as do his *dejaa* in their degree of closeness to him in the segmentary system. A *nabo* carries no such responsibility; he is only a friendly person. There is no likelihood of severe quarrelling between *nabo* and so this wide dispersal in space of his *nabo* provides a man with many potential friends in potentially hostile areas. Further, in a quarrel a *nabo* tries to quieten it, to avert serious fighting.

The effect of these ties of matrilateral kinship is to counteract the isolation of structures based on agnation, to link individual to individual widely over the country; they also tend to increase the number of persons with whom a man may not fight and create a category of men who will seek to keep each other out of a serious fight and who, by refusing to come unquestioningly to each other's side in a quarrel, inhibit the outbreak of fighting. These ties between individuals cross the barriers between tribes and even between peoples. They therefore, in a small measure, tend to mitigate the endless war between tribes.

VIII. The Tribal System

A KONKOMBA tribe is the sum of its component clans. The tribes are territorial units in that the tribal territory is the totality of the districts of one tribe. Many tribes, but not all, are distinguished by different face marks. Clans of the same tribe stand in ritual partnership and kithship to each other, both relations of ritual assistance. Clans of the same tribe accept the rite of *Bi sub tibwar* to end a feud. Finally, clans of the same tribe come to each other's assistance in a fight against members of another tribe and there is no end to inter-tribal fighting. We may therefore speak of feud between clans and of war between tribes.

It is not always possible to distinguish a tribe by the face marks alone. Some of the outlying Konkomba refer to those of the Oti plain as the Bemwatib, the River people. Of these the Betshabob, Bemokpem, Nakpantib and Besangma have the same mark.

I do not know the total number of Konkomba tribes. I have visited members of a dozen but that is not to say that there are no more of which I have no knowledge. No Konkomba knows all the other tribes but most Konkomba know of the Betshabob, the Bemokpem, the Benafiab, the Begbem, the Besangma and the Bekwom. Of these the Betshabob and Bemokpem must each number more than 6,000 and of each some 3,000 live in Ghana on the west bank of the Oti. These are the two largest tribes. The Nakpantib and the Kpaltib number not more than 2,000 each.

There are very wide dialectal variations in Konkomba language. The dialects of the neighbouring Betshabob, Bemokpem, Begbem and Nakpantib are close enough so a speaker of one of them may communicate easily with a speaker of another. Speech between a Betshabob and a Benafiab is difficult even though the tribes are separated at the nearest point by only sixteen miles. Speech between the River people and the Bekwom of northern Gushiego is so difficult that they communicate, when possible, in Dagbane.

Tribes are not corporate bodies though in Konkombaland proper they are localized units. There are no tribal rites such that all or many clans come together; there are no corporate activities. It is only in inter-tribal war that tribal unity is to be observed.

By war I do not here mean an organized calling out of regiments to fight in a battle line until one or other side yields. I mean a permanent state of hostility which intermittently breaks out in small fights. This state of mutual hostility need not even be markedly apparent. It is seen, for example, in the attitude of reserve, a tendency to stand a little apart in small groups in a market owned and run by another tribe; or in the strict adherence to formality observed by a party of Betshabob seeking a bride from a Nakpantib clan, a formality all the more necessary because even on such a mission clubs are carried. Between persons of different tribe, except those who are linked by kinship, this reserve, almost a wariness, is always apparent. Especially is this so in the period which follows a clash between members of two tribes, even though the fighting and killing have been far off. Both tribes after a fight are for long wary and on edge. Any small infringement by either side is likely at such a time to renew the fighting and to embroil more and more clans.

In these days fighting is less frequent than in the past but when it does occur it is swift and bloody. In inter-tribal war there is no intervention of elders to avert combat, no hesitation of young men reluctant to fight with neighbours. Instead there is a swift line-up and a sense of kill or be killed. Of all inter-tribal fighting the most severe has been between the Betshabob and the Bemokpem. This may be partly due to the fact that they are the two largest tribes. They are not contiguous at many points and their principal centres, that of the Betshabob around Saboba and that of the Bemokpem around Saambwer, are separated from each other by clans of the Nakpantib. There has been no outbreak of serious fighting in these regions for some years.

In the summer of 1950 a man of the Kumwatiak district of the Betshabob tribe caught a man of the Bemokpem tribe with his wife and killed him. There were no immediate reprisals though men of both tribes were ready for an outbreak of fighting. It came in Buya in Krachi where many of the Kumwatiak people now live. A Betshabob man, Windam of the Bekujom clan, bought a chewing stick in Buja market and asked a Bemokpem girl to take it home for him. She was met by a clansman of hers, Jajuen, who took it from her and cut off part of it. When she told Windam what Jajuen had done he became angry and went to Jajuen who was now joined by his brother Bukari. Jajuen and Bukari together shouted that the Betshabob need a lesson (*Betshabob a la tshe*) and then Bukari struck Windam. From blows with fists the fight passed to blows with matchets, the outcome of which was that Bukari killed Windam. Tigene, a 'brother' of Windam's, fetched his arrows and he with some other of his clansmen, all armed with bows and arrows, killed Bukari. The Bemokpem men hurriedly retreated and took refuge in the hamlet of a clan of Nakpantib tribe where they were temporarily safe. The Betshabob then went to the hamlet where Bukari and Jajuen lived and killed the elder where he sat in his room. The fight was now over and police arrived shortly after.

This fight was explicitly a continuation of the killing of the Bemokpem man in Kumwatiak: *Ke Kumwatiakanib nanku bani, nimale bi mu be keku tie*—'they say "the Kumwatiak people killed their man, that is why they too want to kill theirs".' The husband who killed his wife's lover was of Bemwatiak clan and the Bemokpem tried to take their revenge on the Bekujom clan. Revenge for inter-tribal killings can be taken on any man of the killer's tribe and not merely on the man himself or on one of his close kinsmen. I do not know the clan affiliations of all the Bemokpem involved but I do not think that they all came from Lagea, the clan of the man killed by his lover's husband. That is, revenge in inter-tribal warfare may be taken by any clan of the same tribe.

The Bemokpem, who have lost three men to the Betshabob's one, are waiting until an occasion presents itself on which they outnumber the Betshabob and then they will take their revenge.

In describing such fights a Konkomba knows the clans of his own tribe involved in the fight. Their opponents are not known in detail, but are merely the 'Bemokpem' or the 'Betshabob'; the opposing tribe is known, not its clans. It is only in inter-tribal warfare that Konkomba clans join against a common enemy. In warfare, diversity of clan status is merged in identity of tribal status against a unit of the same order. This junction of parts, this coalescence of diverse groups, can be seen at all levels of organization on the occasion of brawls and fights. A man looks first to his *naabo*, 'mother's child', then to his *taabo*, his 'father's child', for assistance; then to a member of his own minor lineage for help against a man of another clan. The next stage is the calling in of men of his major lineage and then of his clan. This same conjunction of segments is observed in brawls and fights between clans of one tribe and it operates in feud between clans. The conjunction of clans of one tribe is only seen in inter-tribal fights when any man must go to the help of his fellow tribesman. As was noted earlier in the fight between the Betshabob of Kitiak and the Bemokpem of Lagea and again in the fight just described, retreating foes who take refuge with men of a third tribe are temporarily safe.

It is possible to conceive of a yet wider association, of all Konkomba tribes against the Dagomba. There is no evidence that the tribes ever did join in international warfare. This is one reason for the ease with which the Dagomba carried out their invasion. Further, when the Benafiab killed the Dzagberi Na, no other Konkomba tribe thought of itself as involved and the Betshabob bitterly resented their inclusion in the punishment imposed by the Government on the Benafiab.

Konkomba tribes are, like the clans, probably impermanent though much longer enduring than the clans. Because of the high mobility on the ground of Konkomba, whole clans can break up and it is possible that tribes may also do the same. The Begbem were once numerous and occupied a compact region between Demon and Gnani. This is now empty bush and only a few Begbem clans are to be found to the west of the Demon–Saboba road, especially near Wapul. It is probable that many of them have moved away to northern Krachi, a region I was unable to study. On the other hand, new tribes come into being. The Nakpantib tribe is probably of more recent growth than the Betshabob, Bemokpem and Bekwom tribes. The last three tribes date themselves, at the latest, from the time of the Dagomba invasion and probably from before the invasion. The Nakpantib have no migration legend. They appear to have spread by extra-district fission from Nakpando-Proper over a fairly compact region. The spread of the Nakpantib is part of the westward drift of Konkomba. If this is so, then the relations between neighbouring clans as they formed would be parental/filial relations, which in the course of time could become relations of ritual partnership and kithship once the precise relation of affiliation was forgotten. It is clear enough, today, that the Betshabob regard the Nakpantib as *bibaba*, 'by themselves', and that neighbours of either group do not attend each other's rites.

Earlier, in discussing the spread of the Benalog from Nalogni into Nalog, Waju, Kugar and other districts, I noted that these clans describe themselves as Benalog and not as Betshabob, while the parent clan does describe itself as Betshabob. Unlike the spread of the Nakpantib from Nakpando-Proper, the spread of the Benalog from Nalogni did not take place over a compact region; the Benalog went to the south-west and to the north-east of the original settlement but not one of their clans is contiguous with the parent clan. Similarly with the offshoots of the Benangmam of Kitiak and the Bekumbwam of Saboba; when extra-district fission took segments from these parent clans, the new segments were settled at a distance both from the parent clans and from each other. Fission that took place in this way did not lead to the formation of new tribes.

If it is through extra-district fission over a compact area that new tribes come into being the process is certainly a slow one. Not all the fission that takes place is from the point of first settlement and many generations must be allowed to permit the process of population increase and lineage fission to take place in the new settlements. In any case the Nakpantib must have attained tribal status slowly, at the earliest some time after the Dagomba invasion.

The structure of Konkomba society is then a system of relations between units of different duration through time. From the temporary, interstitial structures, the nuclear lineages, to the long-enduring but not necessarily permanent tribes, every unit of the structure is in its own degree transient; each may break up and disappear to give place to a new structure of the same form. Particular units of organization disappear but the form endures. Therefore, underlying the slightly varying form of lineage, clan and tribe at any point in time, there are certain principles of organization which persist. It is in virtue of these principles that new lineage segments, new clans, and new tribes repeat the pattern of lineages, clans and tribes now broken up and lost.

IX. The Political System: Conclusion

THE social structure of a society is, in part, a function of its ecology. The Oti plain, flooded in the wet season and burned in the dry, provides permanent sites for habitation only along its ridges. The population of any given hamlet must be small or else the inhabitants must go far to their bush farms. It is the case that some farms lie between seven and ten miles from the compounds of their owners. Population increase in a settlement means that there is not enough land for all and fission takes place and settlers seek new lands. This was expressed by one elder thus:

'The Konkomba too come and get here to stay. They severally get up and go across the river to stay. They divide thus to stay by themselves because there is no land to hoe (grow) food and eat. They divide and stay by themselves, stay alone, they too stay by themselves.'

Land shortage and lineage fission in this environment appear severely to restrict aggregations of people and to produce a small-scale segmentary society. But this hypothesis cannot be taken as proven without comparative studies among the Konkomba of Mamprusi and the Basare of the hills. The former appear to have a social structure alike in scale and in form to that of the Konkomba of the plain, though theirs is a very different environment. The latter have a social structure which appears to be like that of Konkomba in form but unlike it in scale, again in a different and upland environment.

Until further data on these two groups can be obtained we can look only to the data now available. There is good reason to suppose that the size of Konkomba clans is at the present time greatly reduced in numbers as against the size of forty to fifty years ago. The number of empty and ruined houses in many Konkomba hamlets is quite astonishing. At Saambwer, Kedzabo, Lagea and Nakpando-Proper it is plain to see that the population has been reduced by more than half. According to Afa Abubukari, the leader of the Muslim hierarchy in Yendi, there were once nearly 500 compounds in Saboba. It is impossible to be quite sure what he means by Saboba but he certainly includes the clans of the Bekumbwam and Benasom, the Bemwatiak, the Bwakwintib and the Bekujom. The total number of compounds now occupied by these clans is about 100. Within a dozen miles radius of Saboba three whole clans have been lost to the region and all the others have lost population. Not all the people who moved moved out of Konkombaland; the Bekujom, for example, are for the most part now settled east of the Oti. But most of the people who moved went to Krachi, to the Kulpene Valley, or to Gonja around Salaga. The pacification of the country in the present century has enabled many peoples in this area to move more freely and to seek fresh lands distant from their natal districts. In the special instance of Konkomba this move has also often been a move outside the sphere of Dagomba influence. We need not suppose that the larger scale of Basare society entails a very radical change from the principles of Konkomba organization, though it would be reasonable to expect a more complex segmentation of their larger clans than is now found in the smaller clans of present-day Konkomba. It is certain that, forty years ago, many of the clans of the plains were much larger than they are at present. If they were larger, the system of segmentation may have been more complex than it is today. Indications of this are found at Kukwin and at Saangul; these two clans have quadruple and triple segmentation respectively, in place of the more common bifurcation of a clan into two major lineages. These larger, more segmented clans are found on the higher lands of the plain where flooding is less severe and larger areas of unflooded land are found. Kukwin, Saangul and Saambwer all stand on eminences that for this region are quite considerable. All lie to the west of the ancient river terraces along the western edge of the plain.

The influence of their environment on the social structure of Konkomba is undeniable. The floods, while they do not determine, yet greatly influence the size of Konkomba settlements. Given that environment, then, in the absence of strong ancestor and Earth cults binding men closely to agnatic kinsmen and patrimonial land, there is nothing in their culture on which larger structures could be based. Forde's[1] hypothesis, that poverty of habitat and of productive technology tends to inhibit the development of unilateral descent groups

---

[1] D. Forde, 'The Anthropological Approach in Social Science', in *The Advancement of Science*, iv, 1947, pp. 213–224.

by limiting the scale and stability of settlement, receives further support from this society. Konkomba values are those of small and isolated agnatic kin-groups which in certain contexts can join to produce larger units. The units of the Konkomba structure are minor lineages, major lineages, clans and tribes. Minor lineages join to form major lineages; major lineages join to form clans and clans to form tribes. All these are localized structures and all save tribes are corporate bodies. Throughout the system run the complementary processes of conjunction and segmentation. A lineage segments to form two structures of lower order. The segments of any order, except the most inclusive, can temporarily join together to form a unit of higher order.

I therefore regard what has been written above as a prologue to further analysis, as the essential first step in an analysis of Konkomba society. I have tried to lay out the segments of this society and to indicate some contexts in which the conjunction of segments takes place.

Minor lineages join with other minor lineages to form one major lineage on ritual and economic occasions, for example, in the performance of certain rites. Major lineages join to form a clan on economic, ritual and jural occasions, for example, in sacrifices to the clan land. Clans, since tribes are not corporate bodies, join only on warlike occasions when yet another of an infinite series of fights between two tribes has broken out.

Within the tribe there are forms of linkage which bind together clans which, taken singly, are numerically few and spatially limited. The conjunction of lineages within the clan, the linkages between clans and the conjunction of clans within the tribe are especially relevant to those contexts which may be called political.

Political activities are those which concern good order within a unit of the political system and which concern the independence of that unit *vis-à-vis* other units of like order. Those activities which are concerned with the steady running of the clan, the unit of political organization, I called jural activities; they centre upon theft, brawls and quarrels between fellow-clansmen, succession to farming rights, the destruction of crops, and so on. In such contexts the authority of the elders, based on seniority and ritual power, is commonly sufficient to command restraint and the peaceable settlement of disputes, though fellow clansmen may restrain their kinsman by force or subject him to ostracism. Between clans of one tribe there is no high moral authority to command respect and the sanction on good behaviour between men of different clans of one tribe is the threat of force and the danger of beginning a feud. The situations in which inter-clan fighting commonly breaks out are in quarrels over love-affairs and transgression by one clan of another clan's hunting and fishing rights.

Between men of different tribes the sanction on good behaviour is again that of force, the threat of a recrudescence of inter-tribal warfare.

To mitigate these relations of perennial hostility there are the ritual linkages between *mantotib*, between kith, and between any clan and another clan of the same tribe which accepts the rite of 'They bury the fight'. These linkages are most effective where most needed, that is between clans that are near to each other in ecological distance. In addition, the links of matrilateral kinship work, in lower intensity but greater extension than do inter-clan ritual links, to mitigate hostility between individuals of different clan, tribe or people.

This system of structures expresses the values of Konkomba society, the paramount values of loyalty to the clan and love of its territory, for no Konkomba will ever admit that his harsh country is in any way inferior to surrounding lands.

PART II
THE DOMESTIC ORGANIZATION

X. The Family, Household and Minor Lineage

THIS chapter first seeks to show how far the actual forms of the Konkomba family and household coincide with their forms as conceived by the people themselves. The second part analyses some of the functions of those units of organization. By function, I mean the relation of the household to certain aspects of Konkomba life: namely, the household as a unit of production and consumption, as a unit of social control, as a ritual unit, and so on. The term 'household' refers to the total group of persons living together in one compound (*letʃeni*), which is a cluster of round houses distributed about a central space and linked by a low wall (see Fig. 16). The head of a household (*letʃendaa*) is the senior man, the husband and the father of the family that is the nucleus of the household. This may be an elementary or a polygynous family; or it may be an expanded family, consisting of a number of brothers and their wives, sons, and unmarried daughters; or it may be an extended family, consisting of a man, his wives, their sons, sons' wives and children, and their unmarried daughters. To this nucleus other kin are added and it will be shown that these additional members are always either members of the minor lineage group of the household head or wives or widows of members. For the household is part of a larger grouping, the minor lineage group, which consists of all men of the minor patrilineal segment plus their wives and their unmarried daughters.

To analyse the form of the household and to consider to what extent the ideal and the actual forms coincide, I first state the Konkomba ideal pattern of the household and test statistically its conformity

[1]This chapter appeared in two parts in *Africa*, vol. xxvi, nos. 3 and 4, July and October 1956, under the title of 'The Family, Household, and Minor Lineage of the Konkomba'.

with the actual; I turn then to the functions of the household, and again state ideal patterns and again compare actual activities with them.

As has been indicated, households vary from an elementary family to a quite large group of kin all related to the household head. The elementary family, through time, gives rise to a larger structure which may be called an extended house (p. 100). The Konkomba word '*do*' has two meanings: it refers to an existing compound and the group of kin which occupies that compound, but it also refers to a structural unit which comprises all the descendants of one man through two generations. The principal function of the extended house is found in the rules governing marriage, since between any two such units only one marriage is possible.

In the Konkomba system all structures from the family to the clan are unstable, though the major lineages and clans, at least, are conceived as permanent. They have political functions. The elementary family seldom endures more than half a dozen years before becoming a polygynous family. The simple household rapidly becomes complex by the addition of other kin of the household head. The extended house endures for only one generation. The rate of change in the minor lineage lies somewhere between these extremes.

KONKOMBA MARRIAGE

Change in all these structures is, however, retarded by the long duration of a Konkomba generation. Because men in their early twenties are betrothed to infant girls, few men marry much before the age of 35–40. The generations, then, if calculated in the male line, must be put at not less than forty years and perhaps more to allow for a rising polygyny rate as men age. Thus, even a three- to four-generation genealogy, if regarded as an accurate statement of descent, gives a time depth of not less than 120–160 years counting from the heads of households. This feature of marriage, then, profoundly affects not only the family and household, but the total social system.

Because of this late age of marriage few men live to see their sons marry and to see their sons' sons. For this reason, the extended family does not occur in the form in which it is found in other societies in the region.[1] Among Konkomba it is only found when both father and son marry unusually young: some apparent instances

[1] See M. Fortes, *The Web of Kinship among the Tallensi*, 1949; J. R. Goody, *The Social Organization of the LoWiili*, 1956, also the author's unpublished material on the Dagomba.

of the extended family disappeared on closer investigation which showed the supposed 'son' to be an older brother's son.

A man should be betrothed for the first time in his early twenties and again not more than ten years later. Konkomba do not distinguish between fiancée and wife: both are referred to as '*pu*'. A betrothal is spoken of as *Bi twi opi* (lit. 'they promise a woman') by both the girl's father and the youth's father: *Bi twi opi* therefore means that a contract has been entered into to exchange a girl against goods and services. The prospective husband pays services and corn to her father over the years of the girl's growth. Though Konkomba do not verbally distinguish these statuses it will be convenient to refer to the promised bride as 'fiancée' and to the woman who has joined her husband as 'wife'. Further, there is nothing in Konkomba that can properly be called a 'wedding'.

Konkomba say that a woman *tʃa tɔ tʃar*, that is, goes to her husband, or that a husband *ga o pu*, gets his wife. There is, however, a term for a newly arrived wife, *otʃakpe*, literally, one who comes fresh. When a wife arrives at her husband's hamlet she stays one week in the household of the elder of the major lineage; this may be taken as a symbolic union between the lineage and the bride. Other ceremonies mark her arrival. Yet from the time of betrothal she is spoken of as *pu* and the lineage group of the man to whom she is betrothed will claim her even should the first fiancé die.

There is no possibility of confusing mere love affairs with marriage. All fiancées have love affairs with members of clans other than that of the fiancé. Yet Konkomba love affairs are, in theory, hidden except from members of the girl's household; lovers cannot live together as man and wife except by running away together, and if a man runs away with a woman he cannot later repudiate her and return her to her father's house. (An exception is referred to below at p. 181.) After they have run away the man will approach the girl's father through an intermediary, usually his own brother, to offer the father the proper gifts which will make the runaway union into an acceptable one. If the father agrees, as he always does, then the marriage is valid. But such unions lead to reprisals on the part of the lineage group that has lost a wife and may, even today, lead to an outbreak of feud. If the clan that has lost a promised wife in a runaway union has in turn promised a wife to either one of the other two clans involved, that girl will be withheld and given elsewhere in an exchange marriage.

As a result of the love affairs mentioned earlier, it sometimes happens that a girl is pregnant when she goes to join her husband.

Children born to a woman by a lover belong to the woman's husband and are accepted by him as his children. I know of no differentiation between children begotten by a lover and those begotten by the husband. There is a term, *abombo*, which means 'a child that doesn't know its father': but it can, I think, be applied only to children borne by a girl who, for one reason or another, was not betrothed in infancy.

When a fiancée is considered old enough to go to her husband, at about eighteen or when she is pregnant, whichever is the earlier, she joins him in his hamlet where the pair will live together. If it is the husband's second or later marriage, the bride will join him in his compound. If it is the groom's first marriage and his father, that is his genitor, is alive, the married pair will live in the groom's genitor's compound. If the groom was previously living with a guardian, then it is likely that he will set up his own compound at once and will certainly do so in a very short time. Another form of marriage occurs, a marriage by purchase. Very occasionally men buy wives—Konkomba think and speak of it as 'buying'—from the neighbouring Kabre. The current payment is four cows. Such marriages are infrequent and are regarded as emergency marriages. A wife so obtained is a replacement for a runaway wife or for a dead wife when a man has no other wife to care for the dead woman's children.

The ideal family is polygynous, or more precisely duogynous, for it is thought of as containing two wives and the household as dual. Women think in terms of two wives to a family. A woman once asked her husband when he was going to get his second wife. What, she asked, would happen to him if she fell ill before he did so? From the point of view of the first wife there are several advantages in the arrival of the second. She attains the added status of a senior wife. Women will boast of being the oldest wife of a family, though the status of senior wife means no more than that she has a younger person to help in the household work, especially in the heavy work of fetching water and wood, and that the husband will keep ritual objects in her room. She does not, as do Dagomba senior wives, organize the household's domestic affairs. In general, a high rate of polygyny is not expressly desired by Konkomba, though there is no rule which prohibits a man from marrying more often than twice and most men of the senior age sets have more than two wives. The highest number of wives I recorded was eight living wives, not one of them inherited as a widow. I never saw this household and it may be significant that the husband had left his native place to settle elsewhere.

THE FAMILY AND HOUSEHOLD

The compound is divided among the wives. Each must have her own room, kitchen, and hearth. Except in the lineage elder's compound, where a room is built for the young men of the lineage group, the compounds are entirely divided among the wives. The wives keep very much to their own parts of the compound, though they may, and older wives often do, use the large entry room which is the principal room of the household head. Only a woman's own children, or motherless children assigned to her, may enter her room uninvited. This rule marks the division of the household into the children of one mother and one room—the *naabim*—within the wider grouping of the children of one father and house—the *taabim*. The compound is therefore literally divided between, and the family segmented into, groups composed of the children of one mother.

The layout of a typical elder's compound is as follows:

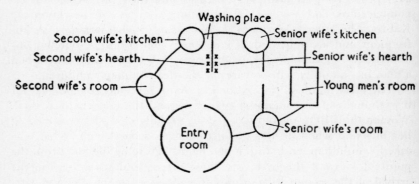

FIG. 16. Plan of a compound

In daily intercourse Konkomba move easily in and out of each other's compounds, although one may not step over a broken wall unless one is a member of the household but must enter through the large entry room. In this, they are in marked contrast with the more formal Dagomba who do not often go beyond the entry room. But since Konkomba speak of the lineage very vaguely, only examination of actual cases can show just which lineage span is involved in this easy coming and going.

The data of the following analysis are a sample of ninety-eight households take from three contiguous clans. The clans can be taken as typical of Konkomba, or at least of the riverain Konkomba, for I have stayed in many places besides these, and have seen no marked

TABLE V

Composition of households in three clans: Banaŋmam, Betʃabob, Banalɔg

Clan segments	Extended house kin															Minor Lineage Kin		Wives of Minor Lineage Kin	Relationship unknown	Tot.	Com-pound
	CH	M	Ws	Ss	Ds	SW	SS	SD	YB	YBW	YBS	YBD	EBS	EBD	Sis	△	O	O	△		
Kotodo	14	2	28	22	32	—	—	—	6	4	15	4	2	—	2	4	2	—	2	139	14
Ɗmaŋeado	7	1	14	11	3	—	—	—	4	—	2	—	4	2	—	2	—	—	—	50	7
BENAƊMAM	21	3	42	33	35	—	—	—	10	4	17	4	6	2	2	6	2	—	2	189	21
Bakumbwam	25	1	52	61	45	13	6	7	—	—	1	—	10	2	—	1	1	—	—	225	26
Banasom	19	—	30	39	30	—	—	—	—	—	7	—	5	2	—	—	—	—	—	132	19
BETƩABOB	44	1	82	100	75	13	6	7	—	—	8	—	15	4	—	1	1	—	—	357	45
Makpadado	8	1	15	21	16	—	—	—	4	2	—	—	1	—	—	5	—	—	—	73	9
Kotiendo	12	1	29	23	21	—	1	—	1	2	4	3	8	—	—	6	—	2	7	120	12
Bwarado	11	—	21	30	12	2	1	—	3	2	—	—	2	1	—	1	—	1	—	87	11
BENALƆG	31	2	65	74	49	3	1	—	8	6	4	3	11	1	—	12	—	3	7	280	32
Total	96	6	189	207	159	16	7	7	18	10	29	7	32	7	2	19	3	3	9	826	98

Key: CH = Compound Head
M = Mother of Compound Head
Ws = Wives of Compound Head
Ss = Sons
Ds = Daughters
SW = Son's wife (of Compound Head)
SS = Son's son

SD = Son's daughter
YB = Younger brother (of Compound Head)
YBW = Younger brother's wife
YBS = Younger brother's son
YBD = Younger brother's daughter
EB = Elder brother (of Compound Head)
EBS = Elder brother's son
EBD = Elder brother's daughter

difference in the size and form of the household. More important, clans intermarry not only within a narrow radius, but with clans perhaps forty miles away to the east and sixteen miles to the north, west, and south. We can therefore take it that the marriage system is uniform in its main features throughout the area and, if the relation between family structure and lineage structure is as close as I take it to be, then the total social system must be uniform also. The system, in fact, runs beyond the boundaries of the Konkomba to the southeast among the Basare and to the north among the Komba.

The data given in the tables were collected in the following way. First, genealogies were recorded in all the clans studied. Then a household survey was taken and the genealogies and the composition of households checked against each other. All discrepancies were investigated until all persons appearing in either record were accounted for.[1]

These figures are set out in Table V. The sample shows that there is no household that contains a child living with his or her maternal grandfather. Indeed, in the whole sample there is only one household in which the sisters of the head were living. They were unmarried at the time the sample was taken but have since moved out to join their husbands. The family is therefore very strictly patrilocal.

Of the ninety-six household heads:

TABLE VI

33 men, that is 34.4 per cent, had 1 wife,	a total of 33 wives
40 men, that is 41.6 per cent, had 2 wives,	a total of 80 wives
16 men, that is 16.6 per cent, had 3 wives,	a total of 48 wives
7 men, that is 7.3 per cent, had 4 wives,	a total of 28 wives
96 men had a total of	189 wives

It will be shown later that, as might be expected, there is a tendency for the men with only one wife to be in the youngest age set.

[1] It might appear that a dead wife could be omitted. This is possible but I do not think it occurred frequently. A childless wife might have been omitted but even this is unlikely: the long period of bride service is an effective reminder. Further, no other marriages are possible between the extended house of even a childless dead woman and the extended house of her husband. Certainly no woman who left children could be omitted, though it may have happened that women have been treated only as wives and not also as inherited widows when they were in fact so inherited. This could happen in the case of a woman who had borne children only to the second husband and whose first husband had not lived long with her. Or a husband might have been inclined to conceal a runaway wife: but again, the genealogies were always collected with most of the members of the hamlet present, making such concealment difficult. Nevertheless, I do not claim 100 per cent accuracy in any table.

The duogynous family appears, from the above figures, to be the type most frequently occurring at a point in time. However, many men have married more frequently than the figures show. Ninety of them, whose marital history is fully known, had, in 1951, a total of 158 wives and had had, during their lives, a total of 180 wives (Table VII). This tabulation yields, as crude averages:

From Table   V 1.96 wives per man in 1951
From Table   VI 1.75 wives per man in 1951
From Table VII 2.0 marriages per man up to 1951

Only one instance of a runaway marriage and only two instances of marriage by purchase occur in the sample, so that runaway marriages have an incidence of about 0.5 per cent and marriages by purchase an incidence of about 1 per cent. On the other hand, out of the total of 158 living wives, thirty-four had previously been married to another husband, giving a percentage of 23.6. Of all marriages recorded for these men, forty, that is 22.2 per cent, were to widows.

It is probable that more men than have been recorded had, at some

TABLE VII

Marriages of men of three clans showing first marriages and remarriages of women alive and dead

N = 90 husbands

	Alive					Dead					Total		
	Wives	Widows	Lovers	Bought	Total	Wives	Widows	Lovers	Bought	Total	Wives	Widows	Total
Bənaŋmam													
Kotodo	16	14	—	1	31	5	—	—	1	6	23	14	37
Ŋmaŋeado	5	8	—	—	13	1	—	—	—	1	6	8	14
Bəkumbwam													
Durdo	19	—	—	—	19	2	—	—	—	2	21	—	21
Gurdo	14	1	—	—	15	3	3	—	—	6	17	4	21
Kpalib	4	4	—	—	8	—	—	—	—	—	4	4	8
Bənaləg													
Makpadado	15	1	—	—	16	3	—	—	—	3	18	1	19
Kotiendo	26	5	1	—	32	1	—	—	—	1	28	5	33
Bwarado	23	1	—	—	24	—	3	—	—	3	23	4	27
	122	34	1	1	158	15	6	—	1	22	140	40	180

Total of married men:

Bənaŋmam 26
Bəkumbwam   40
Bənaləg   24

time or another, been married to a widow. More than half the marriages of widows are recorded in one clan. The possible omission of
a widow from the list of a man's wives has already been explained.
It should be said that a woman's status as inherited widow or wife
does not affect her seniority in the household of her present husband.
A woman married as a widow may become the senior wife in the household in which she is inherited if she has children; a childless woman
may be the wife first married to her first husband and yet lose the
status of senior wife. Motherhood and status, it must be emphasized,
are in no way linked to the bearing of sons. At least one senior wife
in the sample had no surviving sons.

In this sample, one of the widows inherited was the wife of a
runaway marriage, but none the less she was inherited. This is an
indication that a runaway bride will in time achieve the status of a
lineage wife and the security that widow inheritance give a woman.

I know of no marked disabilities under which runaway wives suffer
in the clans of their irregularly gotten husbands. Certainly they
receive the full rites of burial, though this might be taken as an
indication of their status as mothers. All wives are excluded from the
husband's clan shrines, but a runaway wife may suffer other ritual
disabilities; she does not, for example, undergo the ceremonies that
follow the arrival of a bride in her husband's home. One ceremony
omitted is the bride's stay of one week in the house of the elder of her
husband's lineage, a symbolic union of the bride and the lineage.
Another ceremony, in which the bride is made to kneel at the hearth
that is to be hers and is threatened with a beating unless she confesses
the name of her lover, would be pointless after a runaway marriage.
It is also true that, even in later life, a husband looks rather shame-
faced when he admits to a runaway marriage. The position is perhaps
best stated thus: in the early days of such a marriage, even one
regularized by the formal visit to the girl's father to apologize (*ke te
gba njopu*) and make payments for the bride, there is some insecurity.
The diffuse sense of irregularity apart, there is danger of retaliation
on the part of the clan that has lost a wife; that is, the husband has
endangered the peace of his clan. Further, the ceremonies of marriage
have been omitted and the woman is perhaps not fully a lineage wife.
Yet she does acquire the status of inheritability as a widow and that
of an elder, no doubt because she has given children to the lineage.
No suggestion has been made that her children suffer any disability.
It seems, then, that in the early years of the marriage a runaway wife's
position may be insecure but that, in time, she achieves security.

WIDOW INHERITANCE

Table VIII shows the relation of the first husband to the widow's second husband. No instance is found of the inheritance of a widow by a man of the same major lineage or clan but of a different minor lineage group from that of the previous husband. We may take it that when a woman marries, she marries a minor lineage. Nor does a father inherit from his son or a father's brother from a brother's son. In general, a widow of child-bearing age is usually passed down to a younger man from an older man. In two cases in Table VIII, on the contrary, men inherited widows from younger brothers. In sum, a woman can be inherited by a man older or younger than her dead husband, and of the same or a younger generation, never by a man of a higher generation.

TABLE VIII

Relation of first husband to second in widow inheritance
N = 40

	Father	E-B	Y-B	Son	F.EB	F.YB	Minor lineage	Major lineage	Clan
	7	11	2	—	1	4	15	—	—
%	17.5	27.5	5	—	2.5	10	37.5	—	—

These figures may be grouped in percentage figures with respect to kin within the family, the extended house, and the minor lineage. Thus:

TABLE IX

	Family	Extended house	Minor lineage
Percentage	50	12.5	37.5
Cumulative total per cent	50	62.5	100

These figures show that most widows are inherited within the family and extended house; yet a considerable percentage are inherited within the minor lineage beyond them. Two principles are at work. First, a woman is inherited within a minor lineage; secondly, she is inherited by a man junior to her late husband but one as closely related to him as possible. Two cases may exemplify the principles. A man died leaving two wives and he had no true brother. One wife, a middle-aged woman, went to a man whose three wives had died leaving him with young children; the other, a young woman, went to the oldest of the unmarried men of the minor lineage. In the second example, when a very old man died (he was probably over ninety), his three old wives went to live with their sons and the fourth, a young woman, went to a young man of the same minor lineage not previously married. In this case all the dead man's sons were married at least once. In general, the needs of individual members of the lineage are considered; those of the women are not. It sometimes happens, of course, that a woman is inherited more than once; no such case falls within the sample.

I would say that the marriages that give rise to the closest personal relations between husband and wife are marriages by inheritance which bring together a man and a woman of about the same age.

DISPARITY OF AGE BETWEEN HUSBAND AND WIFE

My original material on disparity of age between husband and wife proved inadequate, so a further small sample of ninety-three wives was taken. Each person knows his or her place in the age-set system exactly, but each age set refers only to one clan. Thus the age sets even of contiguous clans do not necessarily coincide though there is an approximation between them. The women married into two clans at the present time (April 1955) were asked to say what men of their husband's clans they would regard as age mates. The husbands' age sets were already known and a simple sum gives the disparity between husband and wife. The central dates of each set were taken, but this leaves room for further error in that one of a pair might be the oldest in the set and the other the youngest, giving an error of about four years. Further, the oldest men are only known to be over sixty and there can be no close calculation beyond that point.

The expected pattern would work out somewhat as follows: a young man of about 20–24 is betrothed to a newly born girl; he is betrothed again to a second girl some years later, say at about 30, and probably again at about 35–40. The disparity of age between husband and first wife is therefore over twenty years; that between husband and second wife is about thirty years; while that between husband and third wife is about thirty-five to forty years. Deaths among betrothed girls will tend to increase this disparity because the husband grows older as he seeks a replacement. On the other hand, deaths among the men diminish the disparity because women tend to be inherited by younger men.

The disparities collected were stratified by age set of the husband in six columns for first, second, third etc. wife. Dead wives were inserted to keep the order, though their ages are not known. Wives who could not give an age mate—Kabre women and others who had come from a distance—were tabulated as 'not known'. Averages were then calculated for the wives in order by age set of the husband, first, for all marriages; secondly, for first marriages of the women, and thirdly, for remarriages of widows (Tables X, XI, and XII).

The range of disparities is enormous. It ranges from + 20, the wife (she was a remarried widow) being twenty years older than her husband, to − 40, the wife being forty years junior to her husband.

TABLE X

Disparity of age between husband and wife: all marriages
No. of wives 93

Age set	1	2	3	4	5	6
I	−13.3 plus*	−20 plus	−30.6 plus	−28 plus	—	—
II	− 8	−16.8	−22	−28	−24	−28
III	−16	−18.4	−12	−26	—	—
IV	−14.8	−23.2	−16	—	—	—
V	−13.5	−24	−12	—	—	—
VI	− 6.4	−16	−20	—	—	—
VII	−12	—	—	—	—	—
Average	−11.5	−19.8	−18.7	−30	−24	−28

TABLE XI

Disparity of age between husband and wife:
first marriages only of the wives

Age set	1	2	3	4	5	6
I	−13.3 plus*	−25.3 plus	−30.6 plus	−28 plus	—	—
II	− 8	−17	−22	−28	−24	−28
III	−21.3	−18.5	−16	−26	—	—
IV	−18	−23.2	−16	−36	—	—
V	−18	−28	−12	—	—	—
VI	−18	−13.3	−20	—	—	—
VII	−20	—	—	—	—	—
Average	−16.6	−20.8	−22.8	−29.5	−24	−28

TABLE XII
*Disparity of age between husband and wife:
remarried widows only*

Age set	1	2	3	4	5	6
I	—	− 4 plus*	—	—	—	—
II	− 8	−16	—	—	—	—
III	− 9.3	—	—	—	—	—
IV	plus 4	—	—	—	—	—
V	plus 2	—	—	—	—	—
VI	plus 7.2	−20	—	—	—	—
VII	− 4	—	—	—	—	—
Average	−1.35	−12	—	—	—	—

*The ages of men in the senior age set are not known accurately, but they are known to be over 60. The disparity of age in this set is therefore more than −13.3, etc.

The average disparities for all marriages are much below the expected ones.

	1W	2W	3W	4W	5W	6W
All sets	−11.5	−19.8	−18.7	−30	−24	−28

This table is greatly affected by the inheritance of widows. The table for first marriages only of women is as follows:

	1W	2W	3W	4W	5W	6W
All sets	−16.6	−20.8	−22.8	−29.5	−24	−28

Here we find a gradual rise in disparity of age between husband and wife in the succession of wives. The fifth and sixth wives may be ignored since few men marry more than four wives. Yet even here the disparity is below the expected level. This result is obtained, of course, because we are here dealing with women who survived to marry but of whom some must surely have been inherited as fiancées by men junior to the original fiancé. The range of variability here is from −8 to −36. No case occurs of a woman at her first marriage marrying a man junior to herself.

Finally, the figures for remarriages of widows are:

	1W	2W
All sets	−1.35	−12

This confirms the earlier statement that widows go to men junior to their first husbands and demonstrates the assertion that widows

who become first wives to their second husbands differ little from
them in age. Yet the range is again very considerable, as appears on
Table XII.

On the whole, then, allowance being made for the incalculable
factor, the deaths of fiancées and fiancés, the figures obtained are not
far from those we might expect from the betrothal pattern of Konkomba.

Of all Konkomba structures the age set is the least firmly defined.
It groups together all men and all women born in a four-year period,
but if a man moves away or dies, the gap he leaves tends to close.
Whole sets have been lost in all these clans by lineage fission and even
a gap of this size closes. Consequently, I have eliminated from this
sample all men of whose age set I am doubtful and instead use a
group of fifty-one men whose age, status, and marital history are
known.

I took these figures and tabulated them by age set of the men and
then reduced the age sets to a common basis of ten men per age set.
These figures are shown in Table XIII and Graph I.

This graph shows a gradual rise in marriages as the sets age. The
jump in age set IV is to be explained thus: it contains two men who
are ex-soldiers, both of whom have married more often than the
average for the most senior set. The variation in the curve of total
marriages is caused by inheritance of widows. The line is fairly
constant except for age set II, that is, men of 57–60. Above I pointed
out that there is a tendency for widows to be inherited by men
junior to the late husband and so by a man of less markedly disparate
age. When a man dies, his wives are distributed over the minor
lineage, his young wives going to the younger men, his middle-aged
wives going to the older men and his elderly wives entering the households of their married sons; or the elderly wives may enter the households of the elderly men, though not always with the full status of a
wife, or they may be set up in small houses of their own. These 'Old
Women's Houses' are a delightful feature of Konkomba hamlet life.
They are single rooms enclosed in a small compound and are always
kept spotlessly clean by the old ladies. The occupants of these houses
are usually women who are without sons and who are maintained by
the minor lineage group of their former husbands. I have not included
'Old Women's Houses' in the sample, though the women themselves
appeared as wives and inherited widows. Graph II shows that the
peak for mothers staying in the households of their sons is in age set
IV, that is, in the households of men of 49–52. After that point no

TABLE XIII

Marriage frequencies of men by age sets
N = 51 husbands and 180 wives

Age set	Alive					Dead					Total		
	Wives	Widows	Lovers	Bought	Total	Wives	Widows	Lovers	Bought	Total	Wives	Widows	Total
I	28	6	—	—	34	2	—	—	—	2	30	6	36
II	20	12.5	—	—	32.5	2.5	2.5	—	—	5	22.5	15	37.5
III	11	6	—	1	18	5	—	—	1	6	18	6	24
IV	18.26	4.98	—	—	23.24	—	1.66	—	—	1.66	18.26	6.64	24.92
V	11.25	3.75	1.25	—	16.25	—	—	—	—	—	12.5	3.75	16.25
VI	7.75	5	—	—	12.75	—	0.25	—	—	0.25	7.75	5.25	13
VII	7.5	2.5	—	—	10.0	—	—	—	—	—	7.5	2.5	10

TABLE XV

All marriages and betrothals of men of one major lineage by age sets of men
N = 101 women

Age set	Wives			Widows			Fiancées			Total	Men	Living Spouses	Wives and Fiancées
	Alive	Dead	Total	Alive	Dead	Total	Alive	Dead	Total				
I	10	0	10	10	—	10	10	—	10	30	10	20	20
II	10	0	10	15	—	15	15	—	15	40	10	25	25
III	8	10	18	10	—	10	16	14	30	58	10	24	48
IV	15	0	15	5	—	5	15	—	15	35	10	30	30
V	13.2	—	13.2	6.6	—	6.6	13.2	3.3	16.5	36.3	10	26.4	29.7
VI	6.6	—	6.6	6.6	—	6.6	26.4	9.9	36.3	49.5	10	33	42.9
VII	—	—	—	—	—	—	15.3	3.4	18.7	18.7	10	15.3	18.7
VIII	—	—	—	—	—	—	10	—	10	10	10	10	10
IX	—	—	—	—	—	—	—	—	10	10	10	10	10
X	—	—	—	—	—	—	20	5	25	25	10	20	25
XI	—	—	—	—	—	—	4.2	1.4	5.6	5.6	10	4.2	5.6

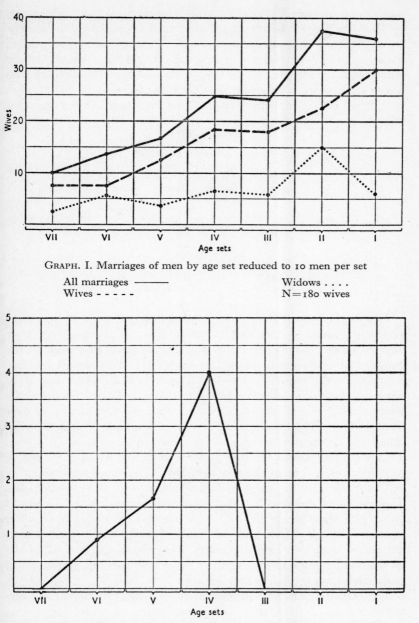

GRAPH. I. Marriages of men by age set reduced to 10 men per set

All marriages ———   Widows . . . .
Wives - - - - -   N = 180 wives

GRAPH II. Mothers of compound heads in households by age set of heads

K.N.G.—N

mothers are recorded. It may be, then, that the peak in Graph I at age set II in the curve for inheritance of widows is caused by the assigning of elderly widows to the households of elderly men. The peak in the curve for all marriages is perhaps due to the same cause. On the other hand, the sample for this set is small and contains one man who has never married a wife but has only inherited widows. This point would not, of course, help to account for the rise in all marriages for this set.

TABLE XIV

Range of marriages by age set
N = 180 marriages

Age set	Highest	Mean	Lowest
I	5	3.6	2
II	5	3.75	2
III	6	2.4	1
IV	4	2.5	1
V	3	1.7	1
VI	2	1.4	1
VII	1	0.2	0

Graph III from Table XIV shows the actual range of marriages against the mean. We see that no man of the two upper age sets ever marries more than five wives or fewer than two. The peak in the curve of all marriages is reached in age set III. This remarkable rise is caused by the six marriages of one man. He had three wives, all of whom died suddenly, leaving him with young children. He hurriedly bought a Kabre and inherited the first available widow to take over his household. The buying of a Kabre is an example of what I earlier called an 'emergency marriage'. He later inherited another widow. The graph also shows that the polygyny rate of the older age sets is well above two. The question arises: How is this rate maintained?

Unfortunately, my data on betrothals proved to be inadequate. Though I had realized that men continued to betroth themselves to infant girls throughout life, I had not grasped the extent to which it is done. Though elderly and old men so betroth themselves, it does not follow that they actually marry the girls themselves when the girls are old enough to marry. They often pass them on to the oldest unmarried man of their minor lineages.

I got the betrothals to all girls living and dead for all men of one major lineage. I hope later to be able to increase the size of this sample. To these figures I added all marriages up to 1951, both to

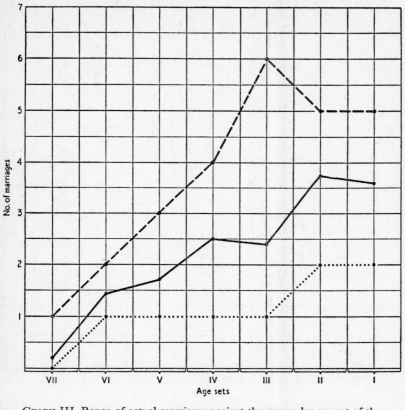

GRAPH III. Range of actual marriages against the mean: by age set of the husbands

Mean ———— Lowest number . . . . .
Highest number - - - - - - N = 180 marriages

new wives and to widows, for all these men and converted the resulting table to one on a common basis of ten men to an age set. The figures are set out in Table XV and in Graph IV. The curves show the following three groups of data: first, the total marriages of all kinds plus all betrothals for men of this major lineage; secondly, it shows the total first wives plus inherited widows plus betrothals for these men; and thirdly, it shows wives alive and fiancées alive. In the second curve we get something near to a continuous rise in the line as the men grow towards middle age and a fall in the later age sets. Perhaps it may be said that this graph suggests that a larger sample

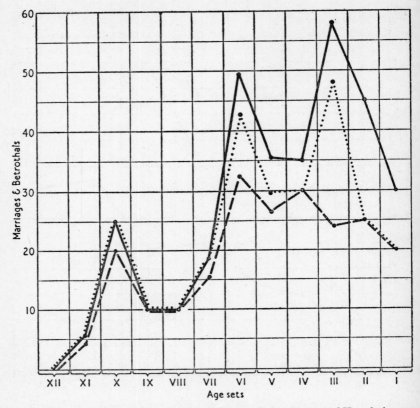

GRAPH IV. Showing all marriages and all betrothals for the men of Kotodo by age set on a common basis of 10 men per set, against all living wives and fiancées and inherited widows, and against all wives and fiancées

All marriages and betrothals ————
All wives, inherited widows and fiancées alive - - - - -
All wives and fiancées . . . . . .
N = 101 women

would give us a curve that would reach its peak in the middle age sets.

There is an effort, I think, to maintain a flow of wives into each lineage; if a man loses one fiancée he at once seeks another; if he is left wifeless he buys a Kabre; men in middle life betroth themselves to infant girls whom they will pass on as wives to young men of the lineage, and some men betroth themselves on behalf of absent

brothers. Therefore the curve of total betrothals is likely to be ir-
regular since deaths may, by chance, affect one age set more than
another. Only a large sample would smooth out this line. But the
total number of living women and girls married or betrothed to a
lineage is likely to be constant through time or, rather, to vary with
the number of males in the lineage; and at any point in time the distribution of the women over the men of the lineage will vary with the
age of the men.

The crude average figure is : 2.8 wives and fiancées per man over
21. The crude number of wives in the large sample of men over 37, it
will be remembered, was 1.96. The betrothal figures are, perhaps, not
too far out.

It may be thought[1] that this pattern of betrothals is best explained
by saying that infant betrothal 'helps to establish claims on the future
fertility of the woman for a particular lineage'. Or, using Bohannan's
terms, we might say that infant betrothal helps to establish a claim to
rights *in genetricem* over the woman. But I do not think the division
into rights *in genetricem* and rights *in uxorem* is valid for Konkomba
society. It is the case that the husband has the right to a child conceived by his fiancée before marriage by another man. Konkomba
define the 'father' (*te*) of a child as 'the husband of the mother'; the
genitor may be distinguished in the phrase 'he who begot the child',
oni o mɛ obo na. But what of the claim to children of a runaway wife?
All claims, it seems, lapse. I know of no case of a deserted fiancé or
husband successfully claiming the children his former fiancée bore
elsewhere. One Konkomba husband appealed to the Native Authority
Court in Yendi for the return of his wife and was given the children
only; the members of the bench were all Dagomba and applied
Dagomba rules. A second woman, a widow, sent her children to her
late husband's elder and then ran away. These cases apart, no deserted husband has established a claim on his wife's fertility unless
the wife were either living with him or ready to do so. (But see below,
p. 181.) And this is consistent with what Konkomba say about the
duties of a wife: these are 'to cook food to give her husband, to lie
with him and bear children to give her husband', *kɔtɔmwam bisa ti o
tʃar kɔtɔti u lɔmwɔr mɛ obo ti o tʃar*. In this statement of a wife's duties
the two rights of the husband are expressly conjoined and they are, I
think, inseparable in Konkomba thought.

The relatively high figure of wives and fiancées is maintained by
distributing all living females over the male population aged over

[1] It was suggested to me by Professor Fortes.

21 and by the buying of wives from outside Konkombaland. Yet even the number of fiancées assigned to men in their twenties is below unity and it only passes unity as they enter their thirties. This is consonant with the appearance of polygyny in age sets III and IV (see Graph I). It also suggests that the age of marriage may be tending to rise among Konkomba.

I do not see how this can be proved or disproved. The average figures for actual marriages, including inheritances of widows, for each of three generations were calculated for three of the major lineages of the sample. The central generation is the generation of the oldest men now living. The figures are:

Generation	1	2	3
Wives	1	1.73	2.48

The figures might be taken to suggest that polygyny is, in fact, declining. In this calculation the count included all recorded marriages of men who lived to marriageable age in all three generations; but the men of generation 3 are all dead and we cannot be sure either that all men were remembered or that all their marriages were accurately recalled. Indeed, we can take it as almost certain that a number of men have been omitted from the record because they never lived to have sons; their wives were then inherited, and this would exaggerate the *per capita* marriages of their generation.

STABILITY OF MARRIAGE

Stability of marriage, regarded by Konkomba as absolute, is in fact remarkably high among them. This statement holds whether we speak of the stability of the jural relationship or of the stability of the conjugal relationship, that is, of cohabitation. Further, there is no reason to suppose that there has been any change in the nature of the jural relationship until very recent times.[1] Change in the jural nature of the relationship may soon come, since one woman has now successfully appealed to the Government Agent's Court against what the Government Agent regarded as a forced marriage.

There is no divorce in Konkomba: neither the husband nor the wife can divorce the other in the sense of any formal legal or ritual ending of the marriage. Husbands have been known to repudiate a wife and wives have been known to run away from their husbands.

[1] Cf. Schneider, D. M., 'A note on Bridewealth and the stability of Marriage', *Man*, liii, 75.

By repudiation I here mean that the husband refused to accept the wife when she came to him and not that he sent her away after some years of marriage. Within this sample three men sought to repudiate a wife but only one was successful. In the second instance the kinsmen of the husband insisted that he accept the wife of the lineage group and she was returned to him with a child that she had in the meantime borne to a lover. The third instance is less clear; the woman is mentally deficient and it is probably incorrect to speak here of repudiation. Physical disability, however, is never accepted as grounds for refusing a wife.

Wives cannot repudiate a husband but they can break their marriages by running away. Four women in the sample have run away, in all cases soon after, and in one case only a few weeks after, the establishment of the marriage. Three were accused of sorcery before they ran away and they were all young and childless. Of only one of these women is the later history known. Most Konkomba runaway wives go far away and are vaguely thought of as joining up somewhere, say in Kumasi, with a Konkomba who is serving in the police or the army. But one young woman went first to her father's house, where pressure was exerted on her to return to her husband. This was in April 1951. She ran away from her father's house and joined her lover some ten miles away across the river. We do not know what happened there but we do know that she turned up in her father's house less than a year later. Since then she has lived there, a constant source of trouble to her family. She has borne one child by an unknown lover; she is now (May 1955) pregnant again. It is rumoured that she is thinking of asking her husband to take her back and, while he has not committed himself on that, he has said that he will claim any children she bears. But it should be noted that no one else is claiming them.

In all six cases of broken marriages the jural and conjugal relationships of husband and wife were never fully established. They are 3.3 per cent of all marriages in the sample. It is difficult, because of the small sample, to connect broken marriages with the relative ages of the husband and wife. But in no instance was the disparity less than about twenty-five to thirty years and in the instance given at length above it was about forty years.

Only one woman in the sample successfully refused to accept the inheritor assigned to her. She and her first husband had left the husband's natal hamlet and were living far from their kin. On the death of her husband she refused to return to that hamlet, though she sent her children. She went off by herself. Since the total number of inherited widows in the sample was forty, this instance gives us a rate of about 2 per cent.

We may take it, then, that the jural relation of marriage is stable. It should not, however, be thought that women go happily to their husbands. All are reluctant to go, most of them seek to delay their going, and in the end they go weeping bitterly. The low rate of broken marriages is due to the controls exerted over both spouses and is in no way due, in the early years of marriage, to happy and close personal relationships. Husbands, on the other hand, are usually delighted to receive a wife. Below I refer to the impression one gets of a close-knit, happy household among Konkomba. It is, I think, a just impression though it may appear to conflict with the fact of the obvious unhappiness, even misery, of a bride. In the cases we have of runaway wives the women were all brides or women who had not long been in their husbands' homes. I know of no measurement of happiness. If we compare individual households we see that one appears happier than others, one markedly less happy than most—both examples being a reflection of the personality of the husband. Another household is disturbed by a restless wife whose restlessness is shown in her visits to any hamlet in which something is going on. She visits more burials than an anthropologist. Again, the factor that has proved difficult to assess—the disparity of age between husband and wife—may and probably does operate. I am inclined to think that a bride adjusts herself most rapidly in the households of the younger married men and of the much older men. The younger men are proud and excited to be in the process of establishing themselves as household heads and are not yet harassed by the demands of a large household. The older men are often secure and sure of themselves with grown children around them. It may be significant that most of the runaway wives in the sample were in fact married to men in late middle age. In most cases a woman seems to settle down in her husband's home after she has children. Her links with her father's home are weakened by time and by the dispersal of her clan sisters in marriage; as her previous ties crumble she forms new ones among her co-wives. Above all, it is in her children that a woman's interests lie and from whom she derives status. I take the decline of a bride's unhappiness to be often slow though, in the end, usually effective. The contrast between a lonely, unhappy bride and a cherished, interested, elderly lineage mother is a sharp one: but the bride will, in time, achieve that change. A Konkomba woman may suffer when she first marries, yet the system gives all the security and care to her and her children that the culture can offer.

The conjugal relation between husband and wife is also stable. In the entire sample no instance occurred of a man or a woman living apart from his or her spouse. Of the runaway wives noted only one went to her kin; the destinations of the other women are unknown. The agnates of a runaway wife will accept her for a short period only and will then return her to her husband. To remain free the wife must run away from her agnates too. Wives do, of course, visit their own kin; they pay visits only on special occasions if they are far away, but not much more frequently even if they are close. Only a bride goes home often and she may not go at all during the first three weeks of marriage.

No preferential treatment of one wife over the other is permitted. Wives largely provide their own clothes by trading; food is issued daily to each wife to cook for the household or for herself. The husband sleeps one week (a six-day week) in each wife's room in rotation and he does so even if the wife is menstruating, though sexual relations are then forbidden. The husband also sleeps in the room of a wife who has borne a child, from the third or fourth day after the birth, in the case of a boy and a girl respectively, even though sexual relations between them are forbidden until the child can walk. The rotation of the husband among the wives is disrupted as little as possible and, while sexual relations between husband and wife may be interrupted, personal relations are not.

We may conclude, then, that Konkomba marriage at present shows a high degree of stability.

THE FORM OF THE HOUSEHOLD

The household is referred to by Konkomba as *ti do*, 'our house', and by the head as *ma do*, 'my house'. The head may also speak of *ma nib*, 'my people'. The word *do* may also be translated as 'family' and Konkomba do not distinguish between family and household as I have done here. In relation to the household head only two statuses are possible within the household—his wife or his child (with the rare addition of son's wife). Anyone brought into the household is assigned one of these statuses, and between a child begotten by the head and one inherited no difference of status or treatment is discernible. Konkomba, then, conceive the household as composed of the married partners and their children. A man invariably begins his married life with one wife, either a bride or an inherited widow, and this small

unit is expected to grow by the addition of other wives and the birth
of children. A man is expected to behave as a young man, and is so
treated, until his wife comes to him. It is true that there is gradation
by age among the young men themselves, yet no young man (*Onat-
shipwã*) can achieve the status of a householder. Because of the
betrothal system a man is a young man up to the age 35–40, i.e. until
he has obtained a wife. He is then expected to put aside the things
suitable to a young man; he ceases to carry an axe or club; he should
now cease to carry on love affairs though not all young married men
do so; he no longer dances the ritual dances though he may now
drum for the dancers.

In short, marriage and especially the setting up of an independent
household is thought of as the major change in status that a man
undergoes until he becomes an elder. For women the change in
status is more gradual and it is motherhood rather than wifehood
that marks the change.

In the large sample we have 826 persons in ninety-eight households (Table V). In only nine cases is the exact relationship of a
person to the head of the household doubtful or not known. The
majority of kin in the household belong to the polygynous family of
the head, but we also find members drawn from his extended house
and minor lineage group or persons married to members of these
units.

In the sample the following forms of family may usefully be distinguished: the elementary family, that is, husband and wife and
their children; the duogynous family, that is, husband and two wives
and their children; the polygynous family, husband, more than two
wives and their children; the extended family, that is, husband, his
wives and their children and his son or sons with their wives; and
the expanded family, that is, the husband and his wife or wives and
their children and his brothers and their wives and children. Their
occurrence may be tabulated thus:

Elementary family	19
Duogynous family	20
Polygynous family	6
Extended family	5
Expanded family	1

There was one household that consisted of a mother and her sons
whose father was dead: the father had not at the time had his 'Second
Burial'. The eldest son was regarded as the head of the household.

The remaining forty-six households are all more complex groupings
that contain kin of the extended house and minor lineage.

From the large sample I took the households of those men whose
age set is accurately known and grouped them by the age set of the
head (Table XVI) and calculated the coefficients of variation in size.
Variation is lowest in the oldest age sets. I also calculated the mean,
S.D., and range of the household sizes by age set of the head, but
S.D. is of so little value in so small and so variable a sample that it is
now omitted, nor did it appear worth while to calculate the significance of the difference between two means. The figures of Table
XVI were then reduced to a common basis of ten men per age set in
Table XVII. Graph V shows the mean size of the household against
the range by age set of the head. Graph VI shows the means of
family, extended house, and minor lineage members of the household
by age set of the head. From these graphs it will be seen that the
family steadily increases in size as the heads age, with a slight fall in

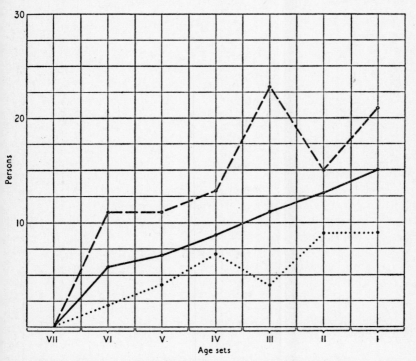

GRAPH V. Mean size of household against the range by age set of the heads
Mean ———————   Maximum - - - - -   Minimum . . . . . .

TABLE XVI

Households grouped by age set of the head

MM=married men

Age set	MM	CH	M	Ws	Ss	Ds	SWs	SSs	SDs	YB	YBW	YBSs	YBDs	EBS	EBDs	EBWs	Sis	Minor Lineage Kin ▽	Minor Lineage Kin O	Wives of MLK	Non-kin ▽	Non-kin O	Total
I	5	5	—	16	22	7	2	1	—	1	2	9	3	3	—	—	—	2	—	1	1	—	75
II	4	4	—	13	12	8	—	—	—	—	—	6	—	5	—	—	—	1	1	—	1	—	51
III	12	10	—	20	28	29	—	—	—	3	4	4	3	5	—	—	—	2	—	2	—	—	110
IV	6	5	2	13	7	6	—	—	—	4	—	2	1	—	—	1	—	2	—	—	1	—	44
V	8	6	1	12	4	5	—	—	—	4	2	—	1	—	—	—	—	5	1	—	—	—	41
VI	14	11	1	15	6	8	—	—	—	2	—	—	—	8	2	—	2	1	1	—	5	—	62
VII	4	—	—	—	—	—	—	—	—	—	—	—	—	—	—	—	—	—	—	—	—	—	—
Total	53	41	4	89	79	63	2	1	—	14	8	21	8	21	2	1	2	13	3	3	8	—	383

TABLE XVII

Composition of households on a common basis of 10 households per age set

N=41 households

Age set	CHs	Ms	Ws	Ss	Ds	SWs	SSs	SDs	YBs	YBWs	YBSs	YBDs	EBSs	EBDs	EBWs	Sis	Minor Lineage Kin		Wives of MLK	Non-kin		Total
																	▽	O	—	▽	O	
I	10	—	32	44	14	4	2	—	2	4	18	6	6	—	—	—	4	—	2	2	—	150
II	10	—	32.5	30	20	—	—	—	—	—	15	—	12.5	—	—	—	2.5	2.5	—	2.5	—	127.5
III	10	—	20	28	29	—	—	—	3	4	4	3	5	—	—	—	2	—	2	—	—	110
IV	10	4	26	14	12	—	—	—	8	—	4	2	—	—	2	—	4	—	—	2	—	88
V	10	1.67	20	6.7	8.3	—	—	—	6.7	3.3	—	1.7	—	—	—	—	8.3	1.7	—	—	—	68.37
VI	10	0.91	13.7	5.5	7.3	—	—	—	1.82	—	—	—	7.3	1.8	—	1.8	0.9	0.9	—	4.55	—	56.48
VII	—	—	—	—	—	—	—	—	—	—	—	—	—	—	—	—	—	—	—	—	—	—
Total	60	6.58	144.2	128.2	90.6	4	2	—	21.52	11.3	41	12.7	30.8	1.8	2	1.8	21.7	5.1	4	11.05	—	600.35

Key: as Table V

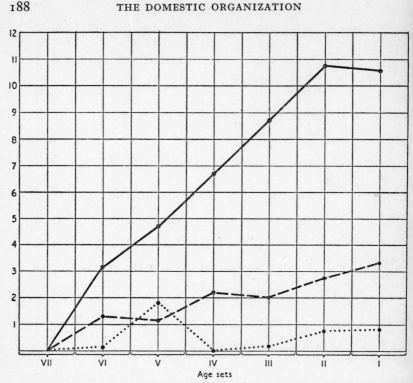

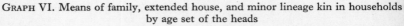

GRAPH VI. Means of family, extended house, and minor lineage kin in households
by age set of the heads

Family ———   Extended house kin - - - - -   Minor lineage kin . . . . . .

the final age set. This fall will be explained below. The extended
house kin in the household also increases steadily as men take in the
children of their dead brothers. The minor lineage kin in the household shows a more variable curve which reaches its peak in age set V,
falls again, and rises slightly to age set I. The peak is due to the
redistribution of young men and women whose fathers are dead. The
reason for its appearance in this particular age set needs further
discussion.

From the large sample the households of those men whose age set
was known were taken, grouped by age set and reduced to a common
basis of ten men per age set. These data were then grouped into
members of the family, the extended house, the minor lineage and
other kin of the household head in cumulative totals. (Table XVIII
and Graph VII.) In general terms we may say that the household

early assumes the form it will keep throughout its existence. The growth of the household appears to be an absolute growth in all its component parts.

TABLE XVIII

Kin of household head: cumulative totals

Age sets	Family	Extended House	Minor lineage	Total
I	106	142.0	148	150
II	92.5	120.0	125.5	127.5
III	87	106	110	110
IV	66	82	84	88
V	46.7	58.4	68.4	68.4
VI	37.3	50.0	51.9	56.4
VII	—	—	—	—

Within the overall growth, however, there is some variation in the rate of growth of the parts. The numbers of family, extended house, and minor lineage kin were then expressed as cumulative percentages of the total in Table XIX; they are shown in Graph VIII. We see that no man of the most junior age set has his own compound, but that by the age of 40–44 men are establishing their own compounds and households which rapidly become more complex units than elementary or polygynous families.

TABLE XIX

Kin of household head: percentages of total

Age sets	Family	Extended House	Minor lineage	Total
I	70.7	94.7	98.7	100
II	72.6	94.1	98.5	100
III	79	96.5	100	100
IV	76	93.3	95.4	100
V	66.9	85.4	100	100
VI	66.2	88.9	91.4	100
VII	—	—	—	—

Consider first the percentage of male minor lineage kin in the households. This is at its greatest in age set V, that is, the men of 45–48. The explanation of this is that the men of this age set are those with young children but no grown sons or sons of an age to go to the farm or daughters able to assist in such heavy work as collecting wood or fetching water. Young men and women whose fathers are dead are assigned to these men as 'sons' and 'daughters' to help to main-tain the household. In time, these young men and women marry, the women first, and go to new households of their own. By this time the

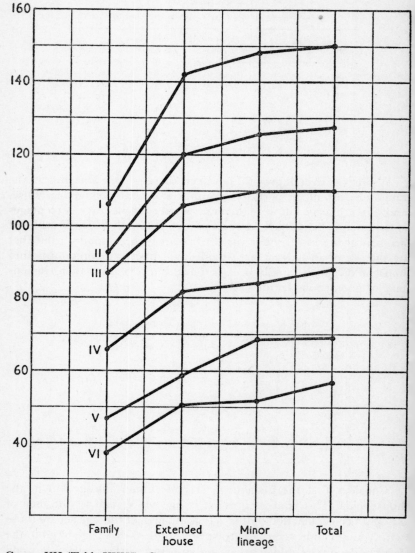

GRAPH VII (Table XVIII). Cumulative totals of family, extended house, minor lineage, and total kin in households by age set of the heads

children of the household head will be grown and able to take over their full work.

Graph IX from Table XVII confirms this. This shows the fluctuation of minor lineage kin through the households, by age set of the head. Such kin can also, of course, be inherited with a widow. The rise of the curve for males in the oldest set may be due to another factor. Widowed women and fatherless children are in the care of the lineage elder unless he assigns them to one or another household. If there is no man with a special need for the assistance of a young man or woman, then any such available persons will remain in the household and care of the elder.

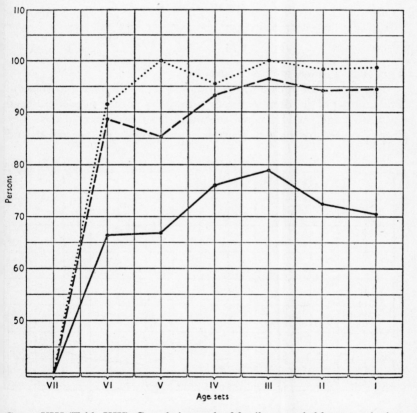

GRAPH VIII (Table XIX). Cumulative totals of family, extended house, and minor lineage kin shown as percentage of total household by age set of the heads

Family ———   Extended house kin - - - - -   Minor lineage kin . . . . . .

The fluctuations in the family may be taken next. Graph X (from Table XVI) shows the numbers of wives, sons, and daughters in the households by age set of the head. The drop in the number of wives for age set III needs some explanation. I have already said that the mean number of the marriages of age set IV is thrown a little high by the inclusion in that set of two ex-soldiers. Age set III is thrown on the low side by the inclusion of a blind man who is, perhaps, fortunate to have even one wife, and by another man who lost a number of betrothed wives. These are the oldest men in the sample to have only one wife. In a larger but less accurate sample I got an average rate of all marriages by age set as follows:

TABLE XX

Age set	VI	V	IV	III	II	I
No. of wives	1.2	1.75	1.9	2.3	2.3	3.2

This gives a much smoother curve.

The curves for sons and daughters also need a little explanation. The number of children increases with the age of the household head until after age set III, when the number of daughters drops. The drop is caused by the girls marrying out between the ages of 16 and 20.

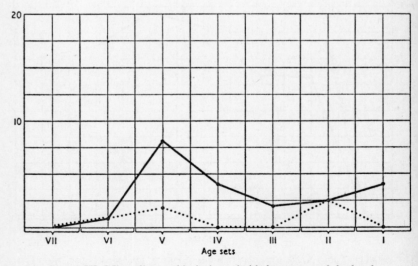

GRAPH IX. Minor lineage kin in households by age set of the heads

Males ──────   Females . . . . . .

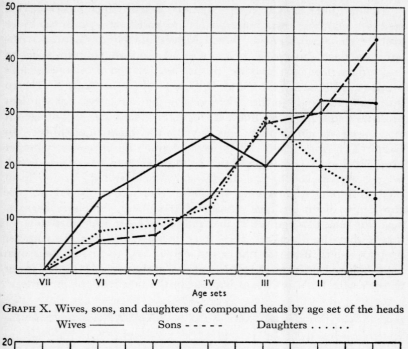

GRAPH X. Wives, sons, and daughters of compound heads by age set of the heads

Wives ———   Sons - - - - -   Daughters . . . . . .

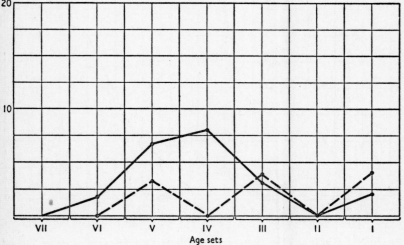

GRAPH XI (Table XVII). Younger brothers and their wives in households by age set of the heads

Younger brothers ———   Younger brothers' wives - - - - -

Finally, then, the kin of the extended house. Since most married men set up their own households and rarely stay with an elder brother, the graph showing these relatives is likely to fluctuate without very clear reason. In the younger age sets we should expect to find unmarried men staying in the household of married elder brothers. This is, in fact, shown in Graph XI (from Table XVII). In this graph it is only in the older age sets that the curves for younger brothers and their wives fluctuate together. The final peak in age set I is caused by one man who has stayed on with his elder brother. In Graph XII from Table XVII we find that the curves of younger brothers' sons and daughters rise in the older age sets, a rise which is no doubt caused by the deaths of brothers and the taking in of their children by surviving brothers. The graph also shows the curves for elder brothers' sons and daughters, which reaches its peak for males in age set II and falls in age set I. The reason for this is that the elder brothers' sons, being older than the younger brothers' sons, begin to marry out earlier and to set up their own households. In Graph XII the curve for the girls is always lower than that for boys, no doubt because of the marriages of the girls.

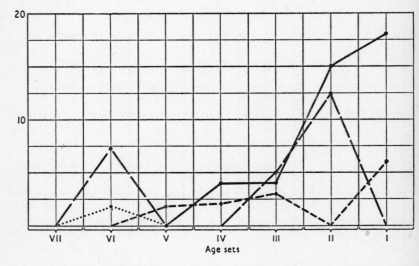

GRAPH XII (Table XVII). Sons and daughters of younger brothers and elder brothers in households by age set of the heads

Younger brothers' sons———   Elder brothers' sons— — —
   ,,   ,,   daughters- - - -   ,,   ,,   daughters . . . . . .

The Konkomba household may then be summarized as follows. It is patrilocal and patrilineal. It is seldom, and never for long, a simple elementary or simple polygynous family but includes kin of the head and inherited widows. The widest segment from which the latter members are drawn is the minor lineage of the head.

We may say that the household operates within the framework of the minor lineage group, which is the unit of widow inheritance, of succession to land rights, the most important unit of co-operative farming, and the unit of succession to the lowest ritual office. The minor lineage group is not significantly a political unit; the major lineage group and the clan are the political units of the Konkomba system, while the minor lineage groups, which seldom exceed eight or ten households, are the largest units of domestic organization.

THE DEVELOPMENT OF THE HOUSEHOLD

The full sequence of household growth would run as follows. It usually begins as a single elementary family which soon becomes a polygynous one. But an elementary family may for a time be part of a larger household before it splits off to start a new compound and household. To such households, in which there are young children and few adults, adolescents or young adults of both sexes are assigned to reinforce the existing members of the household on the farm and in housework. Girls so assigned do not remain long, since, once past adolescence, they too will marry and leave their natal hamlets to enter their husbands' households elsewhere. But by this time daughters of the household are growing up and can begin to take a share in the work of the house: it is some years later that the sons will begin to go to farm. The young men assigned to help in a house will in turn leave it to marry; but, while assigned girls seldom stay in such a household for more than eight to ten years, boys may stay for more than twenty years before they marry. Some wives married to the household head may die, other new wives will arrive and be integrated into the household. The final phase is usually the marriage out of the older daughters of the household head though, very occasionally, a head may live to see his sons marry and start their own families within his household. With the death of the head himself the household comes to an end and breaks up, its members are distributed over other households, themselves in different stages of this sequence.

To a great extent the ideal pattern of growth is confirmed by the data set out above. The core of any household at any point in the sequence is a family of one or another type. Moreover, despite variation in the actual relations with other members of a household, those relations are assimilated to marital and paternal/filial relations. Therefore the household must be thought of as a familial unit and the relations of its members as relations of affinity and descent. When, later, we speak of the authority of the household head we speak of conjugal and paternal authority; when we speak of the rights of a young male member of a household we speak of filial rights.

Late in life a man will speak in terms of affection of two men as his 'father', though neither was his genitor; they are men who brought him up at different times. And this follows from the fact that children assigned to a 'father' or 'mother' on the deaths of their own are not differentiated either in affection or in status from the begotten children of the step-parent.

This is not to say that no difference at all exists in the relation between a father and his child and a step-father and his step-child. While I could see no obvious differences in personality between an actual son and a step-son, provided that the transfer took place when the child was young, there may be such differences between men who have children of their own and those who have only inherited children.[1]

I also think it likely that adolescents are not so easily absorbed into a new household as are either young children or young adults. Adolescent girls, certainly, do not seem to develop very close relations with a step-mother and, if the step-father is fairly young, he will be absorbed in his own small children. On the whole, though, the effect of equating household with familial ties is to create a close-knit and happy unit in which a bereaved child can find new ties of love and security.

THE FUNCTIONS OF THE HOUSEHOLD

Since the household contains members drawn from the larger minor lineage group, we may expect to find that it functions within the framework of the latter. This is indeed the way in which Konkomba think of the household—as part of something larger, as something that is now isolated from and now merged in the larger group.

---

[1]For example, an elderly man, he is second to the elder of his lineage, has a large household of grown 'sons' and young 'daughters'. He has never married a bride but has only inherited widows. None of the children is his own. His domestic situation is regarded by some persons as something of a joke, for he is laughed at behind his back. On the other hand there are many other variables to be considered in personality, and while his domestic situation undoubtedly affects this man, the major traumatic event of his life was probably several years' forced labour under the Germans when he was little more than a boy.

The phrase *Ti je mfum mba* (we are one) may refer to a household, a minor lineage group, a major lineage group, a clan, a tribe or the whole Konkomba people. When speaking of co-operation they speak in terms of the minor lineage group rather than in terms of the household. We shall try to differentiate the role of the household as a unit of reciprocal help, of social control, and of instruction, etc.

PRODUCTION AND CONSUMPTION

The possession of land for three kinds of farm is the right of every household head. These are: compound land (*lenampar*), land beyond the compound land (*duu*), and bush land (*timwoni*). These rights may be acquired gradually, since a married man living in his father's or guardian's or brother's household takes in bush land for yam, bean, cotton, and groundnut crops but has no grain land, since that is controlled by household heads. Bush land is not closely controlled and a man may take in as much land as he can work; a young man may make a farm of his own there and grow a cash crop. Compound land and the land that lies beyond the compound farms is strictly controlled and tends to pass down lines of descent. If there are no sons to inherit this land it passes to others within the minor lineage. All household heads, but only these, are entitled to compound land.

All land is worked collectively by the household head, his sons, and those assigned to him as 'sons'. The bush farms are worked by the members of the household unaided; the compound farms and *duu* farms are worked on the system of work parties whereby a household head invites helpers and pays them in beer and food. The greatest degree of reciprocal help is given within the minor lineage. That is, the turnout from any one household is greatest to help their minor lineage kin; it decreases for major lineage kin, and the elder is the only member of another major lineage of the same clan who receives help. Married women help in farm work only within the minor lineage group; that is, they help potential husbands.

Unmarried men too have land rights. Any young man may, should he wish, farm extra land for himself to raise a cash crop, though only once have I known a young man do so. Others have raised cash crops for their mistresses. Unmarried girls have the same right to a small plot of groundnuts or pepper, and many girls have such plots on their own clan lands, sometimes worked for them by their lovers. Married women have the right to groundnut and pepper plots on the husband's land of their husbands' clans worked for them by their husbands and sons. From this plot they supply the household needs for groundnuts and pepper with, usually, a small surplus for sale.

Game killed in communal hunts is divided between major lineage elders, who divide it among their minor lineage elders who divide it among their household heads.

Fishing is either an individual or a household affair. The dry-season fishing expeditions are individual—each persons keeps his or her catch. Fish trapping is done by households on dams that are owned by household heads and are inherited.

The household is not exclusively the unit of consumption. Cooking is done in the households by the wives of the head in rotation, with meat bought by the head or caught by members of the household and with grain or yams from the household granary or store. But the young men, and to a smaller extent the young women, of the minor lineage group often eat in other households as well as their own. In the evening the young men of the minor lineage group gather in the compound of the elder and eat there with the sons of that household. When this food is eaten the young men scatter in twos and threes taking with them the elder's sons to eat again in their own houses. Sometimes a young man will eat at three houses in one evening. Thus, the household is a unit of production and consumption only within the framework of the minor lineage. The minor lineage group is seen as a unit, composed of co-operating households.

SOCIAL CONTROL

The status of a household head within the compound is not unlike that of the lineage or clan elder within the hamlet or district. There should be no quarrelling, voices should not be raised in anger in the compound and in the presence of the household head. The head has the right to beat a member of the household, though there are few recorded instances of one doing so. He has, it is said, the right to beat his wife. The wife, however, is likely to retaliate by going to her father's home and staying there for an indefinite period. Usually, a man who beats his wife is stopped fairly soon by neighbouring household heads. On one occasion, on the other hand, all the young wives of a minor lineage group, some of whom were suspected of carrying on love affairs, were beaten at about the same time on one afternoon by their indignant husbands, so that on this occasion there was no one left to prevent the beatings.

Children are sometimes beaten by their mothers for misbehaviour inside the compound, but for any misdemeanour outside the compound a boy should be taken to his father for punishment: a boy should not be beaten by the person who happened to catch him.

The household head would deal only with relatively minor offences within the household; anything more serious—for example, a theft whether thought to be committed by a member of the household or not—must be taken to the major lineage elder. The household is, then, a unit of social control in minor offences and to the extent of a husband's control over his wives and a father's control over his children.

This is true to a slighter extent of the status of a head who has younger brothers or men of his minor lineage staying in his compound. In one instance within the sample, a man of over 50 still had no farms of his own but 'farmed for the head'. He was the oldest man in the sample who was living in the compound of another man. Few married men stay for long in the household of a guardian. In one instance, in which two younger married brothers were staying with their elder brother in 1950, the original compound had, by 1955, gradually become two compounds and a third was appearing, by the gradual addition of rooms and the building of separating walls. There will soon be three quite separate compounds. The physical division of one compound into three and the decline of the senior brother's authority have gone on *pari passu*.

INSTRUCTION

Children are trained in the skills they will need in adult life and the control exercised over them is part of the training process. Girls work with their mothers from about the age of eight; at the same time, or a little later, boys begin to learn farm work though it is some years before they start the heavy labour of hoeing. Children learn only on the lands and in the compound of their parents. Only youths and adults join in the reciprocal work parties of the sowing season. The cattle, however, are herded together and those of an entire clan may be seen in the care of boys (and sometimes of a few girls) drawn from every household whose head possesses cows.

THE HOUSEHOLD IN RITUAL

The household is not important in ritual. The most important shrines—those devoted to the land, water, and the fertility of women —are all clan shrines. The major lineage has its ritual symbol *dzambuna*, to which sacrifice is sometimes offered, and the minor lineage has its *igi*, which is not an object of sacrifice, a medicine horn which protects a homicide from the ghost of his victim. At all rites in the clan shrines the minor lineage is represented by an elder who joins the other elders of minor and major lineages in sacrifice.

Sacrifices for a new wife and at a birth are carried out in clan shrines by clan elders. It is only in the New Yam rites that the households appear as ritual units. New Yam rites are carried out in the separate households by the heads on a day fixed by the elder of the minor lineage. The rite is a simple sacrifice to the spirit of the household head.

Other household rites—for example, a sacrifice to the spirit of a member of the household, or for the general welfare of the house on the wall of the senior wife's room, are celebrated on the advice of a diviner.

The bows and staves of the dead forefathers of the household head are always stuck into the thatch above the door of the room that gives access to the compound. Medicines, charms, and skulls of game caught in past hunts are also put there. But no sacrifice is offered to them, since the ancestors are invoked at the shrines. Earth from the entry door is sometimes used medicinally or ritually. This doorway is an important ritual place and above it there is often painted a cross, the sign of fertility, and a hoe blade is often placed in it, forming a kind of lintel.

One important rite is always carried out, at least in part, in the compound. This is the ritual which follows the discovery that a person has been 'sent into the world' by a dead ancestor. Many Konkomba are so sent, though the relation between the living and the dead is not so close as is the *nani* relation of the Dogon.

Children are born in the room of the mother and close to the *kakaambũ*, which is a hole in the floor of the hut, covered with a ground, flat stone, into which young children urinate and into which runs the blood of birth. The *kakaambũ* is therefore associated with birth. When a person undergoes the rites which link him or her with a dead ancestor the subject stands astride the sacrificial animal beside the *kakaambũ* of the senior wife's room. The blood of the sacrificial animal runs into the *kakaambũ*. The whole rite may be regarded as a rebirth and the *kakaambũ* of the senior wife as the centre of birth of the polygynous family.

In general the household is not a very important ritual unit. The major personal sacrifices—rites of propitiation, purification, rites in fulfilment of a vow, rites of the spirit cult—are all removed outside the compound and household and take place at clan shrines in the bush. It is the thank-offerings that take place in the compound—the rites of joyful occasions. That is to say, rites which express anxiety are the concern of the larger units of organization: the principal cults—that of the ancestors and that of the land (Earth shrine)—which have political implications, are solely the concern of the elders of the clan, the major lineage and the minor lineage. These elders are also responsible for sowing rites, rites to purify the land, and rites of propitiation, in short, all rites expressive of doubt and anxiety. These take place in the bush and do not concern the households as distinct units.

THE HOUSEHOLD AND INCEST

The agnatic unit within which love affairs are forbidden is the minor lineage. Members of different minor lineages within the same major lineage may be lovers. Yet there are degrees even within the minor lineage. The incestuous relation that arouses the greatest possible repugnance is that between the son and daughter of one woman: it is unspeakable. It would be a defilement of the closest relation known to Konkomba, that between *naabim*, and would disrupt the smallest unit of organization, the room (*kədig*). Second only to incest between *naabim* comes that between *taabim*, the children of one father. Such a liaison would disrupt the second smallest unit of organization, the house (*do*). I know of no certain instances of incest within these units, either brother-sister or parent-child incest: persons who committed this offence, it is said, would die because 'God does not tolerate such behaviour'.

Within the minor lineage sexual relations between two members may, perhaps, occur. In one of the minor lineages used in this sample it was rumoured that the young men and women were having love affairs. This minor lineage is large and these love affairs, if they in fact occur, may be taken as one of a number of signs of approaching fission).

The household, then, is a unit within which sexual relations other than marital ones are incestuous and can never be condoned. Within the minor lineage too, such relations are incestuous but may occur and so necessitate the segmentation of the lineage. Common membership of one lineage and sexual relations between two persons are incompatible. The minor lineage and household are therefore units which are protected from the tensions of love affairs which may only occur outside them.

THE HOUSEHOLD AND EXOGAMY

The major lineage is invariably exogamous and so, *a fortiori*, are the minor lineage group and family. Further, a man may not marry into the minor lineage of his mother and a girl may not marry into the major lineage of her mother and the minor lineage of her mother's mother. Within these general rules the units used in calculations of eligibility for marriage are the extended houses, and a further rule is that between any two extended houses only one marriage is possible, except for an exchange marriage.

Thus the household is not a primary unit used in calculations of marriage, since it may contain members of different extended houses of one minor lineage group. It is theoretically possible, then, that in one household two members could marry into the same extended house without infringement of the strict rule of marriage. But it is unlikely that they would be permitted to do so in practice, since, because of the equation of all relations within the household with marital and parent-child relations, all members of the household tend to be regarded as members of the extended house of the household head, despite the fact that the extended house is, strictly speaking, a small descent group. But there are other reasons for the avoidance of the marriages of two members of one household into one extended family. It must be remembered that, within the minor lineage group, any man of the proper age and status may wish to inherit or may be called upon to inherit any other man's widow. But a man may not marry sisters or two women of one extended house. Yet such marriages could be necessitated by inheritance should two men of one minor lineage group marry sisters. Consequently such marriages are to some extent avoided because of the limitations and complications they may impose on widow inheritance. They occur, of course, and there is even an example, in the sample, of two brothers marrying two sisters. These marriages came about in the following way: one sister was betrothed to one of the brothers and the other sister was betrothed to another man of the same minor lineage group who later died; she was then inherited as a fiancée by the second brother. This situation required consideration. The marriages were finally agreed to because both the brothers and the sisters were *taabim*, children of one father, not *naabim*, children of one mother. On the principle that *Bi jakanjɛni kɔdig kɔba, na ákwo* (If they don't come from one room (mother), it doesn't matter) the marriage was permitted, but on the express condition that neither brother may inherit his brother's widow.

The household, then, is exogamous. Further, the households tend to be units between which, and outside the prohibited degrees, only one marriage is possible and the minor lineage groups are groups between which, allowance made for the prohibited degrees, few marriages take place lest complications should arise over inheritance of widows.

AVOIDANCES WITHIN THE HOUSEHOLD

I have already said that members of the household can freely enter only their own mother's room and the large entry room. Women tend to keep to their own sides of the compound and do not enter the young men's room.

There is no tabu on an eldest son's looking into his father's granary, as there is among the Tallensi, or on his moving freely about the compound, as there is among Dagomba. The eldest son may be, and when the sons are grown, one son always is, in charge of the household granary each year, to measure out the grain for the women to cook and to receive and store grain payments of bride corn.

But no man may grow a beard during the life-time of his father. No unmarried woman may eat meat. No man at the burial of a man, and no woman at the burial of a woman, may, during the lifetime of his father or of her mother, eat the flesh of the burial sacrifices. To do so is tantamount to wishing that parent to die. Thus is expressed the opposition of proximate generations in the Konkomba household.

These avoidances are extended from the actual genitor and genitrix to the guardians, male and female, within the minor lineage, in that a youth or girl assigned to a household as a son or daughter observes the tabus for the household head or for the woman assigned as a 'mother'. The avoidance of funeral meats may, indeed, be extended to all classificatory 'fathers' and 'mothers' within the minor lineage, since all such persons are potential 'fathers' and 'mothers' to the younger members of the lineage.

The household is a unit of ritual avoidance within the framework of the minor lineage which is the largest unit of these avoidances.

The household is also a unit of prescriptions. Wives keep to their own rooms and parts of the compound and are followed in this by their children. Husbands keep to the large entry room by day, for the most part, and go to a wife's room only after dark. To speak to the household head the younger members, at least, squat on their heels, an attitude also adopted by young wives, though the older ones, with whom the husband has close personal relations, do not.

Towards the father, and also to a lesser extent the mother, a quiet voice and demeanour should be observed.

These avoidances and prescriptions help to obviate quarrels. This is not to say that quarrels, even brawls, never occur; they do. Women sometimes snatch up a piece of firewood for use as a weapon and scream with rage in household quarrels. But they are over soon enough and I have never seen fighting break out in a compound.

THE HOUSEHOLD AND SORCERY

It is now well established that accusations of witchcraft and sorcery tend to be directed according to clear patterns within the framework of the social structure. For example, the Tallensi and Ewe ascription of the inheritance of witchcraft to the uterine line of descent protects the agnatic lineage from disruption but exposes the family and household to it. The Dagomba ascription of witchcraft to the father's sister similarly exposes the Dagomba household to accusations since there is, in Dagomba, no widow-inheritance and widows return to their paternal homes from which they may or may not remarry.

Not a great many actual cases of sorcery, that is, covert or overt accusations, can be discovered in a population of such low density as that of Konkomba. I have in all some twenty instances, not including vague accusations of unknown persons. This gives a rate of accusation of all kinds of about 1 per cent per annum. Many of the accusations fall within the sample used above (p. 165).

There are a number of general beliefs about sorcery that must first be stated. Konkomba do not believe that sorcerers' powers are inherited in either line of descent; on the contrary, it is held that anyone may be a sorcerer or sorceress and any sorcerer may teach a would-be, though always a younger, sorcerer. There is a likelihood that males usually teach males and females females. Instances are given of a father teaching his son and a mother her daughter and there are reported instances of persons teaching others of no known relationship. There is one instance of a woman being accused of learning her sorcery from a lover.

A second important belief is that sorcerers may attack anyone. They are evil and attack for the sheer joy of destruction. On the other hand, it is also believed that sorcerers may kill in order to inherit from an older person and that men may even kill their older brothers in order to inherit wives, goods, and status, and sisters kill their older sisters in order to inherit goods.

The first two general beliefs might lead one to suppose that there will be no pattern in the accusations Konkomba bring, or that accusations will be an expression of purely personal antipathies. These two beliefs do not suggest that accusations of sorcery are so directed that particular social groups are either exposed to disruption or specially protected against it. The third belief would lead us to expect a pattern of accusation between brothers and sisters: but I know of no case of a brother accusing his brother or a sister her sister, though I have instances of a diviner accusing a brother of killing his brother, or a sister of killing her sister.

In considering accusations of sorcery we have to distinguish two general relations: that which may be called the accuser-sorcerer relation, and that which may be called the victim-sorcerer relation. The two may overlap, as when a man supposes himself to be attacked and himself accuses someone of sorcery; accuser and victim are then one. But a man may accuse someone of attacking a third person, and this is the case when a diviner makes the accusation.

One striking feature of Konkomba sorcery is that no woman is known to have made an accusation either covertly or overtly. That is to say that, unlike the Zulu[1], for example, accusations of sorcery do not enter into domestic or other quarrels between women.[2] This is not to say that women never induce their husbands or others to make accusations, but they do not themselves make open accusations and no trace has been found of their making covert ones.

A second striking feature of Konkomba sorcery is that no accusation, covert or overt, is known to have been made by one member of a household against another. On one occasion, and one only, a diviner detected sorcery when a woman had died and implicated the dead woman's young co-wife. But the final stages of divination partly cleared the young woman: tension between these two wives was admitted but sorcery on the part of the younger wife was 'not proven'. That is, the victim-sorcerer relation may be held by an outsider to fall within the household, but in this instance means were found to turn the accusation aside.

Further, there is no instance of an accusation between two male members of one minor lineage. Few accusations have been made by a member of a minor lineage against a woman married into it. Most

---

[1] M. Gluckman, *Rituals of Rebellion in South-East Africa*, 1954.
[2] During part of my own time in Konkombaland I tried to find examples of accusations by women. For eighteen months since then a field assistant has listened to gossip and sought for an example. Not one has been found.

precise accusations have been between members of one clan or major lineage but of different minor segments, or by a man against a woman married into a minor segment other than his own within his own major lineage. Thus, the accuser-sorcerer relation occurs between those political segments of a clan within which the resort to force is forbidden and is prevented by rigorous ritual sanctions. The household and, less certainly, the minor lineage are not disrupted by the accuser-sorcerer relation.

This is not to say that there is no connexion between sorcery and the household. Though internal tensions in the household are not, it seems, expressed in mutual accusations between members of the same household, it may be that accusations of sorcery are made by men who are discontented with their household and marital status. Briefly, accusations seem to be made by the older unmarried men either against young women married into a minor lineage other than the accuser's but of the same major lineage, or against the husbands of such women. That is, men in their thirties or early forties, who are not yet settled as family heads and men of some substance, seem to accuse their more fortunate seniors or the wives of such men.

Of five openly accused women, four were young married women and in each case they were accused by a younger, unmarried kinsman of the husband. By unmarried I here mean that none had married a wife himself as opposed to inheriting a widow. One man had, in fact, inherited a widow past childbearing age. Two of the accused women were Kabre women, 'bought' as wives. All of them ran away when accused. Two were accused by men òf a different minor lineage from that of the husband; three were accused within the minor lineage span, but the lineages concerned were large ones which showed signs of becoming segmented major lineages, and the accuser and accused were in different potential segments which were already in separate hamlets. With one exception the women were young and three were childless.

We must conclude that, whatever may be the pattern of the accuser-sorcerer or victim-sorcerer relation, their incidence falls wholly outside the household and largely outside the minor lineage. I believe sorcery to operate, on the whole, within the clan and major lineage and to be connected with the relative age and status of victim and accused. In so far as household and minor lineage are concerned, in every case recorded in which the victim-sorcerer relation seemed to fall within these units, further divinational inquiry either cast doubt on the accusation or brought in other persons from outside and confused the charge.

Accusations of sorcery, taking the accuser-sorcerer and the victim-sorcerer relations together, appear to show two trends. First, younger men accuse their seniors. To accuse an older man of the minor lineage or household would be to accuse a potential 'father'. The relation of father-son is markedly one of respect. It is very rare indeed for an elderly or old woman to be accused by anyone, but to accuse such a woman married into the accuser's minor lineage would be to accuse a 'mother' and the relation of mother-son is one of affectionate respect. Furthermore, the pattern of authority in Konkomba is that the senior person of any group exercises authority over those of the same sex. Accusations of sorcery within the household and minor lineage, in which the greater part of life is passed, would, in units of so small a scale, seriously disrupt the flow of daily living. Secondly, there is a tendency for men of about forty, the younger married men or the older unmarried men, to accuse young women married into the clan. To do so within the minor lineage would be to accuse a potential wife. The relation between two such persons is a joking relationship; that is, a means for the mitigation or avoidance of tension is already provided, and so perhaps the possibility of tension reaching the point of an accusation of sorcery is eliminated.

The actual patterns of accusations of sorcery are not, then, in agreement with the ideal patterns as conceived by Konkomba. Two of the general beliefs suggest that the actual patterns could be random; the third suggested that accusations would fall within the family. In the event, other cultural mechanisms enter into play to direct accusations outside the family and household. If the inheritance of sorcery were linked to agnatic descent then it would disrupt all agnatic structures. If it were linked with uterine descent it would disrupt the household. If accusations of sorcery were random, some accusations between co-wives would surely occur. The canalization of accusations which causes them to occur between members of different minor lineages or between a member of one minor lineage and the wife of a member of a different minor lineage of the same clan protects the household and minor lineage.

CONCLUSION

The form and function of the Konkomba household is as follows. It is centred on a family. This family begins as an elementary one but grows through time to become a polygynous one: only rarely does the extended or expanded family appear. In this development the household is not for long merely a family of greater or smaller complexity but soon begins to include other members drawn from the minor lineage group of the head. The household usually comes into being with the first marriage of a man and usually ends with his death. Occasionally two or more brothers may, for a time, inhabit one compound under the headship of an older brother; such households, however, do not endure for long but break up in time into two or more compounds. That is to say that the household has a life span of, at the most, some thirty years. During this period it increases in size to reach its maximum as the head reaches the senior age set. But, since there is much shifting of people between the households of one minor lineage group, the household is a unit that operates within and cannot wholly be separated from the minor lineage group.

The projection of ritual and sorcery outside the minor lineage protects that lineage and its component parts from disruption. The system of avoidances and prescriptions and the prohibition of incest within the minor lineage group and household mitigate tensions within those units, reinforce the pattern of authority and help to integrate the group. The practices of distributing the young men and women of this lineage group among the several households, of cooperative work on the farms and of sharing in consumption, prevent the household from becoming an isolated economic and working unit; both work and benefits are shared.

All this helps to explain the unhappiness of the Konkomba when some business takes them away from home. To a Konkomba the world is divided into two parts, *ŋɔtɔmbu*, the houses, and *timwoni*, the bush. The bush begins a few yards from the compound door, and even one setting out for Kumasi or any other large town is spoken of as 'going into the bush'. The safe, the sure place is found in that close, intensely co-operating group, the household and the dozen households that form a minor lineage group.

The growth of the household and its relation to the extended house is in turn related to the growth and segmentation (splitting, ed.) of the minor lineage. The family, household, and extended house are numbers of precisely known persons who stand in known relations of agnation and affinity. The minor lineage differs qualitatively because it is an abstraction. Unlike the persons appearing in the lower segments of a genealogy, the wives of the apical ancestor of the minor lineage are unknown. At this level the wives are irrelevant because they would not affect the marriages of living persons: at lower levels of segmentation the kinship connexions of wives must be known because they affect future marriages. Fully to consider this would require a full discussion of the system of marriage, a discussion that cannot be carried out here.[1] It is perhaps sufficient to say that the apical ancestor of the minor lineage is the first abstract figure that we find in this segmentary system; nothing is known of him yet he serves as a common point of reference for the heads of the component households of that lineage group.

[1] A fuller account is given in Chapter V.

XI. Friendship Relations[1]

I AM concerned here with dyadic relations between individuals. The relations I discuss are symmetrical: by that I mean that the obligations of one person are the same as the reciprocal obligations of his partner. These relations are not joking partnerships nor are they joking relationships: Goody, in *The Social Organization of the LoWiili* (1956), emphasized a distinction between these two forms of relationship: a joking partnership arises from a relation between groups, whereas a joking relationship holds between individuals who stand in kinship categories to each other. The joking partnership implies important reciprocal ritual services and it is cathartic in Griaule's sense of 'alliance cathartique'.[2] Nor are these relations of the same nature as blood-brotherhood.[3] Another form of friendship was discussed by Radcliffe-Brown in 'A Further Note on Joking Relationships' (*Africa*, xix, 2, 1949): it is found in the Andamans and in southern Australia and is one in which two boys who are initiated together or born within a day or two of each other into different hordes do not speak to each other. This link Radcliffe-Brown called 'friendship'.

The relations of amity with which I am concerned are all relations between two persons who help each other in many situations, not merely in ritual ones. By relations of amity I shall mean any form of friendship between two persons. Amity, however, may be voluntary: that is, the two friends may be such by an act of choice. Or the amity may be non-voluntary: that is to say that the relationship is not entered into voluntarily but is ascribed to the two persons by kinship. These two modes of friendship include the total range of dyadic,

---

[1]This chapter appeared in *African Studies*, xiii, 2, 1954, under the title of 'Konkomba Friendship Relations'.
[2]*Africa*, xviii, 4, 1948.
[3]E. E. Evans-Pritchard, 'Zande Blood-brotherhood'. *Africa*, vi, 4, 1933.

reciprocal relations of amity between individuals which vary from the tie between uterine siblings to that between men who were once total strangers. By the term 'amity' I refer to the nature of the relation between two persons of the same or of different sex; by 'friendship' I mean only the voluntary relation of amity between individuals of the same sex.

In Konkomba men and women cannot be friends. They may be kin; they may stand in a joking relationship; they may be lovers; otherwise they must be as strangers. Relations of friendship are therefore relations between people of the same sex. Let us consider these in the context of the political structure. Among the Konkomba clans are linked to each other in a tribal system. There are a number of criteria which define a clan but the most important one is this: between clans of the same tribe feud can be ended in a rite while between clans of different tribes occasional fighting is part of the endless warfare between tribes. Within one tribe clans are linked by several kinds of link. Two clans may stand to each other as *mantotib*: that is, they are ritual partners. Two clans may stand to each other as parent and filial clans: that is, that at some time in the past, lineage fission has led to the location of a new clan not far from the parental one, and there are ritual ties between such clans. Both these relations inhibit feud between clans. Thirdly, any one clan has three or four clans that can be called its 'kith'. That is, there are many ties of neighbourliness, friendship and kinship between them and also a ritual link in that they attend each other's rites. While kithship does not inhibit feud between clans, it makes feud unlikely since between kith a rite can prevent the development of feud even after a homicide.

Thus one clan stands in close relations of ritual co-operation or kithship with not more than six other clans and in relations of potential or perennial hostility to all other clans.

The isolation of the agnatic clan is reduced by ties of *manto*, common descent, kithship and membership of a common tribe. This isolation is further reduced on the level of relations between individuals by the ties of matrilateral and affinal kinship. It is further reduced again by the ties of involuntary amity that arise from certain kinship categories and by the voluntary links of friendship.

There are five kinds of friendship relation between men to be considered. Of these the first is that which unites the children of one mother: this is called *naabo*, that is, *na a bo*, literally 'mother's child'. Secondly, there is that link between children of one father: this is called *taabo*, that is, *te a bo*, literally 'father's child'. Thirdly, there is the link between sons of women of the same clan: this is called *nabo*, that is, *na bo*, literally 'mother child'. Fourthly, there is the link between men who have married clan-sisters: this is called *nato*, a word for which there is no obvious translation. Fifthly, there is the term *dzo* which refers to men of two different clans who are friends.

Women use the terms, or terms comparable to those, given above. They use *naabo*, *taabo* and *nabo*; but where men use the term *nato*, women can stand in a comparable relation to each other which is called *juan*; and where men use the term *dzo*, women use *nakwoo*.

The term *naabo* (pl. *naabim*) denotes the closest tie between individuals known to Konkomba. It holds between two uterine brothers, sisters or between brother and sister and it implies the closest affection and reciprocal help. Sexual relations between members of one minor lineage are evil enough but between *naabim* they are unspeakable. Fortes discusses the *soog* tie among the Tallensi. *Soog* and *naabo* are closely similar concepts and indeed Konkomba and Tallensi are closely similar in culture. But Konkomba do not extend the relationship in the same way as do the Tallensi.

Naabim help each other in all activities. The closeness of the relation begins with their earliest memories since they have a privilege that is not extended even to their fathers; they may enter their mother's room in her absence. *Taabim* may not enter each other's rooms; the only occasion on which a person may enter the room of his mother's co-wife is for a rite in the room of the senior wife of the compound. He only enters then as it were by invitation. It is in the mother's room that *naabim* keep their most cherished possessions. They are the children of that room (*kedig*) and, with their half-brothers and -sisters they are also the children of one house (*do*).[1] It is to the *naabo* that a young man or woman first looks for assistance in love affairs, payment of bride service or in any undertaking; they share common ritual obligations to their matrilateral kin. The Konkomba household is not large and on the death of the head of a household the sons seldom stay together in one house. But when they do, they tend to be *naabim*. On the other hand hamlet fission is frequent among Konkomba and the groups of brothers who move out to settle elsewhere are often *naabim*.

----

[1]The effect of early conditioning on kinship extensions has been considered very fully by Fortes (*The Web of Kinship*) 1949, and by others, e.g. Malinowski ('Kinship', *Man*, xxx, 17, 1930), Radcliffe-Brown ('The Mother's Brother in South Africa', 1924; reprinted in *Structure and Function*, 1952), and by Evans-Pritchard ('The Nature of Kinship Extensions', *Man*, xxxii, 7, 1932).

Second only to the tie of *naabim* in importance and warmth of feeling comes that between *taabim* (s. *taabo*), children of one father. This close tie operates in all the contexts in which that of *naabo* does, but it acts less markedly. There is good reason why this should be so since the children are separated from earliest infancy into distinct rooms, organized around different women. *Taabim* do often, in fact, move together from their natal hamlets to settle elsewhere and this is facilitated by the fact that they have a common father who, though dead, is their intermediary to the more remote ancestors.

But there is one very marked difference between *naabim* and *taabim*. It is possible and it sometimes happens, that the grand-children of *taabim* may marry, It is rare, of course, but it is condoned on the grounds that the married pair do not spring from 'one room'; their common ancestor was a man, not a woman, and at no known point in their common ancestry has the *naabo* tie occurred.

The relation is the same in both these relationships—between two men, two women or between a man and a woman except, of course, that the help given by *naabim* varies with the sex of the helper and the helped. But the contexts in which help is given do not necessarily vary. In any case, the binding compulsory nature of the response to the tie between the two persons does not change; nor does its warmth and affection.

Nabo (pl. *nabim*), literally, 'mother child', is primarily the term applied to the children of the mother's sister. The mother's elder sister is called *nakper*, mother's older sibling or possibly older mother, while the mother's younger sister is called *nawa*. Unlike *nakper*, which implies a respect relationship, *nawa* implies a joking relationship. Further, *nawa* is extended to all women of the mother's clan younger than the mother. In turn, the term *nabo* is extended by men of men and by women of women to the child of a woman ad-dressed as *nawa*, and indeed, to the child of any woman of the mother's clan.

Nabim do not owe each other help in their concerns and private affairs; there are no formal duties implied by the relationship. All that is implied is amity. One can see two such men who have never before met, greeting each other with every appearance of high delight. One would take them for intimates meeting after a long separation. They do, of course, share common ritual duties to members of one clan since they have the same clan as their *umwetib*, mother's clan. But they owe each other no ritual duties.

The tie of *naabo* and *taabo* links even more closely people who are already of necessity linked in clanship (*dejo*, clansman, man speaking, *mindza*, woman speaking). This follows from the strict application of rules of widow inheritance, because widows never pass out of the minor lineage of the late husband. The link between *nabim* is usually, though not invariably, one between persons of different clan and it is thought of as such a link since the ties of closer kinship override the more distant ones where they overlap. That *naabim* are, in fact, usually of different clan arises from the rules governing marriage which, in effect, disperse the women of a clan widely among other clans, often clans of a different tribe. The *nabo* link, then, is the first of the links of amity between individual members of different clans other than those arising from a group relationship or from the joking relationships. It is a tie that arises in matrilateral kinship. Put another way, a *nabo* is the child of a joking relative.

The link between two men who have married women of the same clan is called *nato* (pl. *natotib*). Like the children of women of the same clan they too owe ritual duties to the same clan and their children will be *nabo* to each other. Once again, as with *nabim*, there are no reciprocal rights and duties between *natotib*; they are simply men who, when chance brings them together, are compelled to behave to each other in a most friendly manner. The link is the result of affinal ties common to both men. Like *nabim*, *natotib* are usually of different clan and often of different tribe.

Women cannot be *natotib*. All women married into one clan, and especially the women married into one major lineage are *juan* (pl. *juantib*) to each other. The term is best translated as co-wife. Here again, all co-wives are expected to behave in a friendly and co-operative way to each other and to assist each other with their children and in their household and farm work. Especially is this true of the co-wives of one man. While co-wives of one husband can be of the same clan it actually happens rarely enough and they can never, if the rules of marriage be strictly applied, be of the same house. Yet is is considered desirable that a married woman should have one or more clan-sisters living near her in her husband's district. It is noticeable that women who come from afar to their husbands' houses and who have no clan sister near, are, especially when they are young, rather lonely. The link between a woman and her fellow clans-woman married into the same clan is noticeably closer than that between a woman and her other co-wives. At the level of daily work there are no special rights and duties between such women; they are merely closer in amity than are ordinary co-wives. But on ritual occasions they are spoken of as *manto* to each other. A woman there-fore uses this term *manto* in two ways: first, to refer to the clan that stands as *mantotib* to her own clan; and secondly, to refer to a clan-sister and co-wife in a ritual context. When a clan is to carry out a rite a representative of the *mantotib* clan must be present. Women, however, may marry far away and at such a distance that no one of her clan-*mantotib* could be present. The place of her clan-*mantotib* is therefore filled by her clan-sisters who are also co-wives. Where co-wives are also clan-sisters the friendliness and co-operativeness ex-pected of all clan wives is intensified into a reciprocal ritual relation. This is a link that originates in agnation.

Fifthly and finally, there is simple friendship. The word for friend is *dzo* (pl. *dzotib*) between men and *nakwoo* (pl. *nakwotib*) between women. Men and women are never friends with each other. Yet friendship implies, to Konkomba, more than the surface amity that exists between *nabim* and *natotib*. While friendship does not imply ritual duties nor is it a cathartic relationship, yet, in any lengthy rite that requires a heavy expenditure in foodstuffs and beer, material help is given between friends. Any man who is celebrating, for example, the Second Burial of his father, receives perhaps the bulk of the beer he distributes from his friends rather than from his agnates. Since all the Second Burial rites of a clan are carried out simultane-ously, clearly clansmen cannot help each other. The material help comes therefore from matrilateral kin and from friends.

Women friends similarly help each other in providing corn for brewing when a woman has to send beer to the interment or Second Burial of a close agnatic kinsman.

Friendship usually arises between two men in the following way. One young man is carrying on or wishes to carry on a love affair with a girl of another clan. But all girls are betrothed in infancy and there-fore love affairs may and sometimes do arouse the jealousy of a fiancé. In order then to cover the real reason for visiting his mistress' clan, a young man seeks out a contemporary in that clan and asks him to be his friend. But this friendship relation is not a mere cloak in the end, for the love affair though it begins in that way, since the relation involves reciprocal help and may grow into a warm, enduring, even life-long association.

Similarly with girls who are friends. They usually enter into the relation in order to have a person in a lover's clan who can take a message for him. Indeed, one of a pair of friends is often the sister of the other's lover.

But friends do visit each other simply because they are friends. They meet on other than ritual occasions simply to see each other and to talk. They help each other in giving bride service. They go out visiting other places together; they meet in the markets. It is remarkable, however, that no case came to my attention of friends going out of Konkombaland together to work on the southern yam farms or to go to unskilled labour in a town. Young men do go off to farm work together for short periods each year, but they go in groups of *onatship-watotib*, that is, age-mates. The very occasional young man who goes far afield usually goes alone.

The relations of *dzo* and *nakwoo* are choice relations and do not necessarily arise from kinship though there is nothing to prevent, say, *nabim* from being also *dzotib*. They are voluntary relationships in that they are not ascribed by kinship though they are, by definition, relations other than kin relations. Yet they do often give rise to relations of affinal kinship. Especially may *dzotib* exchange daughters as wives either for each other or for their sons. One of the formal courtesies, indeed, for a man's wife to offer to his friend is: 'I want to bear a child to give you (as a wife).'

Women friends cannot similarly exchange daughters nor can they marry the daughter of the one to the son of the other. This is because of the differential age of marriage for men and women in Konkomba; girls marry at about eighteen and men at about forty years of age. Yet a woman friend may give her daughter to a son of her friend's husband by a senior wife.

Friendship therefore often does lead back to affinal and thence to matrilateral kinship, and so completes a circle.

The importance of the relation of friendship is illustrated in the use of a special phrase for a broken friendship. *Kedzatig do* literally means 'friendship finished', that is, the friends have quarrelled. Sometimes *kedzatig* alone is used to mean a parted friend. Similarly the phrase *kebwatig do* refers to lovers who have parted. A parted friend has to be distinguished from an enemy, *odi* (pl. *bedem*). Enmity is a group relation between clans.

The most common reason for a quarrel between friends is that one suspects that the other has revealed his love affair either to the husband of the girl or to another would-be lover. Since the girl is almost certainly carrying on at least one more love affair at the same time, occasions for jealousy and possibly suspicion of a friend are not infrequent. Similarly in a quarrel between two girls who were friends. I have no figures to indicate the frequency of such quarrels, but they may not be very frequent because Konkomba are aware of the tensions in the relation and they do not lightly enter into it. It is the would-be lover who makes the first approach to a man of his mistresses's clan. A man so approached usually considers the matter carefully before agreeing and refusals are common.

Friends are invariably men of different clan and sometimes they are of different tribe though they may, in fact, be *nabim* or *natotib* at the same time. These relations of amity—*nato*, *nabo* and *dzo*—help to reduce the isolation of the agnatic clan. They also help to reduce the incidence of fights and consequently of feud. Whereas, if a man gets into a severe quarrel, his *naabo* and his *taabo* must come unquestioningly to his aid and so may precipitate a fight, his *nabo*, his *nato* and his *dzo* will do their utmost to compose the quarrel and so obviate a fight.

The groups of kin—clansfolk, mother's clan, wife's clan, along with the *mantotib* clan, parental/filial clan and the kith clans—exhaust the groups of Konkomba linked in amity. Other groups may be enemies. The links I have discussed above exhaust a Konkomba's individual links with persons of the same sex. All other persons are strangers, *betsham* (s. *otshã*). But the relation between strangers must not be confused with that between enemies. A stranger is a person to be treated with courtesy: he must be offered water and if there is food ready, he must be offered food. There is a phrase, *tshigr betsham*, which means 'to behave inhospitably to strangers' and it is a term of strong disapproval.

There seem to be two possible ways of looking at these relations of amity as extensions of kinship relations. First we can consider three categories. If we regard as the primary cognatic tie that between parent and child, since the tie is unmediated through any third person, then that between siblings is secondary in that it is mediated through one person, a parent. Other persons are linked in ties of tertiary cognatic kinship in that they are related through two persons; first cousins are so related. These primary, secondary and tertiary cognatic ties can be either uterine or agnatic according to the sex of the persons forming the links.

Yet, between individuals other linkages of kinship occur that are mediated by two or more persons and do not involve cognation. Thus, brothers-in-law are linked in a secondary affinal tie of kinship through the woman who is the wife of one and the sister of the other. This can be thought of as a secondary tie of affinal kinship if the primary affinal tie is that between husband and wife. A tertiary affinal tie is that between two men who marry sisters (cf. Radcliffe-Brown, 1950, p. 6).

In these senses we could describe the tie between *naabim* as a secondary uterine tie; that between *taabim* as a secondary agnatic one; and that between *nabim* is then a tertiary uterine link since it is mediated through two clan-sisters. In the English system of counting, such people would be classed as first, second and up to fifth cousins. It appears to be an extension of the *naabo* tie between two sisters. The tie between *natotib* is a tertiary affinal one and appears also to be an extension of that between sisters who are *naabim*.

The first two relationships, *naabo* and *taabo*, are then secondary and the other two, *nabo* and *nato*, are tertiary. *Dzo* and *nakwoo* are voluntary relations between persons and have no necessary relation with kinship. The relations of *dzo*, *nakwoo* and *bwa*, which transcend the boundaries of clan and kinship categories, may be considered together. The friendship relation *dzo* or *nakwoo* holds between men or women respectively while the lover relation, *bwa*, holds between men and women. In addition to transcending clan and kinship boundaries this relation also transcends certain boundaries which separate men from women. In Konkomba one may not take a lover in one's own minor lineage nor in the minor lineage of one's mother. A love affair with the wife of a man of one's clan would be incestuous. There are no other limitations except the rule that no person should have more than one lover in any one clan. All young men and women have several love affairs going at once. This lover relation, then, is the only voluntary one between the sexes. Even marriage is not a matter of choice since infant girls are betrothed to young men in an arrangement made by the parents of both. Once a girl marries into a lineage she lives out her life as a wife of that lineage. Even today the number of runaway wives is small. It is true that some marriages do arise out of love affairs but they are remarkably few since they may cause fighting or even feud and always draw out some form of retaliation from the lineage that has lost a wife.

The classification given above does not very satisfactorily explain the genesis of the *nabo* and *nato* relations. The five relations of amity are, if looked at in another way, reducible to three. First, *naabo* and *taabo* are links created in birth and *nabo* and *nato* appear to be extensions of them. Secondly, *dzo* or *nakwoo* differs from the other four in that it is voluntary not compulsory.

Fortes (1949, p. 41 ff.) showed the lineal expansion of the *soog* relationship among the Tallensi through at least three generations in the female line from uterine sisters. All Konkomba structures are of lesser genealogical depth than are those of the Tallensi. Whereas the Tallensi maximal lineage goes to twelve generations depth, the longest Konkomba genealogy does not exceed six generations. The Tallensi kind of lineage expansion of the *soog* bond does not appear to occur among Konkomba. What does occur is some kind of lateral expansion.

The primary application of the term *nabo* is, to the child of the mother's sister and this is, in turn, primarily a uterine link since the two women are *naabim*. But, on the principle of the unity of the lineage, the children of all one's mother's clan-sisters are regarded as *nabo* and this is an agnatic extension because the women have all a common male ancestor not a female one. On the other hand it applies only to women and descends from these women to their children; that is, it is transmitted by uterine descent. There seems therefore to be a fusion of agnatic and uterine principles in the extension of kinship that creates the tie between *nabim*. It passes lineally by uterine descent and is extended laterally by agnation.

The relation called *nato* is not dissimilar. *Natotib* are the fathers of *nabim*. They are linked by affinal ties to women of one clan, women linked to each other by agnation. But again, the primary link is between men married to sisters, especially to uterine sisters, and the tie between the women is extended on the principle of the unity of the lineage to equate all women of the lineage and so to create the link between all men married to clan-sisters.

It might be thought that the expansion of the *naabo* tie would occur in accordance with the principle of the equivalence of siblings. If this were so then the tie between *nabim* would hold only between children of women of the same generation and that between *natotib* would hold only between men married to women of the same generation. This might, indeed, be the case though I think not. If the relations between *nabim* and *natotib* are stratified by generation then it is by the generation of the persons who stand in such relations to each other. The simple relation of friendship is one that holds only between persons of approximately the same age. And, while there appears to be no rule that would prevent *nabim* and *natotib* of markedly disparate age from behaving in a friendly manner, their behaviour is also affected by their relative statuses. Between such persons there is amity but there is also seniority and juniority: this modifies the expression of amity.

Among Konkomba then, the ties of *naabo* and *taabo* are of the same generic kind and differ only in degree. Yet the *taabo* tie is the primary one that is extended lineally and laterally in agnatic kinship to give rise to the agnatic lineage and clan and so creates corporate groups. The *naabo* tie between sisters is the primary one that is extended lineally and laterally by agnatic kinship between women of one clan and transmitted lineally by uterine descent in the clans of the husbands of the women of one clan to give rise to the link between *nabim*. The affinal tie between a man and his wife's sister's husband is similarly extended to link the husband in the *nato* tie to all men who have married a woman of his wife's clan. Thus the *naabo* tie gives rise to individual relations between persons in kinship categories and not to corporate groups.

The primary ties are *naabo* and *taabo* and they work within the lineage framework. The extensions of *naabo* in the *nabo* and *nato* relation and the third relation of friendship range widely through Konkombaland to overrun the boundaries of clan and tribe. They express values in some sense opposed to those of lineage and clan which often lead to fights and feuds. They offer points of amity in potentially or actually hostile regions.

PART III

SOME FEATURES OF KONKOMBA
RITUAL INSTITUTIONS

———◦◦———

XII. Divination and Sacrifice

i. The Role of the Diviner[1]

DIVINERS form one of several ritual categories of persons in this society; they are persons sent into the world by dead diviners. One cannot become a diviner by act of choice. A diviner undergoes a testing rite when in his early twenties and thereafter may practise. He reaches his greatest fame during his fifties and continues until he is too old to walk the distances involved in this work. No political power attaches to his office: should he survive to become a lineage elder he will be too aged to continue practice. No diviner works for his own clansmen. He works with an assistant who is not one of a ritual category. Assistant diviners take up the work to increase their prestige or to earn payment. They may work for their own clansmen.

The diviner reads a message from cowrie shells. This message is then tested. The group (or individual) consulting the diviner puts down three sticks on the ground, each stick representing a question to him. He touches one or other stick with his staff to indicate where the truth lies. Any person present may question him and the questions are decided on out of his hearing. But when the sticks are to be touched the diviner holds his staff by one end while his assistant grasps the other; in fact the assistant, who is present when the questions are decided on, could control the touching. Many sets of ques-

[1]This summary of a communication to the Royal Anthropological Institute, given on 9 October 1952 was printed in *Man*, vol. lii, 249, 1952, under the title of 'The Role of the Diviner in Konkomba Society'.

tions are put to a diviner and in this process his original generalities are sharpened to specific statements which in fact reveal the suspicions, conscious or unconscious, of those who consult the diviner.

While Konkomba affect to despise their diviners they often consult them; diviners regard themselves as men with a mission.

Diviners are consulted about future undertakings and about past events. In situations of personal or group doubt about future activities the diviner commonly suggests some small sacrifice to ancestors or shrine which will ensure success. Especially important is his role in lineage fission, for he then not only obtains the agreement of the ancestors to the separation of kinsmen but discovers shrines for the outgoing kin in a new region. He thus assures them of good relations to ancestors and land.

Among past events the diviner deals largely with misfortune, sickness and death. Situations of misfortune include crop failures and hunting failures. These are generally found to be due to ritual omissions.

The Konkomba concept of the causes of sickness differs with the age of the sufferer. Adult sickness is not conceived as unnatural and is treated with medicines. Sickness in children is generally traced to a failure to give sacrifice of thanks to the ancestor who sent the child into the world.

The causes of death also vary with the age of the dead person. Children die because of failure in the lineage to carry out ritual and moral obligations; because of improper treatment or, simply, because 'God took the child'. People past childhood, other than elders, die because of failures within the lineage to meet social obligations either by the dead persons or towards them. Or death may be due to witchcraft towards or by the dead person; that is, death may be a punishment. Elders die only by witchcraft but are never themselves witches.

The role of the diviner is to select from among a limited number of possible causes the particular cause of a particular death. On the widest view diviners are consulted, first, in situations of doubt and, secondly, in situations of unnatural or unfortunate events. As a consequence of their work in situations of doubt the individuals or groups who consult the diviner discover any ritual impediment or impurity which might endanger the success of a proposed undertaking. After carrying out the sacrifices suggested by the diviner they may carry out their proposals with full confidence in a successful outcome.

As a consequence of the diviner's work after unnatural or unfortunate events, ritual action can be taken by the groups concerned to remove any ritual impurity or to correct lapses from standards of behaviour which led to those events. By sacrifice or by repentance the group that has suffered loss or misfortune may be assured of better times to come.

The diviner's role is to point out ritual and moral omissions. He recalls his society to religious and moral duty and by his insistence on avoidance or expiation of offences he releases his fellows from the burden of guilt and gives them security.

ii. Spirits of the Bush[1]

. . . Among the Konkomba there are several religious practices that are private and not group ones. One such private cult is expressed in the beliefs and practices concerned with certain spirits called *benekpib*. The term *benekpib* refers to two kinds of spirit which may or may not be connected. The word itself is a plural form, the plural of the word *onekpel*, elder, which is used in two senses: to denote a senior person and to denote a lineage elder. The plural form also has more than one usage. First, it can refer to a number of senior persons; secondly, it can refer to the ancestors, and therefore to the ancestral ghosts or spirits; and thirdly, it can refer to the spirits of the bush. Since the same term is used for the ancestral ghosts and for these spirits of the bush, it is tempting to suppose that the *benekpib* of the bush, since they are evil, are the ghosts of unworthy ancestors, sorcerers, or other evil-doers, who were either exiled in life from their communities or who were killed for their sins. I shall come back to this point later.

The spirits of the bush pursue and attack selected victims. They do not, as do the Dagomba *kinkiriga*, bedevil and mislead any chance traveller they may encounter. The *benekpib* attack one selected individual and one only, and they continue their attack until either the victim dies or undergoes a series of rites which will thenceforth protect him. The attack of the *benekpib* is to be observed in individuals who undergo a period of mental stress. The sufferer is greatly distressed, is unable to concentrate on his duties and, especially, suffers

---

[1]This paper first appeared in *Universitas*, I, 1, December 1953 under the title of 'Spirits of the Bush: A Note on Personal Religion among the Konkomba'. *Universitas* is a publication of the University College of Ghana, Accra.

from disturbing dreams because of which he is often unable to sleep. It is noteworthy that most persons so attacked are either in adolescence or in young adulthood. Very occasionally a younger person is attacked but only very rarely indeed is a person in middle age attacked, and such cases occur only in special circumstances. In general the phenomenon is one connected with adolescence.

A sufferer first consults a diviner to learn the cause of his distress. There are several possible explanations, for example that some ancestor has been angered by ritual or moral omissions; yet the most frequently occurring explanation of these symptoms is that they are caused by the *benekpib*. Once this decision is reached the sufferer begins a long series of rites which culminate in one in which the spirits are 'caught' in a bag and handed over to the person they attacked, and who is to be their future controller.

Moral and religious phenomena are divided into the two categories *kenjaa*, good, and *kesuo*, evil. But a thing that is at first in one class can be changed to the other, since the effect of the rite of 'catching the spirits' is to transfer them from the category *kesuo* to that of *kenjaa*. The trapped spirits then no longer distress and disturb their new owner but become to him friendly guiding voices. They now advise him in all his concerns, whether these concerns be of his private or of his public life in lineage and clan.

In effect, then, the rites deal with psychological disturbances, especially with disturbances of young persons. In some instances the mental distress of the sufferer may be the result of separation from home—as in the case of a young man who left the close intimacy of a Konkomba village to work in Kumasi. Or it may be the result of inner conflicts arising from sexual drives at this phase of life. The spirits in fact often come in pairs, a male and a female. Even if a young person begins with only one spirit—a male spirit to a youth and a female one to a girl—a second spirit of the other sex will invariably follow and a second period of distress will be undergone. These spirits are conceived as married to each other, and some male spirits have a number of 'wives'. In the course of time the adult spirits produce spirit children, and there is therefore a family of spirits all of whom are controlled by their holder and each of whom can advise him.

However we may conceive this guidance—as a technique of attending to the unconscious or as an institutionalized technique of attending to one's conscience or otherwise—the effect is plain. The individual who holds spirits has spiritual guides in all his personal relations. As he (or she) matures as an individual and as a social personality, so too do his spirit guides mature and multiply. The maturing person is thus made aware of his own physical maturation and has a technique for using it.

The experience of being attacked by spirits is a painful one. It is a long and slow process and the rites which may and usually do end the suffering take between two and three years. It is, then, a period of preparation which ends, if not in a rebirth, in a new integration of the personality of the one who has undergone it. He comes out of it as one who, because he suffered, has attained to a new and developing spiritual power.

I said above that the use of one term for the ancestral spirits and for the bush spirits is puzzling. It might be thought that the bush spirits are the ghosts of evil ancestors who are condemned to the bush in death, as the ancestors were in life. They could then be thought of as earning their admittance to the communion of the dead ancestors by serving their descendants through a period of penitence. There is but slight evidence to support this view. The Konkomba say that a man's evil dies with him even though he was a sorcerer, just as the sorcerer's evil medicine dies with its owner. It is the case, however, that those believed to have been sorcerers do not immediately join their dead forbears; indeed, the kin of a dead sorcerer make special sacrifices for him to the ancestors, at his Second Burial rites, in order to obtain their forgiveness for him. Further investigation may show the period of estrangement for a dead sorcerer to be prolonged, and one that ends only when the ghost has shown penitence through work for the living.

iii. Libation[1]

The religious rites of Konkomba may be classified under the following heads:

(1) Land rites;

(2) Harvest rites;

(3) Purificatory or expiratory rites; these may be personal or communal;

(4) Divinatory rites.

The categories are not, of course, mutually exclusive.

[1]This paper first appeared in the *Bulletin de l'Institut français d'Afrique Noire*, 17, 1–2, 1955, under the title 'The Place of Libation in Konkomba Ritual'. It was written at the request of the Christian Council of the Gold Coast.

Such rites are all primarily religious rites. By that I mean that in them all there is a primary reference to spiritual persons and beings and commonly to God. The Konkomba word *Uumbwar* can only be translated as 'God'. It appears to be cognate with the word *Obwar*, a chief. He, since Uumbwar is probably male, is very vaguely conceived. He is given no precise location in time or in space; he is distant and no man knows where he is or just what is his nature. Yet he is everywhere and enters into all human beings through the *ungwin*. The term '*ungwin*' is best translated as 'spirit' or 'soul': it is defined as 'that part of a man that God gives'. The spirit comes from God and, on death, returns to God. It is true that ancestors and shrines sometimes send children to their descendants or adherents; but they send the body, *owe*, not the *ungwin* which only God can send.

Uumbwar is perhaps to be thought of as a very remote 'father', the most distant of the *benekpib*, the forefathers. A man making sacrifice invokes his dead father, his grandfather and more remote ancestors as they are known and they in turn are invited to take the offering and to share it with 'those they know'. It is the dead who can and do know God for they live in *Uumbwardo*, God's House.

Unlike many peoples Konkomba have no signs of a developed cosmogony. This is no doubt partly the result of their expulsion from their original territory by the Dagomba four centuries ago. Primitive cosmologies tend to trace an unbroken connexion between the living, the land and the first messengers from the Creator. This is impossible for Konkomba. I know no stories of how they came to be in their former location. Time therefore begins with their expulsion by Dagomba. All this increases the distance from Uumbwar.

Nonetheless, Uumbwar is the source of all good. He is himself 'good' and he can and does punish the evildoer. Uumbwar does not for long tolerate the sorcerer who, unless he repents, will die. To the general good, *kenjaa*, that is in the world, a general evil, *kesuo*, stands opposed. The source of evil is not defined. Nor, in effect, is it unitary but is refracted into particular forms of evil—evil spirits, spirits of the bush, evil places in the bush, the burial places of those killed in feud, sorcery and so on. Similarly, the good that comes from Uumbwar is refracted into particular goods—shrines of the Earth, of water, of fertility; the ancestors who continue to watch over their descendants in death as they did in life; the horns and strips of skin from sacrificial animals—all these and more contain something of the good that comes from Uumbwar.

This is not to say that nothing magical enters into the rites to, say, the ancestors. But ancestral sacrifice differs markedly from the rites of preparation and use of a protective medicine. Once made, such a medicine acts directly. Sacrifice to spiritual beings sees a more distant goal: it is not direct, not immediate in its action but placatory and beseeching. A medicine does achieve its end, it is believed; a supplicatory rite may achieve its end but that depends on the ancestors and on Uumbwar. Medicines compel; sacrifice supplicates.

Libation enters only into the religious rites. When medicines are being prepared or used libation does not occur. It is part, therefore, of religion and not of magic.

Rites of sacrifice and supplication must be carried out in a formal, indeed a reverent manner. There must be no noise or movement during the rite; there must be no talk. Further, there are prescribed attitudes. During one rite it was noticed that I was standing upright. There was a pause while the elders considered what should be done. The proper attitude throughout a rite is for the participants to squat on their heels, an attitude I am unable to maintain for long. It was agreed that I should crouch at certain critical points in the rite but might stand at other times.

These critical points are during libation and the invocation that accompanies it and during sacrifice.

The place of libation in the kinds of rite noted above is as follows. Van Gennep pointed out that rites fall into three parts or phases. The first phase is that of separation from the profane world; the second, which he called 'état de marge', occurs while the participants are in contact with the sacred world; the third or closing phase he called 'état d'agrégation' or the return to the profane world from the sacred world. In all Konkomba rites in which libation occurs, except one, it occurs once in the first phase and once in the closing phase.

A rite opens with an invocation to the ancestors and at each name called libation is poured. The liquid used is often water mixed with beer or water alone. Whether the mixture or water alone is used it is always referred to as 'water'. The closing phase of the rite is the pouring of the remainder of this water on to the shrine itself or on to the feathers of sacrificial fowls. Until this final libation is poured no one may speak of matters other than the rite. On one occasion when a rite had to be carried out in two separate places, the second part was done in the compound; the second libation was poured on arrival at the compound to enable the participants to speak. But on the way back from the shrine none responded to the greetings of some travellers we passed.

It may be useful to take the exceptional rite as an example to make the form clear. My example is that of an Earth rite, a sacrifice to the Earth that is purificatory. The clan which carried out the rite is one that consisted of two contraposed major lineages. That is, there is a division of ritual and political roles between the elders of the two contraposed major lineages, such that one, called the *Otindaa*, the Owner of the Earth, is ritually senior to the other who is called the *Onekpel*, or elder, and who is politically senior to the *Otindaa*. Though the *Otindaa* had to be present, the actual sacrificing was done on this occasion by a young man who was 'sent into the world' by the Earth Shrine, *Ntengbe*.

The clan elders must invite their *mantotib* to such a rite. Indeed, at any rite performed by a clan a representative of the *mantotib* clan should be present. The *mantotib* relation is a dyadic, reciprocal relation of ritual help between clans, commonly contiguous clans. The clan that carried out the rite had also invited the elders of other neighbouring clans with whom it stands in the relation of amity I call kithship. There were, then, the elders of three clans gathered together for this rite and others had been invited but had not come.

The rite is neither a harvest rite nor a sowing rite, strictly speaking, but something of both. It is done in January to February, that is, well after the grain harvest of November–December and well before the spring sowing in May–June. It is a sacrifice to the land which asks for rain and crops.

The rite was done, as is usual in this rite, not in the Earth Shrine itself but outside the house of the *Otindaa* and on a patch of ground that had been swept clear of all debris. It opened with a ritual drinking of beer. The beer was poured into calabashes and the elders drank it two together at the same time from one calabash. To drink together from one calabash is a sign of friendship. The *Otindaa* and the *Onekpel* of the host clan first drank together and then with their neighbours and so on round the semi-circle. The *Otindaa* then called on his more remote ancestors and addressed the Earth. He was followed by the other elders. At the name of each ancestor the young man, who had been given a calabash filled with water and beer, poured a small quantity on the earth. At each pause in the address or after a name was called, all participants other than the speaker joined in a chorus of '*Yoo, Yoo*'.

The rite may be set out as follows:

État de séparation

With the elders seated in a sem-circle the *Otindaa* of the host clan begins:

Otindaa: Wapu!

Chorus: Yoo-Yoo and libation

Otindaa: Koto!

Chorus: Yoo-Yoo and libation

Otindaa: Dzange!

Choruso: Yoo-Yoo and libation[1]

Otindaa: All offer in sacrifice for their houses. I too wish to sacrifice today. Shrine *Ntengbe!* Shrine *Kpambwer!* Shrine *Njitshir!* Shrine *Tshan! Kewabo!*[2] You got the water they (the ancestors) held for you. I want the corn to grow; I want the rain to fall; I want food to eat. Those people who went off to Krachi, I want them to come home to their houses.[3] Wapu! (libation) Koto! (libation) Dzange! (libation) Ngmangea! (libation) Tamanazar! (libation).[4]

Onekpel: We who remain here, we want to sacrifice to the Earth. We call Bwagban and Nalogni[5] they too are staying here, we are doing this. If you are *Ntengbe!* we want the rain to fall. Ojaa and Okandza[6]—he must not go home.

Third Elder: Ngagbi![7] they are getting us. They want they kill this land.[8] We too come. If you are *Ntenbge!* you must not eat and finish all the new food. We want rain to fall, food in plenty. People go away, we want them to come back here to have food.

[1]The names that the *Otindaa* called at this point are the names of the ancestors of his own minor lineage only.

[2]The shrines called in this invocation are those of the host clan. They are, in order of calling, the Earth Shrine; a fertility shrine; the water shrine; an ancestor shrine; and, lastly, a shrine that has no special attachment.

[3]The area in which this rite was carried out is one that has suffered from severe depopulation. Many of the people have left and gone to settle not far from Kete Krachi some 200 miles away.

[4]In his second invocation of the ancestors the *Otindaa* has included the ancestors of that major lineage that is contraposed to his own.

[5]These are neighbouring clans, both kith to the host clan.

[6]Ojaa is the elder of the *mantotib* of the host clan. Okandza is myself (literally, Red Man).

[7]Ngagbi is the name of the *Otindaa.*

[8]This reference is obscure. It refers, certainly, to soil exhaustion which causes the emigration of many Konkomba. Just what evil power wants to kill the land is not clear—unless it is that by going away the emigrants leave fewer people to work the land.

Fourth Elder: Ntengbe! you remain, they[1] not sacrifice. When we come we all want rain to fall, they all see food to eat.

Fifth Elder: Ntgenbe! Wapu! We are but children, we know nothing. We rest on you; we rest on you. We want rain. I plant yams but the rain not come, I want rain now. If it rain—food (will) come, people are happy.

Otindaa (while the young man pours libation after every phrase):
Ntengbe!—your water is here.
Natotengbe!—your water is here.
Bwagbatengbe!—your water is here.
Bwakwinatengbe!—your water is here.
Kumwatiakatengbe!—your water is here.[2]

État de marge

This is the phase of actual sacrifice. All persons present had brought a chicken for the offering.

Onepkel (while at each name called the young man kills one of the chickens):
Ntengbe!
Shrine *Kpambwer!*
Shrine *Tshan!*
Shrine *Njitshir!*
Kewabõ!
Nakpatengbe!
Bwakwinatengbe!
Ngwapatengbe!
Kumwatiakatengbe![3]

État d'agrégation

The young man then took the remainder of the water and threw it in the air to land on the cleared earth. Beer was handed round, all drank and the semicircle broke up.

The themes of this simple rite are clear. They are, first, the request for rain and for food; secondly, the hope that kin who have moved out of Konkomba will return to it. There are, thirdly, signs that the emigrants are blamed for going away—a theme that recurs when the cause of deaths of elders is being divined.

---

[1] That is, *Ntengbe* will remain whether or not people sacrifice.

[2] The *Otindaa* here includes the Earth Shrines of a number of neighbouring clans whether there was a representative of the clan present or not.

[3] The *Onekpel* here includes all the shrines of his own clan in the sacrifice but the Earth shrines only of the kith clans.

The rite falls into three phases. First, the opening invocation of the ancestors and shrines which is accompanied by libation. This is continued in a series of addresses to the Earth Shrines. The addresses culminate in an invocation of the shrines, each invocation being marked by a libation. These libations mark the transition to the 'état de marge' which is devoted to sacrifice. The time taken over the sacrifices is longer than would appear from a simple description. With the ending of sacrifice the 'état de marge' gives way to the phase of 'agrégation' in which a general easing of tension is obvious. The throwing of water leads to the final communal drinking of beer before the group breaks its formal attitudes.

Conclusion

The place of libation in these rites is plain. It marks a transition in ritual condition. It is through libation that contact is established with the spiritual beings and powers of the Konkomba cosmology. It is by means of the final libation that contact is broken off.

Libation is therefore an integral part of a religious rite. Each rite is itself part of a sequence of rites that form a system of rites which, with their attendant beliefs, are a religious system. This totality is a Way, a Path and a Life. It lays down for Konkomba a pattern of conduct which, if followed, offers rewards and which, if neglected, brings punishment. It has no theology, in any sense; it has little ritual equipment. It is strongly gerontocratic since children and young persons are generally excluded from the rites. Religion, then, or better, clan religion or public religion, is something of a mystery to the young men and to all women. It is an activity of the elders and senior men and so reinforces their authority.

This again means that religious experience and religious knowledge is something to be attained in the course of life. It is true that special religious powers are given to diviners, to those who 'hold spirits' and to those 'sent by the shrines'. As men pass middle life, however, the importance of their special power diminishes and they cease to be diviners and, in its place, begin to enter into the religious life of the clan shrines. As they age they penetrate more and more into the religion of the shrines and cults. That is, as they draw nearer and nearer to the ancestors and prepare for their return to that distant ancestor, Uumbwar.

XIII. Konkomba Sorcery[1]

THE Konkomba term for sorcerer is *osŭo* (pl. *bɔsuom*).[2] There is no noun that can properly be translated as 'sorcery', but there is a word, *kɔsŭo*, which refers to a class of phenomena that are evil, a class to which the activities of sorcerers belong. Unlike the Azande and the Navaho,[3] the Konkomba include several different kinds of behaviour under one term. There are two main kinds of activity which are ascribed to malevolent, maleficent persons—the *bɔsuom*. These activities may be called 'sorcery' and 'transvection'. I define sorcery as the use of magical medicines to procure the death of a selected victim. The essence of Konkomba sorcery appears to be this use of medicines. Yet, since the Konkomba are not explicit about the preparation of this medicine, it is impossible to say with certainty whether or not the use of spells enters into the technique. The medicine is known simply as *sŭoanjog* or *osŭo a njog*, literally 'sorcerer's medicine'. It is true that spells enter into the preparation of *idabin* (sing. *ndabin*), and these are medicines that are used as protectives against, *inter alia*, *sŭoanjog*. There is, of course, no reason to suppose that anyone ever in fact tries to make sorcerer's medicine, so it cannot definitely be said that spells are or are not used. By transvection I mean the flying by night of a sorcerer to attack a sleeping victim. The flying sorcerer can be seen as a moving light that is known as *sŭoŋmi*, that is 'sorcerer-fire'. This belief that flying sorcerers emit a light was noted by Evans-Pritchard among the Azande, and it is found also among the Akan-speaking peoples and the Tallensi.[4]

[1]This chapter first appeared in the *Journal of the Royal Anthropological Institute*, Vol. 84, 1954, under the title of 'Konkomba Sorcery'.

[2]The form *ŭo* is here used to indicate a sound between *u* and *o* that is nasalized.

[3]E. E. Evans-Pritchard, *Witchcraft, Oracles and Magic among the Azande*, Oxford, 1937, pp. 9–10; C. Kluckhohn, 'Navaho Witchcraft', *Pap. Peabody Mus.*, 22 (2), 1944, p. 18.

[4]E. L. Rapp, tr. 'The African Explains Witchcraft'. XVII. Akan (Dialect of Ɔkwawu). Translated by E. L. Rapp. *Africa*, 8, pp. 553–4, 1935; R. S. Rattray, *Ashanti Proverbs*, Oxford, 1915, p. 48; Meyer Fortes, *The Web of Kinship among the Tallensi*, 1949, p. 33.

Two other methods are occasionally said to be used by Konkomba sorcerers in magical killing. In the first of these, a sorcerer is believed to be able to send snakes to lie in wait on a path until the victim comes along. It is not believed that a chance passer-by will be bitten, since sorcerers kill but they do not kill at random. It is surprising that this technique of sorcery by snake bite is seldom discussed since snake bites, even fatal ones, are not uncommon. The second of the techniques of lesser importance is that the sorcerer, instead of going himself to overlay his victim, sends his shadow to eat the victim's shadow. As the shadow in life is the ghost after death, a man whose shadow is gone dies of a lingering disease. It is probable that this particular belief is invoked only when someone has died of such a disease. The two major techniques of magical killing are both ascribed to one category of person. The technique of bad medicine is indirect in that the sorcerer does not necessarily meet his victim; transvection is direct and involves contact between sorcerer and victim.

Sorcerer's medicine can be transmitted to the victim in three ways: in beer, in a kola-nut, or by being placed on a path. When beer is being passed round in a calabash, the thumb is always kept very carefully out of the beer. It projects above the rim of the calabash and is not depressed in a way that might allow it to dip into the beer. This is because sorcerers are believed to poison their victims by putting the poison under the thumb nail and so transferring it into the beer. The thumb and all the finger-nails are kept very short, except those of the little fingers. I know of no wholly satisfactory explanation of this long nail. The kola-nut splits down the middle. Sorcerer's medicine can be put into this split and so passed to the victim. The Konkomba do not eat kola-nuts given to them by strangers. They accept the nut, thank the giver, and, later, throw it away. Further, when kola-nuts are eaten they are first split and the two parts are eaten separately. There seems to be no protection against the medicine laid on paths. I know of no avoidance designed to help the victim not to step on it. The method is, in any case, less frequently attributed to sorcerers than are the preceding two. Again, it is believed that only the selected victim would tread on the medicine: chance travellers are not so attacked.

As a protection against transvection, the door leading into a compound is always closed at night. Even so, no one within the compound sleeps alone except, perhaps, a childless woman during the period when her husband is with a co-wife. Even then, if there are young girls in the household one or more of them will sleep with her. Any person approaching a compound after dark does so carefully, announcing his presence, since one defence against the wandering sorcerer is to snatch up a flaming stick from the fire and strike him. This drives him away. The Konkomba also put glowing charcoal by the door of the sleeping room, so that anyone entering can be seen. Finally, the Konkomba seldom go out alone after nightfall and then only during the moon's second quarter. On a dark night no Konkomba would come by himself, even a hundred yards, to set me on my way home, lest he should be unaccompanied on the way back; but two would come together. Though sorcerer-fire is greatly feared, and I have known young men turn about and go home claiming that they had seen it, the danger from it is not very clearly stated. The most precisely stated form of attack is by sorcerer's medicine and the precautions most frequently taken are those against its administration. No one would admit to knowing what ingredients go into it or how it is made. From the precautions taken to destroy the exuviae of a dead body, it may be concluded that these are among the necessary ingredients. Before burial, a body is seated on a tiny stool; the head is shaved, the nails are clipped, and the body and mouth are washed. All this is done with ordinary water. The mouth is again rinsed at the side of the grave with a ritual water called *ndzen*. At this second washing the *ndzen* runs down into the grave. After the shaving and washing, the hair and the nail-clippings are carefully burned, the water used is poured away in the bush, the stool on which the corpse sat is also burned, and the pot in which the washing water was held is broken and the pieces are deposited at a crossroads. All these precautions appear to be designed to prevent a sorcerer from getting hold of the exuviae and using them in the preparation of sorcerer's medicine. The Konkomba term for exuviae is *tədz⁰*.

One seldom hears any discussion about sorcerers, nor are accusations often made openly against individuals. More frequent, though by no means common, are general accusations of the following kind. A man discovered that some puppies, which his bitch had borne on the previous day, had disappeared. It was during the dry season and there was no near-by water into which the puppies could conceivably have fallen. The man's house was separated by a stretch of floodplain from other houses. No path passed near his house except that leading to it. He stood before his compound shouting 'It is a sorcerer'. He thought that the puppies had been taken by a sorcerer to prepare medicine. Though the possible use of the puppies in the medicine was never fully explained to me, I believe they were to be an addition to the exuviae, an addition which would connect the active principle of the medicine, the exuviae, with the proposed victim. Now, the man was frightened. He was a big, powerfully-built man in late middle-age; an active man who worked as an assistant diviner. Assistant diviners do not enjoy special ritual powers among Konkomba but are usually men who have picked up the technique in order to earn some payment in beer and meat, or they are men who simply enjoy going about visiting places. While he himself was frightened, the others present, who were all members either of his household or of his lineage, were not. They sat and waited. As he himself became more and more excited and shouted the harder, the others confined themselves to brief and non-commital sentences. Nor would those I asked about the matter say whether or not they thought the puppies had in fact been taken away. The women of his household, as well as his kinsmen, were aloof and went about their business unheeding their husband's or father's shouts. The reason why the sufferer's kin did not join him in his accusations is that they themselves might be accused of sorcery.

There are general protective medicines, the *idabin*, which a man who fears that he may be the object of attack can use in his own defence; but, when once the attack has begun, it is too late to use them. The only protection then is sacrifice for rain, and the rain is asked to kill the sorcerer. The victim in this instance went to the rain-maker and asked him to carry out the necessary sacrifice and to put out the rain-medicine. The practice of sacrificing for rain as a protection against sorcerers is linked with the Konkomba belief that any person killed by a thunderbolt was a sorcerer who has been punished by God for his crimes. In 1917 Sir Alan Cardinall noted that a Konkomba shrine could be invoked to kill an enemy.[1] The only form of invocation known to me in which the aim is to bring about the death of an enemy is this invocation for rain.

An example of the accusation of a close kinsman by someone who thought himself to be attacked by sorcery is as follows. By chance, a young man and a diviner took shelter from the rain together. They took shelter in a village to which neither belonged. The young man consulted the diviner about his general well-being and was told that a sorcerer was trying to kill him. The first step in Konkomba divination is a reading of events from six cowrie shells laid on the ground. The young man asked the diviner to demonstrate to him exactly who

[1] The source of this statement is an undated entry by Sir Alan in the Dagomba District Book, Yendi, Northern Ghana, for the year in question.

was seeking to kill him. This was done in a second process of divination which is conceived by Konkomba as a test of the diviner's first reading. To do it, three sticks are laid on the ground and, in the diviner's absence, three questions are decided upon, each question being represented by one of the sticks. The questions once decided, the diviner is recalled. He touches one stick, and one only, with his staff to indicate that in that particular stick the truth lies—that is, that whatever was asked in the appropriate question is to be answered affirmatively. Since the questions put by this method are always of the form, 'Does the sorcerer live in village X?', it can be seen that a series of questions so put clarifies the generalities of the reading of the cowries. By putting these questions to the diviner, the supposed victim makes precise the diviner's vague accusation. In the case in point, the sorcerer was shown to be a member of the young man's own major lineage, though of a different minor lineage. I have never been present when a male sorcerer was directly accused by a victim of the same minor lineage, but there are reports that it has happened. It is even said that a sorcerer will kill his own brother, though I know of no instance of this. On the other hand, I do know of one in which a number of kinsmen joined together to accuse a sorcerer, and the accusers included one who was half-brother to the accused. The accusation was made after the death of the accused, at his Second Burial rites.

Thus, close agnatic kinsmen may be accused by their kin of being sorcerers. It is possible, then, that, when a man suspects that he is being attacked, the non-committal attitude of his kin arises from the fear that they themselves may be accused. It might be thought that they seek to dissociate themselves, in some degree, from the victim lest they too be attacked. The Konkomba themselves do not confirm this; the only time at which a sorcerer is thought to be at all likely to attack anyone, other than a carefully selected victim, is when he is obstructed by a traveller while flying by night. When a man suspects a close agnate of sorcery he does not rush away to accuse him immediately, but waits and watches the suspect. Should he fall inexplicably ill, that is, contract one of the diseases which the Konkomba do not recognize as such, then he may ascribe the illness to a sorcerer. Moreover, diviners sometimes advise their clients to take no action at once, but to await a further sign. In many instances, no doubt, nothing else happens; for example, in the case of the young man already quoted. I asked him over a year later, whether anything more had happened, and he looked very embarrassed as he muttered that

'It was all nothing'. In the end, however, an accusation may be made, and the sorcerer may be driven from his home to settle elsewhere. In one instance, a man who had been accused several times over a number of years by his clansmen was finally driven from his native district only to find that his reputation had followed him and that he had to move on again.

During my stay in the Konkomba country the number of definite accusations against men was approximately the same as against women. Among the Konkomba, whether the social structure be that of a major or a minor lineage or that of a clan, the local community is always exogamous. Consequently, the wives of that community are always members of other and possibly distant local communities. They may have no kinsmen near at hand to protect them, and certainly they have no kinsmen on the spot. In any case, since kinsmen do accuse one another there is no reason to suppose that a kinsman could or would protect an accused fellow-clanswoman. An example of the accusation of a woman is as follows. When a man of Kitiak village was told by a diviner that a particular woman sought to kill him, he went to her and, in the presence of his clansmen, placed a head of guinea-corn on the ground and an arrow on the corn. At this point the accuser used the first of two possible formulae. One can be translated as 'Eat before you die' and the other as 'Choose life or death'. The accused woman ran away that night and has not been heard of since.

In this instance, another woman also was involved in the accusation. It was believed that a second and older woman had 'given the medicine' to the one who was accused. The implication of the sentence 'She gave her the medicine' is not that the older woman gave the younger the medicine that the younger woman used on that one occasion but that she had taught her the skills of a sorcerer. Thus both the women were sorcerers, but they were not jointly charged with seeking to kill their accuser. Shortly afterwards, the older woman moved out of the village and went with her husband to another place. The husband later died there, and her children, who were young, were brought back to Kitiak, but the mother refused to come and stayed in her new home. She was afraid that, should she return, she would be accused of killing her husband. Her absence makes the likelihood of such an accusation almost a certainty. In the Second Burial rites of a dead man there is a point at which his wives appear before the group assembled to divine the cause of death, as an indication that they have nothing to fear. This woman's absence would probably be interpreted as showing that she dared not appear.

Four wives were similarly accused in 1951 in a group of villages with a total population of about 1,000. Of these women, two were Kabre. The Konkomba sometimes, as they put it, 'buy' wives from the Kabre. Such women are even more alone than other Konkomba brides for they do not speak a Gurma language. In all four cases the women ran away—possibly to their fathers' homes or possibly to the south. On the other hand, some women have stayed on in their husbands' villages after being accused and have lived down an accusation made when they were young. One such woman died in 1951 and was buried with the full rites of an elder. A final example shows that a woman can be accused of killing her sister. An elderly woman had gone to visit her married daughter, and on her way home called at her natal village and died there. Her Second Burial with the rites of divining the cause of death had not been performed when I left, but her husband's clansmen were accusing her younger sister of killing her with *ndabin*. *Ndabin*, as I have said, is a medicine that is dangerous: it is commonly a protective one, yet, should it be misused, it may turn upon its maker. It is significant that the accusation of the younger sister does not yet say that she used sorcerer's medicine, but only *ndabin*. The dead woman was known to have gone in search of medicine for her disease, so that this accusation was more than usually vague and tentative.

All other recent instances in which persons have been directly accused of being sorcerers are similar to those already given. From the accusations recorded it is clear that close relatives, even siblings, spouses, clansmen and clanswomen may be accused of seeking to kill one another. Accusations against women are usually made by men of their husbands' clans. I have never heard of a woman accusing one of her husband's clansmen, but it is not said to be impossible. In Konkomba thought anyone can be a sorcerer and a sorcerer may kill anyone. On the other hand, whereas women are openly threatened with death when they are suspect, kinsmen do not openly accuse one another immediately. They wait for a favourable occasion when feeling is running against the man they suspect. Again, women so threatened may make off at once to be safe. It is probably rare for a man to be driven out of his clan and district, though this does happen. Accusations by men of a clan against women married into it can be seen as an expression of hostility between the in-group of the agnatic clan towards the out-group of the wives. This view is supported by

e evidence of what happened to sorcerers in the past. Before the
rival of the Germans in Togoland all deaths were first investigated
1 the day of death and not only at the Second Burial rites, and the
rcerer was killed on the spot. The investigation was not carried out
y a diviner. In those days the body was tied to a pole and was
rried round the hamlet. A similar custom was practised by the
shanti.[1]

Sorcerers are known by, and only by, certain persons. First, one
rcerer 'knows', that is can see, another; secondly, a dead person
1ows the living sorcerer who killed him, and, finally, a diviner can
int out the sorcerer who has caused, or is seeking to cause, a death.
he diviner's powers are stronger after a death has occurred, because
that case his knowledge comes from the dead person. When the
ad body was carried round the hamlet, it had the opportunity to
int out the sorcerer responsible for the death. Where the corpse
cked a compound wall, there the sorcerer lived. The bearers then
tered the compound and again the corpse would kick the wall of a
om. It is impossible now to know exactly how it was done. Many
ving elders saw this rite when they were boys, and some have seen as
any as three sorcerers discovered and killed. Such killings were not
ibject to retaliation and did not lead to feud. In every recorded
stance the sorcerer so killed was a woman who had married into the
an carrying out the rite. While this fact can probably be taken as an
emplification of hostility between the in-group and the out-group,
might also be argued that it is a result facilitated by the structure of
Konkomba compound. The compound consists of a ring of round
uses. There is a large entry room which is also a byre; behind it a
imber of rooms are arranged in a rough circle connected by walls
enclose the compound. Each wife has a sleeping room and a
tchen. The compound owner has no room other than the large entry
om. Nor are there any other rooms in the compound, unless the
ad of the house has grown sons who may have a 'Young Men's
om'. It is only in the compound of a lineage elder that a 'Young
en's room' is invariably found. When once a house has been selected
 the corpse, it was almost inevitable that it would be one of the
ves who would be exposed as a sorcerer and killed. Nevertheless it
said that, if the 'Young Men's room' were indicated by the corpse,
en the names of the occupants would be called over until the corpse
ain kicked the wall in response to a particular name.

There are no other forms of direct accusation of sorcerers known

[1] R. S. Rattray, *Religion and Art in Ashanti*, Oxford, 1927, pp. 167–70.

K.N.G.–R

to me. The most frequently occurring accusation is the indirect or made by diviners during Second Burial rites. My records of diviner findings at these rites show that the Konkomba conception of th cause of death varies with the age of the dead person. Though th Konkomba say that anyone may be attacked by a sorcerer, no instanc is known to me in which a diviner has found that a child died by th action of a sorcerer, though there is a wide range of causes of deatl among children, most of which are ritual omissions on the part c their parents. Adults may die as the result of the action of sorcere: and, furthermore, may die because they are themselves sorcerer The man mentioned earlier, whose brother accused him of sorcer was believed to have been killed by the ancestors or by God, since sorcerer is not permitted to continue his evil career indefinitel Elders, on the other hand, invariably die as the result of attacks b sorcerers but are never themselves sorcerers, since the ancestors d not permit a sorcerer to attain to the dignity of elderhood.[1]

Though the deaths of elders are invariably ascribed to the actio of sorcerers, the diviners seldom make direct accusations again: individuals. Only once have I heard a diviner name the sorcerer. I this case the accused man was already believed by his kinsmen to b a sorcerer and was spoken of as such. He was a surly fellow who wa also accused of sodomy.[2] During the divination he sat, chin in han apparently unperturbed by the course it was taking. Nor did he, a others did during the long process, put questions to the diviner de signed to clear himself of the accusation. In most other instances s far recorded, only vague accusations were made, or distant person who were safe from any kind of retaliation were accused.

I have so far described the techniques employed in sorcery an have given examples of sorcery. These examples included (1) th case of a man who believed himself to be attacked; (2) the case of youth who was warned by a diviner that he was being attacked

[1] An elder in this sense is defined as a man (or woman) who has a marrie daughter or, if not the parent of a daughter, has a son of such an age that, ha he been a girl, he would have been married.

[2] It is not easy to say whether or not there is a constant association in Konkoml thought between sodomy and the male sorcerer. Sodomites are supposed to cree into the rooms of sleeping youths at night. Sorcerers also are believed to creep int rooms at night. Evans-Pritchard (op. cit., p. 56) pointed out that lesbianism an witchcraft are associated in Azande thought, but I have never heard of lesbia practices among Konkomba women. While I have no certain knowledge that mal indulge in homosexuality, references to it are not uncommon. M. Wilson (Go Company, London, 1951, pp. 88, 196) has pointed out that homosexuality and witcl craft are associated in Nyakyusa thought.

(3) the open accusation of a suspected woman and the covert accusation of her supposed instructor in sorcery; (4) the covert accusation of a suspected woman; and (5) the open accusation of a suspected man. In all, I discovered sixteen open and covert accusations of suspected sorcerers during the fifteen months between October 1950 and December 1951. All such accusations took place in a group of villages with a total population of about 1,000. These figures do not include the vague accusations against unnamed or distant persons. An examination of the accusations shows that, with two exceptions, the accusations are made by the unmarried men against the younger married men, that is, against men who in Konkomba society are between the ages of forty and fifty years, or against young and usually childless married women. No instance is known to me in which a woman accused someone of sorcery.

The Konkomba say that anyone may be a sorcerer and that anyone may be accused of sorcery. In fact, nearly all direct accusations, either overt or covert, take place within the territorial unit that is a district, and they are either accusations against a man in middle life by a junior clansfellow or against a young wife of the lineage by an unmarried man of the lineage.[1] In other words, accusations of sorcery take place within the major unit of the Konkomba social structure. Within this unit, open aggression, conflict, and even loud-voiced quarrelling are prohibited by rigorous ritual sanctions. Fortes (op. cit., pp. 35, 131), speaking of the Tallensi, a people very similar to the Konkomba, pointed out that among them witchcraft is linked with uterine kinship and may be transmitted by uterine descent. This fact, he points out, dissociates witchcraft from agnatic descent and disperses it along the wider ranging lines of uterine kinship. Such a dissociation protects the agnatic lineage from the disruption consequent upon accusation of witchcraft. The Konkomba lineage is not so protected: the possibility of accusing an agnatic kinsman of learning his sorcery from his father exposes that lineage to disruption. The Tallensi polygynous family, on the other hand, can be seriously disrupted by accusations of witchcraft among co-wives. Though tensions between Konkomba co-wives can be very strong, no case is known to me in which a wife accused her co-wife of sorcery.

Konkomba sorcery may be taught by a father to his son or by a mother to her daughter. Instances of both these modes of instruction are known. But other examples show that a sorcerer may learn from

[1] It is an axiom of Konkomba marriage that a 'woman does not marry one man' but a lineage.

K.N.G.–R*

a person who stands in no kinship relation to him or her. The Kon-komba say that not only does one sorcerer 'see' (recognize) another but that a sorcerer can 'see' a potential, commonly a youthful, sorcerer, one who has not yet 'got the medicine'. Moreover, the potential but as yet uninstructed sorcerer can see 'one who has the medicine', and so may ask that person for it. In all known cases, males have instructed males and females have instructed females, and the instructor is always senior to the pupil. There are but the slightest signs in Konkomba thought of a concept of a sorcerers' association. There is no sign at all of an association or corporation of witch-finders such as Nadel found among the Nupe and Field among the Gã.[1] Even Konkomba diviners do not form a corporate body but are a category of ritual persons, each one of whom is 'sent into the world' individually by a dead diviner of the same lineage. Every sorcerer learns from a senior sorcerer by being given sorcerer's medicine. While this medicine is fatal to the ordinary person, the sorcerer east it not merely with impunity but in order to gain power as a sorcerer, While there are a number of categories of ritual persons—diviners. persons 'sent into the world' by the Earth or by a shrine—it does not seem that sorcerers form such a category. There is no suggestion that a sorcerer is 'sent into the world' by a dead sorcerer of his own or any other lineage.

On the other hand, there is no idea among the Konkomba of the unwitting sorcerer or of one who is so because of an inherited physical condition.[2] Sorcery is a technique to be acquired, and the sorcerer kills with full knowledge of his evil intentions. (I return to this point below.) Nor does the sorcerer work in concert with other sorcerers, though it is sometimes suggested that they employ transvection to hold sorcerers' meetings. No one is at all clear as to the purpose of these meetings: there appear to be no sabbath, no feasting, and no rites at them. Nor are they used as occasions for the instruction of novices. No qualifications, such as the murder of a sibling as among the Navaho, are required of a would-be sorcerer. The assembly, such as it is, seems to be no more than a gathering together of sorcerers before each one flies off alone in search of his intended victim. There is thus no suggestion of co-operation between sorcerers. The accusa-tions made by men against the young women married into their lineage can be regarded as an expression of hostility between the in-

---

[1] S. F. Nadel, 'Witchcraft and Anti-witchcraft in Nupe Society'. *Africa*, viii, 1935. M. J. Field, *Religion and Medicine of the Gã People*, London, 1937.
[2] Cf. Field (op. cit., p. 154) who speaks, however, of witches, not of sorcerers.

group and the out-group. The accusations by young men against their seniors can be regarded as an expression of hostility towards men who exercise some authority, are possibly wealthy in cattle, and who have a number of wives but who, at the same time, are not yet senior enough to enjoy the privileges and ritual protection of elderhood.

Motives for their murders are in turn ascribed to sorcerers. I have already pointed out that the death of any elder is attributed to sorcery. In this gerontocratic society the lineage elders control most of the wealth in land, cattle, or money. The sorcerers, therefore, are said to be jealous of the wealth and power of men who are their seniors. When a younger brother is accused of killing his elder brother by sorcery, it is said that this has been done in order that the younger brother should inherit from the elder; and similarly when a woman is accused of killing her elder sister, and a wife of killing her senior co-wife. Conversely, it is dangerous for a man to succeed to a large number of cattle or of wives at an early age, since he would then be in danger of being accused of getting them by sorcery. These are the motives most clearly ascribed to sorcerers; but specific motives are not essential to a sorcerer, because, as conceived by the Konkomba, he is evil and needs no other motive than his desire to destroy.

In these days a sorcerer is no longer killed. Women, it is true, commonly run away when accused in order to be safe. Men, when first accused, do not abandon their native clans; but, under the pressure of repeated accusations, they either move their houses to a separate part of their natal districts or go to live in a new place. The strongest penal sanction on an accused sorcerer is that of ostracism. Clansmen do not assist a suspected sorcerer in his farm work, nor do they speak to him in daily intercourse. A stronger sanction still is a ritual one: an unrelenting sorcerer will be removed by God or the ancestors. On the other hand, the Konkomba have no concept of ghostly vengeance, nor of vengeance by socially approved magic against the sorcerer. The ordinary homicide has the ritual symbol of his lineage as a protection against the ghost of the man he killed. For three nights the homicide sleeps with this symbol and a medicine horn beside him, lest the ghost appear. The sorcerer is protected by his medicine, which is at once the source of his power and a protection against ghostly vengeance. When a sorcerer dies, however, his medicine dies with him and he is buried with no more than the full rites to which his seniority entitles him.[1] Yet, during his Second Burial rites, a ritual impediment

[1] The Tallensi also give a witch an ordinary burial (Fortes, op. cit., p. 34).

to the departure of his spirit may appear, an impediment which can be removed only by sacrifice. This ritual impediment is discovered by the diviner during the rites, and, on one occasion, it was due to the refusal of the ancestors to accept the spirit of the dead sorcerer without special sacrifice. Such an impediment does not always appear, however, and the dead sorcerer may be buried and mourned almost as though his life had been exemplary. In this Konkomba practice contrasts strongly with that of the Ewe of Hohoe, among whom a sorcerer's body is dragged to the grave in ragged clothing and is beaten with sticks before interment. The Ewe believe that sorcerers live apart from ordinary people in the afterworld, and that, were the spirit to arrive there unbeaten, it would be accepted neither by the spirits of ordinary people nor by those of sorcerers. (This information was given to me by students at the University College of Ghana.)

The sorcerer, as I have said, is not an unwitting practitioner; he is not a sufferer from an inherited condition; he is not a person sent specially into the world by a dead sorcerer. Whence, then, comes his sorcery? He is always an individul working alone. He is one who chooses to make a deliberate approach to someone versed in sorcery to learn a technique. He is one who has asked a senior sorcerer to give him the medicine and by an act of will has eaten it in order to gain the mystical knowlege of sorcery.[1] The sorcerer can, if he will, cease to be a sorcerer. Indeed, to avoid the anger of God he must make that decision; and the problem of sorcery is therefore a moral one. Here I am concerned only with the general pattern of sorcery. On another occasion I will try to break up that pattern into smaller units. At present it can be said that the general pattern of accusations of sorcery against men of some position in Konkomba society suggests that the sorcerer is conceived as one who is rich in property or in women, or is of some status, and has used sorcery to acquire these things.

In this poor society, set in a harsh environment and with a low productive technology, there is little differentiation in wealth, and what accumulations exist are in the hands of the lineage elders, who are protected from the jealousy of their juniors by strong ritual sanctions. No means lie open to an ambitious man to achieve economic, ritual, or political power by his own efforts. The lineage elders achieve their status by simple seniority, and in them is vested supreme economic, ritual, and political power. Some ritual power,

[1] Cf. Fortes (op. cit., p. 35), who says that Tallensi mothers may give their children witches' medicine to eat in infancy.

occasionally great, is vested in diviners, in persons 'sent by the Earth', in persons 'sent by' particular shrines, in persons 'sent by' dead ancestors, and in those who now 'hold spirits', that is, who control and use spirits for good, socially approved purposes. All these statuses are conferred by the chances of birth and by other accidents of life. None can be achieved by personal effort. The role of assistant diviner is singular in that it does offer an individual some increase in his status. But, as conceived by the Konkomba, the role is not one of great importance, nor does it in fact lead to much ritual power, and, since even diviners exercise no political power, it is clear that assistant diviners cannot do so either.

The general pattern of accusations against women differs from that of accusations against men. Though women are 'sent by' dead diviners, 'the Earth' etc., the exigencies of their lives prevent them from exercising the roles proper to their ritual status. A woman 'sent by the Earth', for example, marries into a clan where she had no special ritual relation to the Earth; her status holds only in her natal district. She marries into a strange place where she is young, lonely, and of little consequence. Only with the slow passage of time and the birth of her children can she acquire the high privileged status of a cherished lineage mother. Young women accused of sorcery thus belong to a category which the Konkomba recognize as unhappy and dissatisfied. They are persons who are discontented in their personal lives and resentful of their place in society. They are often, then, accused of expressing this resentment by killing, or seeking to kill, members of the clan which is the context of their discontent.

I have suggested in the previous chapter that the Konkomba diviner is cast in the role of a stabilizing agent. He helps to reassure, to preserve stability, to assist continuity in life. As against him the solitary sorcerer is cast in a Faustian role. He is one who seeks to break out of the closed circle of traditional morality. He tries, by his own effort, to achieve the satisfactions of wealth and power.

BIBLIOGRAPHY OF THE KONKOMBA

(excluding publications by David Tait)

Prepared with the help of R. Cornevin and J.-C. Froelich

(a) Publications devoted exclusively to the Konkomba

Cardinall, A. W. (Sir Alan), 1918, 'Some Random Notes on the Customs of the Konkomba', *Journal of the African Society*, 18, 69.

Cornevin, R., 1954, 'L'Enterrement d'un chef Konkomba', *Africa*, 24, 3.
1954, 'Histoire des populations Konkomba', *Encyclopédie Mensuelle d'Outre Mer*, No. 42.

Froelich, J.-C., 1949, 'Les Konkomba du Nord-Togo', *Bull. I.F.A.N.*, II, and 4.
1954, *La Tribu Konkomba du Nord Togo*, Mémoire de l'Institut français d'Afrique noire, No. 37, Dakar.
1958, 'Le Kinan des Konkomba du Nord-Togo', *Notes Afr. I.F.A.N.*, 80, 103–4.

Labadie, Lieut., 1929, 'Les Konkomba', *Togo-Cameroun*.

(b) Publications referring to the Konkomba

Cardinall, A. W. (Sir Alan), 1921, *The Natives of the Northern Territories of the Gold Coast*, London.
1927, *In Ashanti and Beyond*, Philadelphia.

Cornevin, R., 1959, *Histoire du Togo*, Paris.

Klose, H., 1899, *Togo unter deutscher Flagge*, Berlin.

Manoukian, M., 1952, *Tribes of the Northern Territories of the Gold Coast*, London.

Martonne, E. de, 1930, 'Résultats scientifiques de la Mission de délimitation du Togo, Mission Bauche 1927–9', *La Géographie*, Paris.

Metzger, O. F., 1941, *Unsere alte Kolonie Togo*, Neudamm.

Passarge, S., 1914, *Togo (Das deutsche Kolonialreich*, vol. ii, pt. i), Leipzig and Vienna.

Rattray, R. S., 1932, *Tribes of the Ashanti Hinterland*, Oxford.

Tamakloe, E. F., 1931, *A Brief History of the Dagbamba People*, Accra.

Trierenberg, G., 1914, *Togo: Die Erschliessung des Landes*, Berlin.

Zech, Graf von, 1904, 'Land und Leute an der Nordwest Grenze von Togo', *Mitt. deutsch. Schutzgeb.* p. 107, trans. by Rev. Father Neth, *Études Dahoméennes*, 2, 1949.

(c) Unpublished MSS

Anon., 1891, 'Report of the German Mission to the Kulukpène R.', Archives du Cercle de Sokadé, Togo.

Anderson, 1943(?), 'A Report on the Konkombas', Govt. Archives, Accra.

Blair, H. A., 1938(?), 'Some Tribes of the Konkombas', Govt. Archives, Accra; Administrative Reports, Yendi, Ghana.

Cardinall, A. W. (Sir Alan), Administrative Reports, Yendi, Ghana.

Coëz, Lieut., 1919, 'Monographie, Archives du Cercle de Mango', Togo.

Fagalde, Lieut., 1943, 'Monographie', Mission Catholique de Bassari, Togo.

Labadie, Lieut., 1923, *Rapport sur la tournée de police Ier fev. au 2 mars*, 1923, *en pays Konkomba*. dated 1 April, 1923, Mango. Archives du Cercle de Mango, Togo.

Massu, Lieut., 1936, *Rapport sur l'emploi du détachement de milice en pays Konkomba, avril 1935–juillet*, 1936, Bassari, Togo.

Puifouilloux, Captain, 1922, 'Monographie', Archives du Cercle de Mango, Togo.

In addition there are the field notes of David Tait deposited at University College, Accra, Ghana.

A BIBLIOGRAPHY OF THE WRITINGS OF DAVID TAIT

Prepared by J. D. Fage

Formerly Professor of History, University College of Ghana

1. Review of M. Leiris: *La Langue secrète des Dogons de Sanga*. Man, 50, 136, July 1950.
2. 'An Analytical Commentary on the Social Structure of the Dogon', Africa, 20, 3, July 1950, pp. 175–99.
3. Review of *Gold Coast Census of Population*. Man, 51, 220, September 1951.
4. Review of K. A. Busia: *Social Survey of Sekondi-Takoradi*. Man, 51, 291, December 1951.
5. 'The Role of the Diviner in Konkomba Society', Man, 52, 249, November 1952.
6. Review of R. J. H. Pogucki: *Land Tenure in native customary law* . . . Africa, 22, 4, December 1952, pp. 380–2.
7. Review of E. L. R. Meyerowitz: *Akan traditions of origin*. Man, 53, 10, January 1953.
8. 'On the Growth of some Konkomba Markets', *Proceedings of the Annual Conference of the West African Institute of Social and Economic Research*, Sociology Section, March 1953, pp. 38–50.

9. 'The Political System of Konkomba', *Africa*, 23, 3, July 1953, pp. 213–23.

10. 'Spirits of the Bush; a note on personal religion among the Konkomba', *Universitas*, I, 1, December 1953.

11. 'Konkomba Nominal Classes' (with a phonetic commentary by P. D. Strevens), *Africa*, 24, 2, April 1954, pp. 130–48.

12. 'Konkomba Friendship Relations', *African Studies*, 13, 2, 1954, pp. 77–84.

13. 'Konkomba Sorcery', *Journal of the Royal Anthropological Institute*, 84, 1–2, 1954, pp. 66–74.

14. 'Standards of Living; a comment' (with Walter Birmingham), *Universitas*, I, 3 and 4, June and December 1954.

15. 'The Place of Libation in Konkomba Ritual', *Bull. I.F.A.N.*, B, 17, 1–2, January–April 1955, pp. 168–72.

16. 'Language and Social Symbiosis among the Dogon of Sanga', *Bull. I.F.A.N.*, B, 17, 3–4, July–October 1955, pp. 525–7.

17. 'History and Social Organization', *Transactions of the Gold Coast and Togoland Historical Society*, I, 5, 1955, pp. 193–210.

18. 'Konkomba *osuo* [sorcerer]', *Man*, 55, 162, October 1955, pp. 152–3.

19. Review of J. C. Froelich: *La Tribu Konkomba du Nord Togo*. *Africa*, 25, 4, October 1955, pp. 441–2.

20. Article: 'Konkomba', *Encyclopaedia Britannica*, 1955.

21. Review of V. Paques, *Les Bambara*, J. R. Rouch, *Les Songhay*, M. de Lestrange, *Les Coniagui et les Bassari*. *Man*, 56, 83, June 1956.

22. 'The Family, Household, and Minor Lineage of the Konkomba' (two parts), *Africa*, 26, 3 and 4, July and October 1956, pp. 219–49 and 332–42.

23. 'Food in the Northern Territories', *Universitas*, II, 3, June 1956.

24. Introduction (with John Middleton) to *Tribes without Rulers: Studies in African Segmentary Systems* (ed. Middleton & Tait), Routledge and Kegan Paul, London, 1958, pp. 1–31.

25. 'The Territorial Pattern and Lineage System of Konkomba', in *Tribes without Rulers*, 1958, pp. 167–202.

26. *The Konkomba of Northern Ghana* (ed. Jack Goody), O.U.P. for International African Institute and University College of Ghana, London, 1961.

INDEX

Adultery, 66, 86, 96, 144, 147, 148
Affines, 24, 84, 90, 102, 108, 111–12, 133–5, 138, 144, 211, 214, 216–20
Age-sets, 81, 86ff, 124, 170, 173–80, 185–94, 208, 216
Akan, 4, 232
Amity, 24, 210ff, 228
Ancestors, 14, 15, 56, 71, 72ff, 84, 115–16, 120–2, 124–5, 138, 140, 157, 200–1, 208–9, 213, 222, 223, 224–5, 226–31, 240, 243–5
Animals, dangerous, 82
Ashanti, 9, 26, 232, 239
Authority, 14, 47, 50, 61–71, 75, 88, 91, 141, 145–8, 158, 198–9, 207–8, 231
Avoidance, 203–4, 208
Azande, 232

Basare, 2, 4, 7, 9, 10, 22, 23, 28, 53, 54, 156–7, 166
Beard, 203
Beer, 21, 26, 29, 50, 64, 85–86, 93, 131, 136, 138, 140, 147, 197, 215, 227, 228, 230–31, 233
Betrothal, 2, 84, 93–97, 105, 108–10, 114, 142, 162, 170, 173, 176, 178–9, 184, 202
Bimbila, 30
Blacksmiths, 25, 27
Bride, 84–85, 99, 162, 182–3
Bride price, 31, 94–95, 97–98, 168; bride corn, 40, 84, 94–95, 97, 105, 162, 203; bride service, 40, 81, 93–5, 97, 105, 162, 166n, 211, 216
British Administration, 9, 10, 11, 25, 66
Burial rites, 38, 39–41, 42, 55, 81, 128, 130–1, 132, 136ff, 203, 234, 238, 239; dancing at, 89–90, 137, 139; male elder, 82, 90, 137–8; second burial (final funeral), 14, 15, 16, 17, 73, 74, 82, 98, 139, 215, 225, 234, 236, 237, 240, 244; sorcerer, 225, 243; women, 138–9
Bush farms, 14, 30, 48–49, 123–4, 197

Calabash of the dead, 139
Carrying the corpse, 239
Cattle, 14–15, 25, 29, 67, 142, 199, 243
Clan, 18, 21–23, 24, 27, 29–30, 32–35, 38–42, 45–47, 48, 60, 63, 69–73, 84–85, 89–92, 113, 119–21, 123–6, 127ff, 137, 140, 143, 144, 145, 151–5, 156–9, 206, 211, 213–21; compound, 35, 40–41, 45, 49, 69, 72;

contrapuntal, 35–36, 39, 41–45, 49, 52, 58, 60, 69, 72, 76–78, 104, 118–20, 123, 126, 141, 228; unitary, 35, 40–41, 45, 59, 72 (for names, see separate index).
Clan 'daughters', 137, 138
Clan 'sons', 139
Compound, 2, 23, 34, 160–1, 163–4, 195, 199–200 (see also household)
Compound clan (district), 35, 40–41, 45, 49, 69, 72
Compound farms, 14, 30, 48–49, 73, 123, 197
Compound head, 29, 30, 50, 66, 72–73, 77, 183–4, 195, 197–200
Contrapuntal clan (district), 35–36, 39, 41–45, 49, 52, 58, 60, 69, 72, 76–78, 118–20, 123, 126, 141, 228
Co-wives, 66, 98, 182–3, 205, 207, 212, 214–15, 233, 241, 243
Cowries, 29, 68, 95, 221
Crafts, 25, 27, 28
Crops, 14, 15–17, 25, 54, 67, 197–8, 222, 228–30; cash, 197

Dagomba, 1, 4, 6–12, 17, 20, 23, 25–28, 39, 43, 53, 96, 124, 132, 148, 154, 157, 163, 164, 179, 203–4, 223; cavalry, 8, 9, 26–27; elder chiefdoms, 6–7; gates, 6–7; infantry, 8, 10–11; influence, 66; invasions, 4, 8–10, 22, 47; royal chiefdoms, 6–7; and structural distance, 22, 23
Daughters, 138, 189, 192–3, 195, 201, 203, 216, 241; 'daughters', 137–8, 190, 194, 203
Death, cause of, 59, 73, 82, 97, 222, 230, 239–40
District, 32–48, 59–60, 63, 65, 69–71, 73, 120, 123–6, 241 (for names, see separate index)
District shrines, 35, 36, 39, 41–43
Divination, 73, 221–3, 235–7, 239–40, 245
Diviners, 39, 42, 43, 50, 57, 59, 68, 98, 124, 200, 205–6, 221–3, 224, 225, 231, 235–6, 237, 239–40, 242, 244–5
Divorce, 180–1
Dogon, 200
Dreams, 82, 223–4
Drum chants, 4, 9
Drumming, 90, 137
Dry season, 13–14, 15, 67, 91
Dzo, 215–18

Earth, 36, 62–63, 71, 81, 124, 128, 140–
    1, 145, 146, 157, 200–1, 222; sacrifice
    to, 21, 35, 55, 59, 73, 128, 140–1,
    228–30
Earth shrine, 35n, 35–36, 39, 40, 41, 42,
    43, 44, 45, 46, 59, 71, 73, 79–80, 84,
    120, 140, 145, 147, 228–31
Ecological space, 18, 21, 23, 24, 74, 159
Ecological time, 17–18, 21, 23, 24
Ecology, 13ff, 156
Elder, The, 35–36, 47, 48, 49, 50, 53,
    62–63, 74, 75, 77, 82–83, 84, 88,
    91, 135, 137, 143, 146–7, 153, 162,
    191, 198–9, 200–1, 223, 228, 230, 244;
    authority of, 62, 63, 65–67, 70, 75, 141
Elders, 11, 22, 29, 30, 47, 61, 73,
    90, 131, 140, 184, 222, 223, 240;
    authority of, 14, 145–6; burial, 90,
    137–8; compound of, 164
Elder's people, 36, 41, 42, 44, 49, 50, 52,
    54, 77, 119, 120
Elopement, 70, 97, 117, 162, 167–8, 218
Ewe, 204, 244
Exchange marriages, 94, 95–96, 103,
    112–13, 162, 202, 216
Exogamy, 36, 40, 42, 43, 44, 45, 69, 70,
    104, 117, 119, 120, 202–3, 237
Extended house, 77–78, 100ff, 114–15,
    121–2, 125, 133, 161, 166n, 169, 184–
    5, 188–91, 202, 208

Facial marks, 32, 87, 151
Family, 160–2, 169, 184, 189, 195, 207–
    8; duogynous, 163, 166, 184; elemen-
    tary, 160–1, 184, 189, 195, 207; ex-
    panded, 160, 184, 208; extended,
    160–2, 184, 208; polygynous, 160–1,
    184, 189, 195, 200, 207, 241
Farm cycle, 15–17, 21, 48
Farming, 13–17, 21, 25, 33, 48, 49,
    123–4, 137, 156, 197, 199, 208, 222,
    229n
Farms, bush, 14, 30, 48–49, 123, 197
Farms, compound, 14, 17, 30, 48–49, 73,
    123, 197
Farms, women's, 25
Father-daughter, 138
Father-in-law, 95–96, 138, 140
Father's child, 49, 153, 164, 201, 202,
    211–13, 217–20
Father-son 31, 59, 115, 203–4, 207, 241
Ferry, 17, 26, 28, 29, 132
Feud, 24, 32, 43, 47, 60, 63, 66, 67,
    70–71, 81, 89–90, 96, 132, 136, 144–9,
    151, 153, 159, 162, 211, 217–18, 220,
    239
Fiancé, 172–3, 215
Fiancée, 162–3, 172–80, 202
Fighting, 27, 53, 62, 63, 64, 65, 66, 70–
    71, 81, 82–83, 85, 89, 141–50, 152–3,
    159, 204, 217–18, 220

Fire festival, 59
First fruit rites, 56, 58–60, 83, 200
Fishing, 14, 15, 16, 17, 28, 36, 40, 42,
    44, 60, 90, 142–4, 159, 198
Fission, xv, 30, 40–41, 50, 77, 116–21,
    123–6, 155, 156, 173, 201, 208, 212–
    13; extra-district, 77, 88, 121, 123–5,
    131, 154–5, 156, 222; intra-district,
    77, 78, 123, 125–6, 156
Floods, 13–14, 34, 130, 157, 234
Food tabus, 14, 52, 203
Friendship, 210ff, 228; voluntary, 210–
    11, 215–18; ascribed, 210–14
Fulani, 14
Fusion, 23, 116, 121–3, 125, 153–4

Ga, 242
Germans, 4, 8, 196n
Ghost, 82, 200, 223, 225, 233
God, 62, 63, 226, 231, 240, 243
Gonja, 8, 10, 157
Granaries, 17, 48, 49, 203
Grave, 124, 137–9, 226

Hamlet, 13, 14, 23, 32, 34–38, 40–45, 46,
    50, 51, 67, 73, 75, 83, 123, 139 (for
    names, see separate index)
Harmattan, 13, 15
Homicide, 63–64, 82–83, 89, 132, 145–6,
    149, 211, 243
Household, 2, 50, 100, 160ff, esp. 165,
    183ff, 195ff, 198–9, 201–3, 204–7,
    207–9 (see also compound)
Household head, 48, 160, 183–4, 195,
    197–8, 200; authority of, 198–9
Hunting, 14, 15, 16, 33, 51–53, 60, 74,
    81, 82–3, 142–3, 159, 198, 222
Husband-wife, 66, 84, 170, 180ff,
    238; difference in ages of, 170–3,
    181–2, 216

Incest, 65, 107–8, 117, 201, 208, 212,
    218
Inheritance, 14, 48–50, 197–8, 204,
    207, 243; of land, 49–50, 77; of
    widows, 40, 45, 77, 81, 86, 97, 98,
    117, 122, 167–8, 169–70, 173–8, 180–2,
    195, 196n, 202–3, 204, 214
Instruction, 75, 199, 204, 237, 241

Joking relationships, 65, 86, 207, 210,
    213–14
Juan, 212, 214
Jural activities, 60ff, 141ff, 158

Kabre, 2, 4, 10, 22, 23, 28, 53, 97–98,
    163, 176, 178, 206, 238
Kakā, 18, 26, 27, 28, 44, 51, 53–54, 80
Kinship: agnatic, 23, 33, 34–35, 41, 47,
    60, 64, 67, 72ff, 85, 89, 100–3, 105–10,
    112–13, 114ff, 133, 136, 138–9,

149–50, 157–8, 183, 201, 204, 207, 211, 215, 217, 219–20, 236, 238, 241; cognatic, 217; matrilateral, 24, 74, 90, 101–5, 110–13, 123, 132, 133–6, 137–8, 148–50, 159, 211–12, 215–16; uterine, 104, 106–10, 204, 207, 212, 217–20, 241

Kinship terminology, 2, 74, 77, 84, 86, 133–5, 163, 179, 213–14

Kith, 131–3, 138, 140–1, 143–5, 147–9, 151, 154, 159, 211, 217, 228, 229n

Kola nut, 233

Komba, 166

Krachi, 8, 30–31, 35, 38, 43, 45, 49, 124, 152, 157, 229

Kulpene valley, 38, 39, 43, 45, 49, 124, 132, 157

Kumasi, 26, 28

Land rights, 34, 42, 44, 48–50, 122, 142–3, 197

Language, 2, 98, 151; Akan, 2; Gurma, 2, 238; Kabre, 2, 98; Konkomba, 2, 98, 151; Mossi, 2; Tem, 2

Law, 6ff, 141ff

Levirate (absence of), 98

Libation, 227–31

Lineage, 21–24, 40, 47, 69–70, 72ff, 113, 114ff, 158; fission, xv, 30, 40–41, 50, 88, 116–21, 123–6, 155, 156, 173, 201, 208, 212–13, 222; fusion, 116, 121–3, 125, 153–4; segmentation, xv, 40, 84, 88–89, 115–16, 120–1, 123, 125–6, 157–8, 209

Livestock, 15, 25, 27, 67

Love affairs, 96–97, 107–8, 110, 117, 132, 142, 145, 152–3, 159, 162, 181, 184, 201, 215–16, 218

Lover, 49, 66, 85, 96–7, 99, 107–8, 110, 119, 144, 147, 148, 163, 197, 204, 215–18

LoWiili, 161n

Major lineage, 22–23, 32, 35, 40, 42, 45–46, 49, 51, 59–60, 72–80, 82–83, 84–85, 86, 88–89, 97, 102–4, 107, 110–12, 116–19, 120–5, 127, 135–6, 137–8, 140, 143, 153, 158, 162, 169, 198, 199–202, 206, 236

Mamprusi, 2, 4, 156

Mantotib, 38, 41, 42, 90, 99, 127–32, 137–8, 140–1, 143, 148–9, 151, 154, 159, 211, 215, 217, 228; of women, 128, 131, 215

Market cycles, 18–21, 53

Market elder, 54–55, 64, 68

Market prices, 20–21, 26–28, 98

Market produce, 25–27

Market shrine, 54, 80, 147

Market space, 18–21, 24, 53

Market tax, 25, 54

Market time, 17–21, 24

Markets, 11, 18–21, 25–30, 34, 52, 53ff, 73, 137, 147; Basare, 28; Bawku, 29; Galimata, 26, 28, 53; Gushiego, 26; Saambwer, 26, 28; Saboba, 18, 26, 27, 28, 44, 51, 53–54, 80; Tsheriponi, 26; Yendi, 9, 18–21, 26–28, 53

Marriage, 84, 93ff, 119, 161–3, 170ff, 202–3, 206, 208, 213, 214, 218; age of, 29, 95, 96, 108–10, 114, 122, 161, 170, 182, 195, 216; arranging of, 78, 97, 98, 114, 216; exchange, 94, 95–96, 103, 104, 112–13, 162, 202, 216; stability of, 180–3

Marriage by purchase, 97–8, 163, 167, 176, 178, 180, 206

Marriage ceremony, 81, 84–85, 162, 168

Marriage rules, 78, 84–86, 98–99, 100–13, 119, 134, 166n, 202, 213, 214

Medicine, 91, 200, 227; idabin, 235, 238; igi, 81–83, 243; kaalku, 55, 227, njog, 81–82; in sorcery, 225, 232–5, 237–8, 242–4

Migration, 30, 34, 38, 39, 43, 45, 46–47, 49, 124, 154–5, 157, 229–30; see also parent-offshoot districts, and lineage fission

Minor lineage, 50, 51, 60, 64, 72–80, 82–83, 85–86, 89, 98, 107, 110, 114–15, 117–18, 120, 122–3, 125–6, 134, 137, 139–40, 142, 153, 158, 160, 169–70, 173, 176, 184–5, 188–92, 195–203, 205–7, 207–9, 214, 218, 236

Mossi, 2, 11, 26, 132

Mother-daughter, 203–4, 241

Mother's brother, 90, 103, 133, 136, 149

Mother's child, 49, 69, 104, 134, 150, 153, 164, 201, 202, 211–13, 217–20

Mother-son, 165, 173, 175–6, 184, 204, 207

Mother's sister, 103, 105, 138, 140, 213, 219

Muslims, 11, 27, 157

Myths, 46, 47, 76

Naabo, 49, 69, 104, 134, 150, 153, 164, 201, 202, 211–13, 217–20

Nabo, 104, 105, 136, 149–50, 212–14, 217–18

Nakwoo, 215–16, 218

Nanumba, 2, 4

Nato, 212, 214–5, 217–8

Neighbouring clans (kith), 131–3, 138, 140–1, 143–5, 147–9, 151, 154, 159, 211, 217, 228, 229n

New guinea corn rites, 56–57, 59, 83

New yam rites, 58–59, 83, 200

Njog, 81–82; in sorcery, 232–5, 237–8, 242–4

Nuclear lineage, 72ff, 77–80, 85–98, 114–17, 119, 120, 122–3, 125, 136, 139, 155
Nupe, 242

Old women's house, 173
Onekpel, see Elder, The
Onibaa, 33, 35, 36, 41, 72, 73–74, 117
Orphans, 49, 50, 69, 81, 135, 163, 189, 191, 194, 196, 203
Ostracism, 62, 64–65, 91, 141, 243
Osuo, 204–7, 223, 225, 226, 232ff
Otindaa, xv, 35–36, 40, 46, 49, 51, 52, 54, 59, 63, 83, 88, 140, 228–30
Oti Plain, 1, 2, 8, 13, 25, 28, 30, 156–7
Oti River, 1, 4, 8, 11, 13–14, 17, 20, 28, 36, 124
Owner of the Earth, xv, 35–36, 40, 46, 49, 51, 52, 54, 59, 63, 83, 88, 140, 228–30
Owner of the Earth's people, 36, 41, 42, 44, 51, 52, 54, 59, 119, 120

Parent'Filial clans (districts), *see* Parent-Offshoot districts
Parent-Offshoot districts (clans), 23, 36–45 *pass.*, 53, 127, 130–2, 137–8, 140, 148–9, 154, 211, 217
Parents-in-law, 93–98, 133, 135
Peace-making rite, 32, 63, 65, 144, 147, 149, 151, 159, 211
Political relations, 22, 23, 24, 33 *pass.*, 47–71 *pass.*, 90, 125, 127, 133–6, 136–41, 158, 161, 211; and political distance, 22; and structural space, 22; units of political structure, 32–46
Polygyny, 91, 114, 160, 161, 163, 173–80, 243; rate, 166–7, 173ff, 192
Population, 1; decrease, 30, 34, 44, 46, 156–7; growth, 115, 121, 125; increase, 36, 50, 115–16, 123–6, 155–6; of clans, 73, 118, 156–7, 165; of districts, 118; of hamlets, 34, 54–5, 118; of lineages, 118, 121; of tribes, 151
Possession, 139
Pregnancy, 57, 87, 99, 162–3
Private property, 68–69
Proscribed marriages, 78, 84, 98, 99, 100–3, 119, 134, 166n
Protective medicine, 227; *idabin*, 235, 238; *igi* horn, 82–83, 91, 200, 243

Quarrels, 63–66, 141, 143–6, 148, 150, 159, 204, 205, 216–17, 241

Rain, 13, 15, 17, 228–30, 235; medicine, 81, 235
Religious (ritual) sanction, 62–63, 64, 68, 91, 145–6, 148, 201, 226, 235, 240–1, 243–4
Rest days, 21, 52

Restitution, 62
Retaliation, 62, 63, 67, 89, 97, 141–2, 144, 152–3, 162, 168, 218, 239
Rights over children, 99, 122, 163, 179, 181, 189–90, 191, 194–6
Rights over land, 34, 40, 42, 44, 48–50, 90, 122, 124, 142–3, 197
Rights over women, 105, 108, 112–13, 141–2, 179, 180–2, 198–9
Rites, 55–60, 147, 223–8, 230–1; at Earth shrine, 55, 59; at market shrine, 54; "catching the spirits", 58, 59, 60, 224–5; fire festival, 59; new guinea corn, 56–57; new yams, 58–59, 83, 200; peace making, 32, 63, 65, 144, 147, 149, 151, 159, 211; purificatory, 55–56, 57–58, 63, 64, 73, 228
Ritual, 208, 215, 240
Ritual hunts, 51–53, 81, 82
Ritual partners, 38, 41, 42, 90, 99, 127–32, 137–8, 140–1, 143, 148–9, 151, 154, 159, 211, 215, 217, 228
Ritual symbols, 81ff; *dzambuna*, 81–84, 91, 200, 243; *igi*, 81, 83, 91, 200, 243
River rights, 32, 42, 44, 143

Saambwer, 30, 152
Saboba, 30, 44–45, 152
Saboba Na, 11, 44, 66, 96
Sacrifice, 15, 21, 35, 43, 54, 55–60, 65, 73, 74, 83, 124, 138, 139, 140, 145, 200, 203, 222–3, 225, 227–31, 235, 244
Sacrificing together, 60, 65
Salaga, 30, 124, 157
Segmentation, xv, 40, 77–80, 84, 88–89, 115–16, 120–1, 123, 125–6, 157–8, 209
Senior wife, 69, 139, 163, 168, 200, 212, 216
Sexual intercourse, 52, 84, 86, 87, 96, 98, 183, 201–12, 240 and n
Shrines, 15, 35, 40, 74, 80, 81, 127, 199–200, 222, 226–7, 229–31, 245; clan district, 35–36, 39, 41–42, 46, 199–201; Earth, *see* Earth shrine; ferries and fords, 29, 199, 231; household, 2, 200–1; market, 54, 80, 147; medicine, 2, 58; parent-offshoot clans, 130
Siblings, 57, 63, 69, 105, 122, 145, 147, 194, 199, 201–2, 202, 204–5, 208, 211–13, 217–20, 234, 238, 240, 243
Sickness, 233, 236; divination and cause of, 222
Sister's son, 104, 105, 133, 136
Slaves, 9, 10
Social control, 9–11, 60ff, 141ff, 151ff, 198–9
Sodomy, 64, 240 and n
Soil, 13, 15, 30, 123–4, 229n

Son, 122, 161, 189, 192–3, 195, 197–9, 201, 203, 212, 216, 241; eldest, 137–8, 184, 203; 'sons', 125, 139, 162, 190, 194, 197
Son-in-law, 137–8, 140
Sorcerer, 204–7, 223, 225, 226, 232ff; burial of, 225, 243–4; sorcerer's medicine, 225, 232–4, 237–8, 242
Sorcery, xvi, 181, 204–8, 232ff
Sororate (absence of), 84, 105, 202
Space, ecological, 18, 21, 23, 24, 74, 159; market, 18–21, 53; structural, 21–24, 74
Spirit, 56, 57, 159, 200, 226, 244
Spirit calabash, 56–58, 137
Spirit holders, 58–59, 60, 63, 81, 84, 88, 224–5, 231, 245
Spirits of the bush, 223–5
Stability of marriage, 180–3
Step-father, 189, 191, 194–6, 203
Step-mother, 135, 196, 203
Strangers, 77, 211, 217
Structural space (distance), see space, structural

Taabo, 49, 153, 164, 201, 202, 211–13, 217–20
Tax, market, 25, 54; poll and cattle, 10
Tallensi, 35, 161, 203, 204, 212, 218–19, 232, 241, 243n
Tamale, 26, 28
Temperature, 13
Theft, 54, 62, 68–69, 199
Time, 15–17; ecological, 17–18, 21; lunar, 17; market, 17–21, 24, 53; structural 21–22, 24; week, 17–18, 21, 52, 53
Tobote (see Basare), 2
Trade goods, 25–27
Transvection, 232–3, 236, 242
Trees, 81; baobab, 54; dawa dawa, 30, 92; kapok, 30, 54
Tribal marks, 32, 87, 151
Tribe, 5, 20–24 pass., 32, 37, 63, 70–71, 132, 148, 150,151ff, 158, 211

Tshakosi, 2, 8, 53

Ungwin, 56, 57, 226
Unitary clan (district), 35, 45, 59, 72

Wage labour, 14, 17, 30–31, 95, 216
Warfare, 8, 9, 10, 12, 24, 32, 70–71, 150, 151–4, 159, 211
Wars, 4, 8, 10
Weaning, 87
Week days, 17–18, 21, 51–52, 53
Wet season, 13–14, 15, 91, 142
Widows, 98, 137, 173, 179
Widow inheritance, 40, 45, 77, 81, 86, 97, 98, 117, 122, 167–8, 169–70, 173–8, 180–2, 195, 196n, 202–3, 204, 214; age difference between widow and second husband, 171–3
Wife, 40, 50–51, 56, 63, 66–67, 77, 84, 93, 97, 138–9, 141–2, 162, 163–4, 168, 170ff, 180ff, 195n, 198, 203, 207–8, 237–9, 241, 243, 245
Wind storms, 15
Witch, xvi, 97
Witchcraft, 61, 97, 204, 222, 241
Woman's room, 69, 164, 200, 203, 212
Women, burial of, 128, 138–40, 168
Women and mantotib, 128, 131, 215
Women and sorcery, 205–7, 237–9, 241, 243, 245
Women's activities, 25, 28, 29, 51, 85, 163, 197–8, 214
Women's age-sets, 86–88
Women's farms, 25
Work parties, 50–51, 64, 81, 92, 197, 199, 243

Yendi, 1, 4, 6, 25, 54, 55, 146
Yoruba traders, 11, 26, 69
'Young men', 83, 85, 89–91, 137, 145, 147, 184
Young men's room, 83, 91, 164, 203, 239
'Young women', 89, 90

Zulu, 205

INDEX OF KONKOMBA LOCAL AND DESCENT GROUPS

Key: (c) = clan, (d) = district, (h) = hamlet, (mjl) = major lineage, (ml) = minor lineage, (sh) = sub-hamlet, (t) = tribe.

Banjuni (d), 43, 120
Begbem (t), 43, 45, 118, 151, 154
Bejikpab (t), 4
Bekujom (c), 44, 65, 68, 123, 124, 127, 128, 148, 152, 157
Bekumbwam (c), 42, 46, 54, 64, 83, 117–18, 120, 124, 128, 155, 157
Bekumbwam (mjl), 44–45, 48–49, 51, 64, 79, 83, 117–20, 128, 140, 142, 165, Genealogy II
Bekwom (t), 2, 4, 151, 154
Bemokpem (c), 146
Bemokpem (t), 33n, 43, 52, 53, 67, 99, 151–2, 153–4
Bemwatiak (c), 33, 41, 120, 159
Benafiab (t), 10, 53, 148, 151, 154
Benalog (c), 36, 40, 51, 80, 99–100, 117–18, 124, 154–5, 165
Benalog (mjl), 40, 51, 55–57, 58, 80, 83, 117–19, 124, 165, Genealogy III
Benalog (t), 154–5
Benaman (t), 2
Benangmam (c), 33, 41, 43, 46–47, 76, 80, 82, 88, 99–100, 117–20, 124, 127, 128, 140, 144, 148, 155, 165, 228–30, Genealogy I
Benangmin (t), 2
Benasom (c), 120, 128, 157
Benasom (mjl), 44–45, 51, 79, 120, 128, 165
Benjembob (t), 4
Besangma (t), 151
Betshabob (c), 146, 165
Betshabob (t), 4, 20, 33n, 36–38, 43, 44, 51, 53, 99, 146, 151–2, 154
Bewado (d), 41
Botwe (h), 43, 144
Bwagban (c), 229
Bwagban (h), 44, 51, 79
Bwakwin (d), 39, 43, 44, 83, 119
Bwakwintib (c), 46, 118–20, 128–9, 157
Bwakwintib (mjl), 118–20, 136, 142, Genealogy IV
Bwarado (h), 40, 55, 57, 58
Bwarado (ml), 56, 58, 80, 83, 118–19, 165, Genealogy III

Ditshie (sh), 40, 130
Dzakpe (h), 36

Dzangendo (ml), 42, 50, 51, 52, 59, 68, 76–77, 101, 114, 117–18, 122, 228–9, Genealogies I and V
Dzengendo (sh), 42

Fanindo (ml), 42, 49, 50, 52, 59, 76–77, 117–18, Genealogy I

Gbendza (d), 120
Gbiedo (h), 34, 44, 54
Gurdo-Dardo (ml), 48–49, 54, 79, 117–18, Genealogy II

Jabwarape (d), 45, 143
Jatshado (ml), alternative form, Natiedo, 42, 58, 117–18, Genealogy I

Kakpene (h), 44
Kandzo (d), 146
Kandzotib (c), 148
Kedzabo (d), 34, 70, 120, 127, 156
Kesabwini (d), 45
Kitiak (d), 33, 41–3, 44, 46, 50, 51, 52, 58, 75, 76, 118–19, 130
Kitiak (h), 34, 41, 43, 49, 59, 68, 75–78, 237
Kotiendo (h), 40, 51, 55, 57, 58, 59, 60
Kotiendo (ml), 40, 51, 55–57, 58, 59, 80, 83, 117–19, 136, 165, Genealogy III
Kotodo (mjl), 42, 49, 51, 59, 75, 76–78, 101, 117–19, 121, 122, 125, 165, 228, Genealogy I
Kotodo (sh), 42, 75
Kpalib (h), 44, 45
Kpaliba (d), 128–9
Kpalipa (h), 44, 45, 49, 66–67
Kpaltib (c), 47, 128–9
Kpaltib (t), 151
Kpambildo (ml), alternative forms, Kugbedo, Ngkwodo, 42, 117–18, Genealogy I
Kpatab (c), 46, 128–9
Kpatab (d), 45
Kpeo (d), 41, 83
Kpeotib (c), 120
Kugar (d), 36, 38
Kugbedo (ml), alternative forms, Kpambildo, Ngkwodo, 42, 117–18, Genealogy I

Kukwin (d), 35
Kukwintib (c), 120, 157
Kumwatiak (d), 33, 41, 53, 152
Kumwatiak (h), 41
Kuntsha (d), 38
Kuwane (h), 41

Lagea (c), 153–4
Lagea (d), 52, 156
Lefur (d), 41, 53
Lemwagbal (d), 46, 124, 130, 144
Lemwol (d), 18, 20, 52, 143

Makpadado (ml), 56, 80, 117–18, 124, 165, Genealogy III
Mwagban (c), 130–1

Najil (d), 45
Najil (h), 45
Nakpando (d), 43, 43 n, 58, 120, 130, 156
Nakpantib (c), 42–43, 43 n, 99, 128–9, 131
Nakpantib (t), 20, 43n, 45, 46, 52, 99, 118, 131, 151–5
Nalog (d), 36, 38, 41, 43
Nalog (h), 36, 38, 54–55, 119
Nalogni (c), 229
Nalogni (d), 38–40, 41, 43, 51, 55–56, 58–59, 80, 118, 130, 155
Namam (d), 43
Napin (d), 43
Natiedo (ml), alternative form, Jatshado, 42, 58, 117–18, Genealogy I
Nejil Pa (h), 45

Ngkwodo (h), 41, 42, 58, 60
Ngkwodo (ml), alternative forms, Kpambildo, Kugbedo, 42, 58, 117–18, Genealogy I
Ngmangeado (mjl), 42, 51, 52, 58, 59, 75, 76–77, 88, 117–19, 121, 165, 229, Genealogy I
Nimie (d), 41, 53
Ngangen (d), 41, 42, 43
Ntshaponi (h), 44

Saambwer (d), 34, 128, 144, 146, 156, 157
Saambwertib (c), 128–30, 144, 146, 148, 157
Saangul (d), 35, 157
Saangul (h), 34
Saangultib (c), 120, 157
Saboba (d), 18, 34, 44, 50–51, 65, 70, 118, 120, 140, 157
Sobib (d), 18, 120
Sobibtib (c), 46, 83

Tama (d), 38
Tilengbene (h), 34, 42, 43, 44, 52, 124
Tshakpu (d), 53
Tshegban (d), 18, 120
Tshegban (h), 43

Udzado (h), 34, 46
Uwenido (ml), 79, 117–18, Genealogy II

Wadzado (h), 40, 55, 57
Waju (d), 34, 35–36, 38